COLONIAL EDUCATION AND INDIA 1781–1945

COLONIAL EDUCATION AND INDIA 1781–1945

Edited by
Pramod K. Nayar

Volume V

Indian Responses

Routledge
Taylor & Francis Group
LONDON AND NEW YORK

First published 2020
by Routledge
2 Park Square, Milton Park, Abingdon, Oxon OX14 4RN

and by Routledge
52 Vanderbilt Avenue, New York, NY 10017

Routledge is an imprint of the Taylor & Francis Group, an informa business

British Library Cataloguing-in-Publication Data
A catalogue record for this book is available from the British Library

Library of Congress Cataloging-in-Publication Data
A catalog record for this book has been requested

ISBN: 978-0-8153-7655-2 (set)
eISBN: 978-1-351-21216-8 (set)
ISBN: 978-0-8153-8084-9 (Volume V)
eISBN: 978-1-351-21192-5 (Volume V)

Typeset in Times New Roman
by Apex CoVantage, LLC

Publisher's Note
References within each chapter are as they appear in the original complete work.

CONTENTS

VOLUME V INDIAN RESPONSES

1

AUROBINDO GHOSE, EXTRACT FROM *A SYSTEM OF NATIONAL EDUCATION* (MADRAS: TAGORE & CO, 1921), 1–67

I. THE HUMAN MIND

The true basis of Education is the study of the human mind, infant, adolescent, and adult. Any system of Education founded on theories of academic perfection, which ignores the instrument of study, is more likely to hamper and impair intellectual growth than to produce a perfect and perfectly equipped mind. For the Educationist has to do, not with dead material like the artist or sculptor, but with an infinitely subtle and sensitive organism. He cannot shape an educational masterpiece out of human wood or stone; he has to work in the elusive substance of mind and respect the limits imposed by the fragile human body.

There can be no doubt that the Educational System of Europe is a great advance on the many methods of antiquity, but its defects are also palpable. It is based on an in-sufficient knowledge of human psychology and it is only safeguarded in Europe from disastrous results by the refusal of the ordinary student to subject himself to the processes it involves, his habit of studying only so much as he must to avoid punishment or to pass an immediate test, his resort to active habits and vigorous physical exercise. In India the disastrous effects of the system on body, mind and character are only too apparent. The first problem in a National System of Education is to give an Education as comprehensive as the European and more thorough, without the evils of strain and cramming. This can only be done by studying the instruments of knowledge and finding a system of teaching which shall be natural, easy and effective. It is only by strengthening and sharpening these instruments to their utmost capacity that they can be made effective for the increased work which modern conditions require. The muscles of the mind must be thoroughly trained by simple and easy means; then, and not till then, great feats of intellectual strength can be required of them.

The first principle of true teaching is that nothing can be taught. The teacher is not an Instructor or Taskmaster, he is a helper and a guide. His business is to suggest and not to impose. He does not actually train the pupil's mind, he only shows him how to perfect his instruments of knowledge and helps and encourages him in the process. He does not impart knowledge to him, he shows him how to acquire knowledge for himself. He does not call forth the knowledge that is within; he only shows him where it lies and how it can be habituated to rise to the surface. The distinction that reserves this principle for the teaching of adolescent and adult minds and denies its application to the child is a conservative and unintelligent doctrine. Child or man, boy or girl, there is only one sound principle of good teaching. Difference of age only serves to diminish or increase the amount of help and guidance necessary, it does not change its nature.

The second principle is that the mind has to be consulted in its own growth. The idea of hammering the child into the shape desired by the parent or teacher is a barbarous and ignorant superstition. It is he himself who must be induced to expand in accordance with his own nature. There can be no greater error than for the parent to arrange beforehand that his son shall develop particular qualities, capacities, ideas, virtues, or be prepared for a prearranged career. To force the nature, to abandon its own *dharma* is to do it permanent harm, mutilate its growth and deface its perfection. It is a selfish tyranny over a human soul and a wound to the Nation, which loses the benefit of the best that a man could have given it and is forced to accept instead something imperfect and artificial, second rate, perfunctory andcommon. Every one has in him something divine, something his own, a chance of perfection and strength in however small a sphere which God offers him to take or refuse. The task is to find it, develop it and use it. The chief aim of Education should be to help the growing soul to draw out that in itself which is best and make it perfect for a noble use.

The third principle of Education is to work from the near to the far, from that which is to that which shall be. The basis of a man's nature is almost, always, in addition to his soul's past, his heredity, his surroundings, his nationality, his country, the soil from which he draws sustenance, the air which he breathes, the sights, sounds, habits to which he is accustomed. They mould him not the less powerfully because insensibly, from that then we must begin. We must not take up the nature by the roots from the Earth in which it must grow or surround the mind with images and ideas of a life which is alien to that in which it must physically move. If anything has to be brought in from outside, it must be offered, not forced on the mind. A free and natural growth is the condition of genuine development. There are souls which naturally revolt from their surroundings and seem to belong to another age and clime. Let them be free to follow their bent; but the majority languish, become empty, become artificial, if artificially moulded into an alien form. It is God's arrangement that they should belong to a particular nation, age, society, that they should be children of the past, possessors of the present, creators of the future. The past is our foundation, the present our material, the future our aim and summit. Each must have its due and natural place in a National System of Education.

CHAPTER II
THE POWERS OF THE MIND

The instrument of the Educationist is the mind or *antahkarana,* which consists of four layers. The reservoir of past mental impressions, the *chitta* or storehouse of memory, which must be distinguished from the specific act of memory, is the foundation on which all the other layers stand. All experience lies within us as passive or potential memory; active memory selects and takes what it requires from that storehouse. But the active memory is like a man searching among a great mass of locked-up material; sometime he cannot find what he wants; often in his rapid search he stumbles across many things for which he has no immediate need; often too he blunders and thinks he has found the real thing when it is something else irrelevant if not valueless, on which he has laid his hand. The passive memory or *chitta* needs no training, it is automatic and naturally sufficient to its task; there is not the slightest object of knowledge coming within its field which is not secured, placed and faultlessly preserved in that admirable receptacle. It is the active memory, a higher but less perfectly developed function, which is in need of improvement.

The second layer is the mind proper or *manas,* the sixth sense of our Indian Psychology, in which all the others are gathered up. The function of the mind is to receive the images of things translated into sight, sound, smell, taste and touch, the five senses and translate these again into thought-sensations. It receives also images of its own direct grasping and forms them into mental impressions. These sensations and impressions are the material of thought, not thought itself; but it is exceedingly important that thought should work on sufficient and perfect material. It is therefore the first business of the Educationist, to develop in the child the right use of the six senses; to see that they are not stunted or injured by disease, but trained by the child himself under the teacher's direction to that perfect accuracy and keen subtle sensitiveness of which they are capable. In addition, whatever assistance can be gained by the organs of action should be thoroughly employed. The hand, for instance, should be trained to reproduce what the eye sees, and the mind senses. The speech should be trained the perfect expression of the knowledge which the whole *antahkarna* possesses.

The third layer is the intellect or *buddhi,* which is the real instrument of thought and that which orders and disposes of the knowledge acquired by the other parts of the machine. For the purpose of the Educationist this is infinitely the most important of the three I have named. The intellect is an organ composed of several groups of functions, divisible into two important classes, the functions and faculties of the right hand, the functions and the faculties of the left hand. The faculties of the right hand are comprehensive, creative and synthetic; the faculties of the left hand critical and analytic. To the right hand belongs judgment, imagination, memory, observation; to the left hand comparison and reasoning. The critical faculties distinguish, compare, classify, generalise, deduce, infer, conclude;they are the component parts of the logical reason. The right hand faculties comprehend, command, judge in their own right, grasp; hold and manipulate. The right hand mind is the master of the knowledge, the left hand its servant. The left hand touches only the body of knowledge, the right hand penetrates its soul. The left hand limits itself to assertained truth, the right hand grasps that which is still elusive or unascertained. Both are essential to the completeness of the human reason. These important functions of the machine have all to be raised to their highest and finest working-power, if the Education of the child is not to be imperfect and one-sided.

There is a fourth layer of faculty which, not as yet entirely developed in man, is attaining gradually a wider development and more perfect evolution. The powers peculiar to this highest stratum of knowledge are chiefly known to us from the phenomena of genius—sovereign discernment, intuitive perception of truth, plenary inspiration of speech, direct vision of knowledge to an extent often amounting to revelation, making a man a prophet of truth. The powers are rare in their higher development, though many possess them imperfectly or by flashes. They are still greatly distrusted by the critical reason of mankind because of the admixture of error, caprice and a biassed imagination which obstructs and distorts their perfect workings. Yet it is clear that humanity could not have advanced to its present stage if it had not been for the help of these faculties, and it is a question with which Educationists have not yet grappled, what is to be done with this mighty and baffling element, the element of genius in the pupil. The mere instructor does his best to discourage and stifle genius, the more liberal teacher welcoms it. Faculties so important to humanity cannot be left out of our consideration. It is foolish to neglect them. Their imperfect development must be perfected, the admixture of error, caprice and biassed fancifulness must be carefully and wisely removed. But the teacher cannot do it; he would eradicate the good corn as well as the tares if he interfered. Here, as in all educational operations, he can only put the growing soul into the way of its own perfection.

CHAPTER III
THE MORAL NATURE

In the economy of man the mental nature rests upon the moral, and the education of the intellect divorced from the perfection of the moral and emotional nature is injurious to human progress. Yet, while it is easy to arrange some kind of curriculum or syllabus which will do well enough for the training of the mind, it has not yet been found possible to provide under modern conditions a suitable moral training for the School and College. The attempt to make boys moral and religious by the teaching of moral and religious text-books is a vanity and a delusion, precisely because the heart is not the mind and to instruct the mind does not necessarily improve the heart. It would be an error to say that it has no effect. It throws certain seeds of thought into the *antahkarana* and, if these thoughts become habitual, they influence the conduct. But the danger of moral text-books is that they make the thinking of high things mechanical and artificial, and whatever is mechanical and artificial, is inoperative for good.

There are three things which are of the utmost importance in dealing with a man's moral nature, the emotions, the *samskaras* or formed habits and associations, and the *swabhava* or nature. The only way for him to train himself morally is to habituate himself to the right emotions, the noblest associations, the best mental, emotional and physical habits and the following out in right action of the fundamental impulses of his essential nature. You can impose a certain discipline on children, dress them into a certain mould, lash them into a desired path, but unless you can get their hearts and natures on your side, the conformity to this becomes a hypocritical and heartless, often a cowardly compliance. This is what is done in Europe, and it leads to that remarkable phenomenon known as the sowing of wild oats as soon as the yoke of discipline at School and at home is removed, and to the social hypocrisy which is so large a feature of European life. Only what the man admires and accepts, becomes part of himself; the rest is a mask. He conforms to the discipline of society as he conformed to the moral routine of home and school, but considers himself at liberty to guide his real life, inner and private, according to his own likings and passions. On the other hand, to neglect moral and religious Education altogether is to corrupt the race. The notorious moral corruption in our young men previous to the saving touch of the Swadeshi Movement, was the direct result of the purely mental instruction given to them under the English System of Education. The adoption of the English System under an Indian disguise in Institutions like the Central Hindu College is likely to lead to the European result. That it is better than nothing, is all that can be said for it.

As in the education of the mind, so in the education of the heart, the best way is to put the child into the right road to his own perfection and encourage him to follow it, watching, suggesting, helping, but not interfering. The one excellent element in the English Boarding School is that the master at his best stands there as a moral guide and example, leaving the boys largely to influence and help each other in following the path silently shown to them. But the method practised is crude and marred by the excess of outer discipline, for which the pupils have no respect except that of fear, and the exiguity of the inner assistance. The little good that is done is outweighed by much evil. The old Indian System of the *Guru* commanding by his knowledge and sanctity, the implicit obedience, perfect admiration, reverent emulation of the student, was a far superior method of moral discipline. It is impossible to restore that ancient system; but it is not impossible to substitute the wise friend, guide and helper for the hired Instructor or the benevolent Policeman which is all that the European System usually makes of the pedagogue.

The first rule of Moral Training is to suggest and invite, not command or impose. The best method of suggestion is by personal example, daily converse and the books read from day to day. These books should contain, for the younger student, the lofty examples of the past given, not as moral lessons, but as things of supreme human interest, and, for the elder student, the great thoughts of great souls, the passages of literature which set fire to the highest emotions and prompt the highest ideals and aspirations, the records of history and biography which exemplify the living of those great thoughts, noble emotions and aspiring ideals. This is a kind of good company, *satsanga,* which can seldom fail to have effect so long as sententious sermonising is avoided, and becomes of the highest effect if the personal life of the teacher is itself moulded by the great things he places before his pupils. It cannot, however, have full force unless the young life is given an opportunity, within its limited sphere, of embodying in action the moral impulses which rise within it. The thirst of knowledge, the self-devotion, the purity, the renunciation of the Brahmin, the courage, ardour, honour, nobility, chivalry, patriotism of the Kshatriya,—the beneficence, skill, industry, generous enterprise and large openhandedness of the Vaisya,—the self-effacement and loving service of the Sudra,—these are the qualities of the Aryan. They constitute the moral temper we desire in our young men, in the whole Nation. But how can we get them if we do not give opportunities to the young to train themselves in the Aryan tradition, to form by the practice and familiarity of childhood and boyhood the stuff of which their adult lives must be made?

Every boy should, therefore, be given practical opportunity as well as intellectual encouragement to develop all that is best in the nature. If he has bad qualities, bad habits, bad *samskaras* whether of mind or body, he should not be treated harshly as a delinquent, but encouraged to get rid of them by the Rajayogic Method of *Sanyama,* rejection and substitution. He should be encouraged to think of them, not as sins or offences, but as symptoms of a curable disease alterable by a steady and sustained effort of the will, falsehood being rejected whenever it rises into the mind and replaced by truth, fear by courage, selfishness by sacrifice and renunciation, malice by love. Great care will have to be taken that unformed virtues are not rejected as faults. The wildness and recklessness of many young natures are only the overflowings of an excessive strength, greatness and nobility. They should be purified, not discouraged.

I have spoken of morality; it is necessary to speak a word of religious teaching. There is a strange idea prevalent that by merely teaching the dogmas of religion children can be made pious and moral. This is an European error, and its practice leads, either to mechanical acceptance of a creed having no effect on the inner and little on the outer life, or it creates the fanatic, the pietist, the ritualist or the unctuous hypocrite. Religion has to be lived, not learned as a creed. The singular compromise made in the so-called National Education of Bengal making the teaching of religious beliefs compulsory, but forbidding the practice of *anushtana* or religious exercise, is a sample of the ignorant confusion which distracts men's mind on this subject. The prohibition is a sop to secularism declared or concealed. No religious teaching is of any value unless it is lived, and the use of various kinds of *sadhana,* spiritual self-training and exercise, is the only effective preparation for religious living. The ritual of prayer homage, ceremony is craved for by many minds as an essential preparation and, if not made an end in itself, is a great help to spiritual progress; if it is withheld, some other form of meditation, devotion or religious duty must be put in its place. Otherwise, Religious Teaching is of little use and would almost be better ungiven.

But whether distinct teaching in any form of religion is imparted or not, the essence of religion, to live for God, for humanity, for country, for others and for oneself in these, must be made the ideal in every School which calls itself National. It is this spirit of Hinduism pervading our Schools which—far more than the teaching of Indian Subjects, the use of Indian methods or formal instruction in Hindu Beliefs and Hindu Scriptures—should be the essence of Nationalism in our Schools distinguishing them from all others.

CHAPTER IV
SIMULTANEOUS AND SUCCESSIVE TEACHING

A very remarkable feature of modern training which has been subjected in India to a reduction *ad absurdum* is the practice of teaching by snippets. A subject is taught a little at a time, in conjunction with a host of others, with the result that what might be well learnt in a single year is badly learned in seven and the boy goes out ill-equipped, served with imperfect parcels of knowledge, master of none of the great departments of human knowledge. The system of Education adopted by the National Council, an amphibious and twynatured creation, attempts to heighten this practice of teaching by snippets at the bottom and the middle and suddenly change it to a grandiose specialism at the top. This is to base the Triangle on its apex and hope that it will stand.

The old system was to teach one or two subjects well and thoroughly and then proceed to others, and certainly it was a more rational system than the modern. If it did not impart so much varied information, it built up a deeper, nobler and more real culture. Much of the shallowness, discursive lightness and fickle mutability of the average modern mind is due to the vicious principle of teaching by snippets. The one defect that can be alleged against the old system was that the subject earliest learned might fade from the mind of the student while he was mastering his later studies. But the excellent training given to the memory by the ancients obviated the incidence of this defect. In the future Education we need not bind ourselves either by the ancient or the modern system, but select only the most perfect and rapid means of mastering knowledge.

In defence of modern system it is alleged that the attention of children is easily tired and cannot be subjected to the strain of long application to a single subject. The frequent changes of subject gives rest to the mind. The question naturally arises: are the children of modern times then so different from the ancients, and, if so, have we not made them so by discouraging prolonged concentration? A very young child cannot, indeed apply himself; but a very young child is unfit for School teaching of any kind. A child of seven or eight, and that is the earliest permissible age for the commencement of any regular kind of study, is capable of a good deal of concentration if he is interested. Interest is after all, the basis of con-centration. We make his lessons supremely uninteresting and repellent to the child, a harsh compulsion the basis of teaching and then complain of his restless inattention! The substitution of a natural self-Education by the child for the present unnatural system will remove this objection of inability. A child, like a man, if he is interested, much prefers to get to the end of his subject rather than leave it unfinished. To lead him on step by step, interesting and absorbing him in each as it comes, until he has mastered his subject is the true art of teaching.

The first attention of the teacher must be given to the medium and the instruments, and, until these are perfected, to multiply subjects of regular instruction is to waste time and energy. When the mental instruments are sufficiently developed to acquire a language easily and swiftly, that is the time to introduce him to many languages, not when he can only partially understand what he is taught and masters it laboriously and imperfectly. Moreover, one who has mastered his own language, has one very necessary facility for mastering another. With the linguistic faculty unsatisfactorily developed in one's own tongue, to master others is impossible. To study Science with the faculties of observation, judgment, reasoning, and comparison only slightly developed, is to undertake a useless and thankless labour. So it is with all other subjects.

The mother-tongue is the proper medium of Education and therefore the first energies of the child should be directed to the thorough mastering of the medium. Almost every child has an imagination, an instinct for words, a dramatic faculty, a wealth of idea and fancy. These should be interested in the literature and history of the Nation. Instead of stupid and dry spelling and reading books, looked on as a dreary and ungrateful task, he should be introduced by rapidly progressive stages to the most interesting parts of his own literature and the life around him and behind him, and they should be put before him, in such a way as to attract and appeal to the qualities of which I have spoken. All other study at this period should be devoted to the perfection of the mental functions and the moral character. A foundation should be laid at this time for the study of history, science, philosophy, art, but not in an obtrusive and formal manner. Every child is a lover of interesting narrative, a hero-worshipper and a patriot. Appeal to these qualities in him and through him, let him master without knowing it the living and human parts of his Nation's history. Every child is an inquirer, an investigator, analyser, a merciless anatomist. Appeal to those qualities in him and let him acquire without knowing it the right temper and the necessary fundamental knowledge of the Scientist. Every child has an insatiable intellectual curiosity and turn for metaphysical enquiry. Use it to draw him on slowly to an understanding of the world and himself. Every child has the gift of imitation and a touch of imaginative power. Use it to give him the ground work of the faculty of the artist.

It is by allowing Nature to work that we get the benefit of the gifts she has bestowed on us. Humanity in its education of children has chosen to thwart and hamper the rapidity of its onward march. Happily, saner ideas are now beginning to prevail. But the way has not yet been found. The past hangs about our necks with all its prejudices and errors and will not leave us; it enters into our most radical attempts to return to the guidance of the all-wise Mother. We must have the courage to take up clearer knowledge and apply it fearlessly in the interests of posterity. Teaching by snippets must be relegated to the lumber-room of dead sorrows. The first work is to interest the child in life, work and knowledge, to develop his instruments of knowledge with the utmost thoroughness, to give him mastery of the medium he must use. Afterwards, the rapidity with which he will learn, will be found that, where now he learns a few things badly, then he will learn many things thoroughly well.

CHAPTER V
THE TRAINING OF THE MIND

There are six senses which minister to knowledge, sight, hearing, smell, touch and taste, mind, and all of these except the last, look outward and gather the material of thought from outside through the physical nerves and their end-organs, eye, ear, nose, skin, palate. The perfection of the senses as ministers to thought must be one of the first cares of the teachers. The two things that are needed of the senses are accuracy and sensitiveness. We must first understand what are the obstacles to the accuracy and sensitiveness of the senses, in order that we may take the best steps to remove them. The cause of imperfection must be understood by those who desire to bring about perfection.

The senses depend for their accuracy and sensitiveness on the unobstructed activity of the nerves which are the channels of their information and the passive acceptance of the mind which is the recipient. In themselves the organs do their work perfectly. The eye gives the right form, the ear the correct sound, the palate the right taste, the skin the right touch, the nose the right smell. This can easily be understood if we study the action of the eye as a crucial example. A correct image is reproduced automatically on the retina, if there is any error in appreciating it, it is not the fault of the organ, but of something else.

The fault may be with the nerve currents. The nerves are nothing but channels, they have no power in themselves to alter the information given by the organs. But a channel may be obstructed and the obstruction may interfere either with the fullness or the accuracy of the information, not as it reaches the organ where it is necessarily and automatically perfect, but as it reaches the mind. The only exception is in case of a physical defect in the organ as an instrument. That is not a matter for the educationist, but for the physician.

If the obstruction is such as to stop the information reaching the mind at all, the result is an insufficient sensitiveness of the senses. The defects of sight, hearing, smell, touch, taste, anoethesia in its various degrees, are curable when not the effect of physical injury or defect in the organ itself. The obstructions can be removed and the sensitiveness remedied by the purification of the nerve system. The remedy is a simple one which is now becoming more and more popular in Europe for different reasons and objects, the regulation of the breathing. This process inevitably restores the perfect and unobstructed activity of the channels and, if well and thoroughly done, leads to a high activity of the senses. The process is called in Yogic discipline, *nadi-suddhi,* or nerve-purification.

The obstruction in the channel may be such as not absolutely to stop in however small a degree, but to distort the information. A familiar instance of this is the effect of fear or alarm on the sense action. The startled horse takes the sack on the road for a dangerous living thing, the startled man takes a rope for a snake, a waving curtain for a ghostly form. All distortions due to actions in the nervous system can be traced to some kind of emotional disturbance acting in the nerve channels. The only remedy for them is the habit of calm, the habitual steadiness of the nerves. This also can be brought about by *nadi-suddhi* or nerve-purficiation, which quiets the system, gives a deliberate calmness to all the internal processes and prepares the purification of the mind.

If the nerve channels are quiet and clear, the only possible disturbance of the information is from or through the mind. Now the *manas* or sixth sense is in itself a channel like the nerves, a channel for communication: with the *buddhi* or brain-force disturbance may happen either from above or from below. The information outside is first photographed on the end organ, then reproduced at the other end of the nerve system in the *chitta* or passive memory. All the images of sight, sound, smell, touch and taste are deposited there and the *manas* reports them to the *buddhi.* The *manas* is both a sense organ and a channel. As a sense organ it is as automatically perfect as the others, as a channel it is subject to disturbance resulting either in obstruction or distortion.

As a sense organ the mind receives direct thought impressions from outside and from within. These impressions are in themselves perfectly correct, but in their report to the intellect at all or may reach it so distorted as to make a false or partially false impression. The disturbance may effect the impression which attains the information of eye, ear, nose, skin or palate, but it is very slightly powerful here, in its effect on the direct impressions of the mind, it is extremely powerful and the chief source of error. The mind takes direct impressions primarily of thought, but also of form, sound, indeed of all the things for which it usually prefers to depend on the sense organs. The full development of this sensitiveness of the mind is called in our Yogic discipline *Sushmadrishti* or subtle reception of images. Telepathy, clairvoyance, claraudience, presentment, thought-reading, character-reading and many other modern discoveries are very ancient powers of the mind which have been left undeveloped, and they all belong to the *manas.* The development of the sixth sense has never formed part of human training. In a future age it will undoubtedly take a place in the necessary preliminary training of the human instrument. Meanwhile there is no reason why the mind should not be trained to give a correct report to the intellect so that our thought may start with absolutely correct if not with full impressions.

The first obstacle, the nervous emotional, we may suppose to be removed by the purification of the nervous system. The second obstacle is that of the emotions themselves warping the impressions as it comes. Love may do this, hatred may do this, any emotion or desire according to its power and intensity may distort the impression as it travels. This difficulty can only be removed by the discipline of the emotions, the purifying of the moral training and its consideration may be postponed for the moment. The next difficulty is the interference of previous associations formed or ingrained in the *chitta* or passive memory. We have a habitual way of looking at things and the conservative inertia in our nature disposes us to give every new experience the shape and semblance of those to which we are accustomed. It is only more developed minds which can receive first impressions without an unconscious bias against the novelty of novel experience. For instance, if we get a true impression of what is happening and we habitually act on such impressions true or false if it differs from what we are accustomed to expect, the old association meets it in the *chitta* and sends a changed report to the intellect in which either the new impression is overlaid and concealed by the old or mingled with it. To go farther into this subject would be to involve ourselves too deeply into the details of psychology. This typical instance will suffice. To get rid of this obstacle is impossible without *chittasuddhi* or purification of the mental moral habits formed in the *chitta*. This is a preliminary process of Yoga and was effected in our ancient system by various means, but would be considered out of place in a modern system of education.

It is clear, therefore, that unless we revert to our old system in some of its principles, we must be content to allow this source of disturbance to remain. A really national system of education would not allow itself to be controlled by European ideas in this all important matter. And there is a process so simple and momentous that it can easily be made a part of our system.

It consists in bringing about passivity of the restless flood of thought sensations rising of its own momentum from the passive memory independent of our will and control. This passivity liberatest he intellect from the siege of old associations and false impressions. It gives it power to select only what is wanted from the storehouse of the passive memory, automatically brings about the habit of getting right impressions and enables the intellect to dictate so the *chitta* what *samskara* or associations shall be formed or rejected. This is the real office of the intellect to discriminate, choose, select, arrange. But so long as there is not *chitta-suddhi,* instead of doing this office perfectly, it itself remains imperfect and corrupt and adds to the confusion in the mind channel by false judgment, false imagination, false memory, false observation, false comparison, contrast and analogy, false education, induction and inference. The purification of the *chitta* is essential for the liberation, purification and perfect action of the intellect.

CHAPTER VI
SENSE-IMPROVEMENT BY PRACTICE

Another cause of the inefficiency of the senses as gatherers of Knowledge, is insufficient use. We do not observe sufficiently or with sufficient attention and closeness and a sight, sound, smell, even touch or taste knocks in vain at the door for admission. This *tamasic* inertia of the receiving instruments is no doubt due to the inattention of the *buddhi* and therefore its consideration may seem to come properly under the training of the functions of the intellect, but it is more convenient, though less psychologically correct, to notice it here. The student ought to be accustomed to catch the sights, sounds etc, around him, distinguish them, mark their nature, properties and sources and fix them in the *chitta* so that they may be always ready to respond when called for by the memory.

It is a fact which has been proved by minute experiments that the faculty of observation is very imperfectly developed in men, merely from want of care in the use of the sense and the memory. Give twelve men the task of recording from memory something they all saw two hours ago and the accounts will all vary from each other and from the actual occurence. To get rid of this; imperfection will go a long way towards the removal of error. It can be done by training the senses to do their work perfectly which they will do readily enough if they know the *buddhi* requires it of them, and giving sufficient attention to put the facts in their right place and order in memory.

Attention is a factor in knowledge, the importance of which has been always recognised. Attention is the first condition of right memory and of accuracy. To attend to what he is doing, is the first element of discipline required of the student, and, as I have suggested, this can easily be secured if the object of attention is made interesting. This attention to a single thing is called concentration.One truth is however, sometimes overlooked; that concentration on several things at a time is often indispensable. When people talk of concentration, they imply centring the mind on one thing at a time; but it is quite possible to develop the power of double concentration, triple concentration, multiple concentration. When a given incident is happening, it may be made up of several simultaneous happenings or a set of simultaneous circumstances, a sight, a sound, a touch or several sights, sounds, touches occuring at the same moment or in the same short space of time. The tendency of the kind is to fasten on one and mark others vaguely, many not at all or, if compelled to attend to all, to be distracted and mark none perfectly. Yet this can be remedied and the attention equally distributed over a set of circumstances in such a way as to observe and remember each perfectly. It is merely a matter of *abhyasa* or steady natural practice.

It is also very desirable that the hand should be capable of coming to the help of the eye in dealing with the multitudinous objects of its activity so as to ensure accuracy. This is of a use so obvious and imperatively needed, that it need not be dwelt on at length. The practice of imitation by the hand of the thing seen is of use both of detecting the lapses and inaccuracies of the mind in noticing the objects of sense and in registering accurately what has been seen. Imitation by the hand ensures accuracy of observation. This is one of the first uses of drawing and it is sufficient in itself to make the teaching of this subject a necessary part of the training of the organs.

CHAPTER VII
THE TRAINING OF THE MENTAL FACULTIES

The first qualities of the mind that have to be developed are those which can be grouped under observation. We notice some things, ignore others. Even of what we notice, we observe very little. A general perception of an object is what we all usually carry away from a cursory half-attentive glance. A closer attention fixes its place, from nature as distinct from its surroundings. Full concentration of the faculty of observation gives us all the knowledge that the three chief senses can gather about the object, or if we touch or taste, we may gather all that the five senses can tell of its nature and properties. Those who make use of the six senses, the Poet, the Painter, the Yogin, can also gather much that is hidden from the ordinary observer. The Scientist by investigation ascertains other facts open to a minuter observation. These are the components of the faculty of observation, and it is obvious that its basis is attention, which may be only close, or close and minute. We may gather much even from a passing glance at an object, if we have the habit of concentrating the attention and the habit of *Satwic* receptivity. The first the teacher has to do is to accustom the pupil to concentrate attention.

We may take the instance of a flower. Instead of looking casually at it and getting a casual impression of scent, form and colour, he should be encouraged to know the flower—to fix in his mind the exact shade, the peculiar glow, the precise intensity of the scent, the beauty of curve and design in the form. His touch should assure itself of the texture and its peculiarities. Next, the flower should be taken to pieces and its structure examined with the same carefulness of observation. All these should be done not as a task, but as an object of interest by skilfully arranged questions suited to the learner which will draw him on to observe and investigate one thing after the other until he has almost unconsciously mastered the whole.

Memory and judgment are the next qualities that will be called upon, and they should be encouraged in the same unconscious way. The student should not be made to repeat the same lesson over again in order to remember it. That is a mechanical burden-some and unintelligent way of training the memory. A similar but different flower should be put in the hands and he should be encouraged to note it with the same care, but with the avowed object of noting the similarities and differences. By this practice daily repeated the memory will naturally be trained. Not only so, but the mental centres of comparison and contrast will be developed. The learner will begin to observe as a habit the similarities of things and their differences. The teacher should take every care to encourage the perfect growth of this faculty and habit. At the same time, the laws of species and genus will begin to dawn on the mind and by a skilful following and leading of the young developing mind, the scientific habit, the scientific attitude and the fundamental facts of scientific knowledge may in a very short time be made part of its permanent equipment. The observation and comparison of flowers, leaves, plants, trees will lay the foundations of botanical knowledge without loading the mind with names and that dry, set acquisition of informations which is the beginning of cramming and detested by the healthy human mind when it is fresh from nature and unspoiled by natural habits. In the same way by the observation of the stars, astronomy, by the observation of earth, stones, etc., geology by the observation of insects and animals, etymology and zoology may be founded. A little later chemistry may be started by interesting observation of experiments without any formal teaching or heaping on the mind of formulas and book knowledge. There is no scientific object the perfect and natural mastery of which cannot be prepared in early childhood by this training of the faculties to observe, compare, remember and judge various classes of objects. It can be done easily and attended with a supreme and absorbing interest in the mind of the student. Once the taste is created, the boy can be trusted to follow it up with all the enthusiasm of youth in his leisure hours. This will prevent the necessity at a later age of teaching him everything in class.

The judgment will naturally be trained along with the other faculties. At every step the boy will have to decide what is the right idea, measurement, appreciation of colour, sound, scent, etc., and what is wrong. Often the judgments and distinctions made will have to be exceedingly subtle, and delicate. At first many errors will be made, but the learner should be taught to trust his judgment without being attached to its results. It will be found that the judgment will soon begin to respond to the calls made on it, clear itself of all errors and begin to judge correctly and minutely. The best way is to accustom the boy to compare his judgments with those of others. When he is wrong, it should at first be pointed out to him how far he was right and why he went wrong; afterwards he should be encouraged to note these things for itself. Every time he is right, his attention should be prominently and encouragingly called to it so that he may get confidence.

While engaged in comparing and contrasting, another centre is certain to develop, the centre of analogy. The learner will inevitably draw analogies and argue from like to like. He should be encouraged to use his faculty while noticing its limitations and errors. In this way he will be trained to form the habit of correct analogy which is an indispensable and in the acquisition of knowledge.

The one faculty we have omitted, apart from the faculty of direct reasoning, is Imagination. This is a most important and indispensable instrument It may be divided into three functions, the forming of mental images, the power of creating thoughts images and imitations or new combinations of existing thoughts and images, the appreciation of the soul in things, beauty, charm, greatness, hidden suggestiveness, the emotion and spiritual life that prevades the world. This is in every way, as important as the training of the faculties which observe and compare outward things. But I shall deal with it in a subsequent chapter.

The mental faculties should first be exercised on things, afterwards on words and ideas. Our dealings with language are much too perfunctory and the absence of a fine sense for words impoverishes the intellect and limits the fineness and truth of its operations. The mind should be accustomed first to notice the word thoroughly, its form, sound and sense; then to compare the form with other similar forms in the points of similarity and difference, thus forming the foundation of the grammatical sense; then to distinguish between the fine shades of sense of similar words and the formtaion and rhythm of different sentences; thus the formation of the liberty and the syntactical faculties. All this should be done informally drawing on the curiosity and interest, avoiding set-teaching and memorising of rules. The true knowledge takes its base on things, *arthas,* and only when it has mastered the thing, proceeds to formalize its information.

CHAPTER VIII
THE TRAINING OF THE LOGICAL FACULTY

The training of the logical reason but necessarily follows the training of the faculties which collect the material on which the logical reason must work. Not only so but the mind must have some development of the faculty of dealing before it can deal successfully with ideas. The question is, once this preliminary work is done, what is the best way of teaching the boy to think correctly from premises. For the logical reason cannot proceed without premises. It either infers from facts to a conclusion to a fresh one, or from one fact to another. It either induces, deduces or simply infers. I see the Sun rise day after day, I conclude or induce that it rises to a law daily after a varying interval of darkness. I have already ascertained that wherever there is smoke, there is fire. I have induced that general rule from an observation of facts. I deduce that in a particular case of smoke, there is a fire behind. I infer that a man must have let it from the improbability of any other cause under the particular circumstances. I cannot deduce it because fire is not always created by human kindling; it may be volcanic or caused by a stroke of lightening or the sparks from some kind of friction in the neighbourhood.

There are three elements necessary to correct reasoning: first, the correctness of the facts or conclusions I start from, secondly, the completeness as well as the accuracy of the data I start from, thirdly, the elimination of other possible or impossible conclusions from the same facts. The fallibility of the logical reason is due partly to avoidable negligence and looseness in securing these conditions, partly to the difficulty of getting all the facts correct, still more to the difficulty of getting all the facts complete, most of all, to the extreme difficulty of eliminating all possible conclusions except the one which happens to be right. No fact is supposed to be more perfectly established than the universality of the Law of Gravitation as an imperative rule, yet a single new fact inconsistent with it would upset this supposed universality. And such facts exist. Nevertheless by care and keenness the fallibility may be reduced to its minimum.

The usual practice is to train the logical reason by teaching the Science of Logic. This is an instance of the prevalent error by which book knowledge of a thing is made the object of the study instead of the thing itself. The experience of reasoning and its errors should be given to the mind and it should be taught to observe how these work for itself; it should proceed from the example to the rule and from the accumulating harmony of rules to the formal science of the subject, not from the formal science to the rule, and from the rule to the example.

The first step is to make the young mind interest itself in drawing inferences from the facts, tracing cause and effect. It should then be led on to notice its successes and its failures and the reason of the success and of the failure; the incorrectness of the fact started from, the haste in drawing conclusions from insufficient facts, the carlessness in accepting a conclusion which is improbable, little supported by the data or open to doubt, the indolence or prejudice which does wish to consider other possible explanations or conclusions. In this way the mind can be trained to reason as correctly as the fallibility of the human logic will allow, minimising the change of error. The study of formal logic should be postponed to a later period when it can easily be mastered in a very brief period, since it will be only the systematising of the art perfectly well-known to the student.

2

J. GHOSH, EXTRACT FROM *HIGHER EDUCATION IN BENGAL UNDER BRITISH RULE* (CALCUTTA: THE BOOK COMPANY, 1926), 104–197

CHAPTER II

WESTERN EDUCATION

Lord Bentinck's educational policy was warmly reprobated in certain quarters The Asiatic Society of Bengal characterised it as destructive unjust unpopular and impolitic and compared the prospective injury to scholarship from its operation with the incalculable loss caused by the destruction of the Alexandrian Library The Muslim residents of Calcutta implored him to spare the Madrassah and to avoid taking any steps that might lead to the destruction of the literature and the religious system of Islam or to the conversion of the people to the faith of their rulers. He replied on the 9th of March to the effect that such motives never had influenced never could influence the counsels of government And not long after he repeated the assuring observation that any interference with the religious belief of the students any mingling of direct or indirect teaching of Christianity with the system of instruction would be positively forbidden Thus the new scheme of education was to have the negative virtue of complete abstention from spiritual training in flagrant disregard of a cherished tradition of the East which prescribes an indissoluble union between such training and higher education It was also an unprecedented departure from the experience of the West, where up to that time the clergy had taken an active interest in the diffusion of knowledge But the rulers were apparently disinclined to admit the propriety of securing the co-operation of the Maulvis and the Pandits, 'the clergy of India,' though they might have been won over to the cause by a cordial and understanding treatment.[1]

It was also widely and not unreasonably apprehended that the preference given to English as a medium of instruction might stand in the way of a proper cultivation and development of the vernacular The General Committee of Public Instruction tried to allay the suspicion by a clear statement of their views in their annual report for 1835 "They are deeply sensible," so ran the report, "of the importance of encouraging the cultivation of the vernacular languages. They do not conceive that the ordinance of the 7th of March precludes this, and they have constantly acted on this construction. In the discussion which preceded that ordinance, the claims of the vernacular language were broadly and prominently admitted by all parties, and the question submitted for the decision of government only concerned the relative advantage of English on the one side and the learned eastern languages on the other" But their pledge and their explanation did not square with their activities By abolishing from the Government seminaries separate classes for instruction in the vernacular and by leaving the indigenous primary schools to their own devices, the committee withheld from it the patronage which it was sorely in need of.

The establishment of the Medical College in June of the fateful year, 1835, was like another sign-post indicating a turn in the road It was the fruit of an enquiry set on foot by Lord Bentinck into the state of medical knowledge in the metropolis The committee appointed for the purpose had found that the scope of the classes attached to the Madrassah and the Sanskrit College did not extend beyond the diffusion of a smattering of European science and some knowledge of the indigenous art of healing and that the curriculum of the school started for the training of Indian assistants to European medical officers was equally unsatisfactory And they had reported that a knowledge of English should be regarded as a preliminary qualification for students of medicine because that language combined within itself the circle of all the sciences and incalculable wealth of printed works and illustrations circumstances that gave it obvious advantages over the oriental languages in which were to be found only the crudest elements of science or the most irrational substitutes for it"[2] The Government acted on this report and directed the abolition of the medical classes at the Madrassah and the Sanskrit College and of the school for the training of native doctors, which had been started so far back as 1822 It resolved also to set up a new and independent college for teaching medical science on European principles and through the medium of the English language This decision materialised in June 1835 in the form of a noble institution, which has since done much to confer on the people the benefits of a new and scientific mode of the treatment of diseases At its inception grave fears were entertained that the prejudices of the Hindus might compromise its popularity and success Those prejudices proved, however, less intractable than the prejudices of the rulers, which stood in the way of a correlation of western science with the results of centuries of medical experience in the east As embodied in oriental works, they were overlaid, no doubt, with false notions and absurd theories, the degrading contribution of ages in which independent enquiry had been abjured out of a superstitious regard for authority. But they had been obtained by methods of investigation not unlike those which had yielded a rich harvest of new truths in the west. And it was unscientific to exclude their critical study from a course of instruction designed for students who were to apply their knowledge under the tropical conditions of India A juster appreciation of their value had been shown by the Court of Directors so early as 1814 in their observation that "there were many tracts of merit in the Sanskrit language on the virtues of plants and drugs and on the application of them in medicine, the knowledge of which might prove desirable to the European practitioner."

Another innovation in which however, the principle of continuity was set aside with better reason was the supersession of Persian by English and the vernacular in courts and important departments of the State Persian had been the language of culture in Mogul India and was, therefore, gilded with the reflection of a departed glory But the faith and the philosophy of Islam were not enshrined in it, nor, indeed, was it a passport to any of those studies that mark off Muhammadanism from other systems of thought and practice And in the advanced portions of Bengal, it was learnt by the Hindus more largely than by their Muhammadan brethren[3] But its acquisition was a hindrance to the attainment of proficiency in English and the vernacular So the Hindus had every reason for welcoming the change and the Muhammadans had not many cogent ones for disliking it It was introduced in pursuance of an Act passed on the 20th November, 1837 which authorised the Governor-General in Council to dispense with Persian in judicial and revenue proceedings and to delegate the dispensing power to provincial rulers In Bengal no transitional stage was felt to be necessary, and the steps that were taken received the entire approval of the Court of Directors in a despatch of the 11th of July, 1838.

The new scheme of education continued, however, to be viewed with dissatisfaction, if not with alarm, in certain quarters, while the Orientalists who were still on the committee did not slacken their efforts in favour of a reversion to the earlier policy of patronage of the classical languages of India The main grievances were the transfer of appropriations from the Sanskrit College and the Madrassah to the support of English classes under the same roofs and the discontinuance of stipends to the alumni of these institutions, though many of them were too poor to continue their studies without alimentary allowances[4] These causes of discontent appeared weighty enough to Lord Auckland to justify some modification of the principles laid down by Lord Bentinck He carefully considered the question and came to the conclusion that the inadequacy of the funds allotted for the encouragement of indigenous learning was at the root of the discontent and the controversy His finding and the decision based thereon were embodied in a minute dated 24th November 1839 and addressed to the General Committee of Public Instruction It dictated the maintenance of the oriental colleges in full efficiency and the combination of instruction in the vernacular with that in English The Court of Directors endorsed this method of dealing with the situation and declared that the funds assigned to each oriental institution should be employed exclusively for its support.

Lord Auckland's measure did not amount to a reversal of the policy of Lord Bentinck Nor did it aim at a proper synthesis of the rival cultures But it was calculated to allay discontent and to disarm opposition He agreed with Macaulay and Lord Bentinck in thinking that, advanced English education would place instructed native gentlemen on a level with the best European officers and so allowed the committee to establish a system of scholarships for deserving students in English seminaries and to divide the country into nine educational circles for the purpose of setting up a central college in each of them[5] On another point also there was perfect concurrence, for he declared that education in the Government schools must be secular in conformity with the pledges of the past. But the principle of religious neutrality, which he thus reaffirmed, provoked an outburst of indignation from the Christian missionaries in Calcutta, who were then taking an active interest in the education of the people Chief among them was Alexander Duff, who referred to his minute in the following words: "While certain parts of His Lordship's minute have been warmly applauded, others have been warmly reprobated. Of the latter the two great central points are the re-endowment of orientalism, including its false religion and the total exclusion of the true religion from the course of higher instruction in the literature and the science of Europe As the act of a Government which represents the British nation, this is neither more nor less than a national recognition of the false religions of Brahmanism and Muhammadanism and at the same time a national abnegation of the only true religion, that is Christianity Surely, surely this is a great national sin, which if not repented of and removed, may sooner or later draw down the most terrible but righteous retribution at the hands of an offended God.[6]

The pronounced attitude of Duff on the question of religious neutrality appears incompatible at first sight with his genuine sympathy for Indians and the reverence in which his memory is held by them But it was quite in keeping with his character and with the nature of the task that he set before himself He had come out to India in 1829 as the missionary of the General Assembly of Scotland, but unencumbered by vexatious directions about the manner in which he was to proceed with his work. There could have been no better choice of a man for bringing their message to the East, nor could full discretionary power have been more wisely delegated. For in Duff were united a magnetic personality, extraordinary energy and extensive learning with a singleness of purpose and a sincerity of faith that could not be obscured by the diversity of his interests He achieved remarkable success but was never tempted to place success before principle And he was able to reconcile the dogma of religion with the generalisations of philosophy and science So he early conceived the idea of converting a highly literary and scientific education into a means of spreading the gospel In his effort to translate this favourite scheme into a reality he was materially helped at the outset by Raja Ram Mohan Ray but he remained unaffected by the eclecticism of the great Hindu reformer and convinced that the new knowledge of the West must prepare the way for the fire of a new faith which was to rid this ancient society of its manifold abuses and imperfections To the attainment of this object he consecrated his great gifts and they won for him considerable authority of which however the light of truth as he saw it continued to be the very soul It is not strange therefore that the opinion of such a man should have carried great weight in certain quarters But his anathema failed to destroy the equanimity of Lord Auckland who wisely decided to adhere to the policy of his predecessors And it is only to be regretted that he did not go a step further to provide for the discipline of the will and the heart of the Hindu and Muslim students on the lines laid down by their respective creeds.[7]

Lord Auckland resolved not long after that Government should assume direct control of higher education in the country And this decision, which was arrived at on the 12th January 1842, led to certain significant though transitory changes The General Committee of Public Instruction was abolished and a Council of Education was formed in its place with the principal officers in Calcutta as its members and a deputy secretary to Government as its secretary But the new Council was not entrusted with the important administrative functions which had belonged to its predecessor, as the disposal of the funds ear marked for education and the superintendence of the institutions established for imparting it were, except in a few instances, vested in the General Department of the Government of India The arrangement however, proved unsatisfactory, and the council very reasonably complained that by being retained as a consultative and referential body, it was placed in a position of responsibility, but of no real power" So there was a retransfer of administrative functions which gave to it all the controlling influence over education which the defunct committee had possessed And thus strengthened it devoted its energy to the task of extending and popularising western knowledge which it succeeded in accomplishing in Bengal at least, by introducing a system of graded examinations and appointing trained and efficient teachers.

A still more direct and powerful impetus to the acquisition of the exotic learning was sought to be given in Lord Hardinge's resolution of the 10th of October 1844, which aimed at reserving all but the lowest posts under Government for those who distinguished themselves by their proficiency in it[8] But the decision was resented by the Christian missionaries in Calcutta, who apprehended that it might affect the usefulness and importance of the institutions over which they presided And their views and feelings were voiced once more by Duff, who led the opposition. He challenged the competence of the officials who were to conduct the examination for the selection of candidates for the public service and repudiated the implication in the syllabus that secular knowledge was a better test of fitness for it than a mastery over purely Christian literature The Court of Directors also found fault with the scheme because it appeared to be based on the notion that the rare accomplishments of a scholar formed an indispensable qualification for public service And in their reply to Lord Hardinge's letter of the 21st of May, 1845, they emphasised the view that "to require only a moderate and practical knowledge of English with a thorough command of the vernacular languages and testimonies of regularity, steadiness, diligence and good conduct would be the best way to obtain the largest number of candidates competent to become useful officers."

The immediate effect of Lord Hardinge's resolution could not be very striking, because it failed to win the approval of the Court of Directors But the bias of the principal officers of Government towards a thorough European education and the eagerness of Bengali students to receive it led to a tacit acceptance of the principle which it embodied And shortly after the Council of Education submitted a scheme for the establishment of a central university in Calcutta for the purpose of conferring degrees in Arts, Science Law Medicine and Civil Engineering[9] In recommending the proposal to the notice of the Governor-General they expressed the hope that if accepted it would open new avenues to social distinction and material gain for those who were devoting themselves to the acquisition of knowledge and that besides providing the State with competent and faithful servants, it would call into existence an upper class of educated men whose influence might rapidly diffuse a taste for refined and intellectual pursuits in the community Lord Hardinge endorsed the views of the Council regarding the possibilities of such an institution but the Directors stood once more in the way They wrote to him in 1846 to say that after maturely considering the subject they had come to the conclusion that sanction should not be accorded to an ambitious scheme like that laid before them The narrow ideal of education as a preparation for service in certain capacities seems still to have determined their attitude, though men on the spot realised that it could be much more than that and tried to act up to their conviction.

Among the men who thought nobly at this period of education and of the capacity of the Bengali race to profit by it stands out the interesting figure of John Drinkwater Bethune He was an ardent advocate of western learning and lacked probably the capacity and inclination for a just appraisement of what was distinctive in the culture and civilisation of the East. And yet his memory is cherished as a precious bequest even by those Bengalis who have lost their faith in his programme for their regeneration. Much of this appreciation is, indeed, only a natural tribute to the greatness of his character and to his genius for public usefulness But it is due also in some measure to the ardour of his conviction that the Indian people could come to anything considerable only by means of a vigorous and wholesome education What it could do not only for the recipients but also for those who came in contact with them, he took occasion to observe more than once[10] And he rightly stressed the view that it was a sacred trust for the proper use of which the educated were responsible to their less fortunate countrymen It is not for yourselves said he in an address to the students of the Dacca College or for your own sake only that you are educated you are expected to be the instruments of reflecting and diffusing around you the knowledge that you have acquired The individual might claim indeed to be trained to play his proper part in society but this he held should mean making not only a living but also a life as training could not in his opinion be liberal culture unless it succeeded in shifting the centre of interest from petty personal wants to the life and health of the community.

The specific which he recommended was limited in its curative influence Still it had important virtues which were not apparent even to those who were busily engaged in administering it In fact it failed when judged by its ultimate results to attain the objects that were dearest to their hearts Western education so the Christian missionaries thought would enable them to break up the fallow ground and protect them from the mischievous consequences of sowing the precious seed of faith among thorns But the obdurate soil defeated their expectation though it bore a plentiful crop of new thoughts and sentiments under their treatment The secular philanthropist hoped on the other hand that the dissemination of western ideas would lead to the reconstruction of society on western principles and start it on lines of intellectual and material advance which were approved in the West The goal was thus set in perfect confidence, and the race began under encouraging conditions, but it was not steadily pursued. For though the new learning bred in the recipients a spirit of experiment and a yearning for quick advance, yet the impulse did not extend beyond occasional and tentative attempts at social and economic reform[11] Hence in spite of the vagaries of the first students of English literature and the activities of certain sects which ultimately seceded from the pale of orthodoxy Hindu society remained practically unaltered both in its physiognomy and organisation The alien culture failed not only to bring about a break with the past but led to a revival of interest in and loyalty to ancient ideals and ways of thinking though the need was generally recognised of a revision of them.

This apparent failure however was in reality the most signal of triumphs The literature of England could not help inspiring even a dependent population with a certain independence of spirit and some measure of self-respect Those who studied it learnt in course of time that their salvation lay not in servile mimicry but in an honest and manly effort to raise themselves in their own way Hence they heard or supposed that they heard a clear call ringing out of the depths of the past which had been voiceless for generations Here was the origin of the reorientation of aim, which has appeared a mystery to many thoughtful observers The new knowledge sent them back to their old traditions, and they hoped to discover in these a base broad and deepset enough for their reconstructive activity.

Quite different, indeed, was the attitude of the first students of English literature, who believed that their lights were before them, while all behind was shadow But theirs had been a provisional age, an age of assimilation and recuperation marked by the indiscriminate gathering up of the discoveries and assumptions of others Besides, even in it class interests had widened into the consciousness of commanding national concerns, while the golden age had been recognised as lying unrealised in the future A long step forward was taken, however, when educated men appreciated the superiority of initiative and reform to mere imitation as elements of progress The weak adoption of the externals of a foreign civilisation was not indeed given up at once, nor was there a public repudiation of unworthy prejudices, though many scouted them in the privacy of their hearts Still the moral gain was immense in the acceptance of the new principle which was neither wholly retrospective nor based on a supercilious contempt for the past.

This principle may be defined as conservatism tempered by the realised need of keeping an open mind It invaded even the Sanskrit College which had been consecrated as it were to the fatal correctness of an ancient and stereotyped routine Its doors were thrown open to non-Brahmins in the teeth of caste prejudice which had effectually guarded it against such intrusion The needlessly difficult method of learning Sanskrit which seemed to have been designed to perpetuate an artificial monopoly was replaced by a simpler and easier process of acquisition And the arrangements for instruction in English were revised with a view to render it systematic and compulsory These significant reforms were due no doubt, to the foresight of Pandit Iswara Chandra Vidyasagara, and he was severely alone in his effort to introduce them But the thought that the spirit of the age was working with him fortified and encouraged him in the uphill fight in which he was engaged He had early felt the might of the new ideas and they had given him radiant visions of an ever-increasing usefulness for the institution over which he presided[12] Its mission, as conceived by him, was to create pandits who should possess in as full a measure as he himself the austere virtues of their race and the power of adjusting their ancient thought to modern conditions.

There were thus signs on every side of a genuine renascence in which the intellectual elite ceased to be under the spell of irrational doctrines whether new or old and sought the milder but more rational stimulus of reasonable evidence and attainable ideals It was the right time for giving them the benefit of a many sided education in every branch of which the light of truth and not the false glare of fashion or prejudice should be the guide And indeed certain measures were taken by Government which whatever their merits might have been were obviously prompted by the conviction that the occasion had arrived for adjusting the system of instruction to the varied needs of the people The curriculum of the Madrassah was revised with a view to impart to students in the lower forms a knowledge of English and Persian that might enable them to compete for the junior scholarship examination in half a dozen years[13] Beyond this stage they were required to choose between higher English education which had to be sought elsewhere and specialisation in Arabic learning for which there was adequate provision in the Madrassah. It was resolved also to establish a new general college for advanced studies in English in literature, science medicine law and engineering and to merge the Hindu College in it with the concurrence of the patrons This ambitious scheme came, indeed in course of time to be considerably curtailed owing to the decision of Government to maintain separate institutions for professional training But it has a certain interest in so far as it indicates what the authorities considered in the middle of the nineteenth century to be a comprehensive scheme of education for Bengali youths The time will come observed Lord Dalhousie in defining it when the Presidency College having elevated itself by its reputation and being enriched by endowments and scholarhips will extend its sphere of attraction far beyond the local limits which it is now designed to serve and when strengthened by the most distinguished scholars from other cities and united with the Medical College in all its various departments and with other Professorships of practical science and art whose establishment cannot long be postponed it will expand itself into something approaching to the dignity and proportions of an Indian University."

The need of such an expansion came to be felt even outside the limits of the country And this feeling gained in definiteness as a result of the Parliamentary enquiry into educational conditions on the occasion of the renewal of the Company's charter in 1853 A number of distinguished Indian administrators were examined and they gave it as their considered opinion that an attempt should be made at once to acclimatize in India the entire educational system of England, that the lakh of rupees which had formed the annual allotment was quite inadequate for such a purpose and that, therefore, a liberal appropriation from the revenues of the country should be allowed to fulfil it[14] Prominence was also given and that for the first time to the claims of elementary education for the masses on the ground that "popular knowledge was a safer thing to deal with than popular ignorance" And it was unhesitatingly declared that the success of the British administration depended more on a satisfactory solution of the educational problem than on anything else.

The time appeared, therefore, to be ripe for the initiation of a more important experiment than the Presidency College, and so the scheme of a university which had been rejected as premature nine years ago was now taken up and elaborated by the authorities in England As presented in the despatches of 1854 and 1859, it exhibited a definiteness of outline and a copiousness of detail that must have been the result of an extensive survey of existing conditions and of some insight into the requirements of the future[15] But the narrow and unsound view of education to which the Directors had consistently adhered, reappeared in these remarkable documents, though modified in some measure by important considerations of its general utility The diffusion of knowledge was to be encouraged, according to them, because besides benefiting the community in a variety of ways, it would provide an ample field for the selection of capable and honest public servants and stimulate the manufacturing industry of England by fostering a taste for foreign commodities and increasing the output of raw materials[16] They revealed also a lack of appreciation of the vital importance of oriental learning, which was characterised once more as useless knowledge in contrast with the useful knowledge of the West The special institutions for cultivating it were to be tolerated indeed but only because it had a certain value for philological historical and antiquarian purposes Its capacity for linking spiritually the educated Indian with the society of which he was a member and with the traditions which formed his asset if also his encumbrance in certain respects was not even hinted at Thus while education was rightly characterised in these despatches as a powerful lever for raising the people in the scale of civilisation an important side of it which consists in the formation of character was almost entirely ignored.

So far there was a confirmation of the principles on which schools and colleges had been run in Bengal for nearly a quarter of a century But the policy of confining the educational efforts of the State to an influential minority in the hope that knowledge would filter down to the lower classes was set down as narrow and unsatisfactory It had been bequeathed as an official legacy by the defunct Committee of Public Instruction, but its operation had not led to the dissemination of "useful and practical knowledge suited to every station in life among the great mass of the people" The expediency, therefore, of sitting down with folded hands because they made no demand for light was questioned, and a departure was recommended from the system which had enabled only a few to luxuriate on the blessings of a liberal culture and left the rest to starve in ignorance The advantages of higher education were not, indeed, minimised; but it was urged that in some provinces at least, public funds should be drawn on mainly for the benefit of those who could not obtain any education by their unaided efforts Education, they stated, must be the nursery of society and not merely a seed-bed for the special culture of merit It is to be regretted, however, that the financial position of Government led them to enunciate the educational problem as a choice between alternatives, for higher education had not reached that stage anywhere in India at which it could dispense with the watchful care and open-handed liberality of the State Still candour demands the observation that there was every reason for directing the attention of the rulers to the needs of the teeming millions, as the few torches that had been lighted in previous decades had not dispelled in any appreciable degree the surrounding darkness.

Another notable feature of the despatches was the stress that they laid on the cultivation of the vernaculars and the sanguine hopes that they expressed regarding their future 'It is neither our aim nor desire, so ran the despatch of 1854, to substitute the English language for the vernacular dialects of the country These languages and not English have been put by us in the place of Persian in the administration of justice and in the intercourse between the officers of Government and the people It is indispensable, therefore that in any general system of education the study of them should be assiduously attended to' How this was to be done was also made abundantly clear by the statement that they should rank by the side of English as media for the diffusion of European knowledge and be cultivated along with it in the high schools in the country And lastly there was the confident forecast that when their merits and possibilities were rightly appreciated, they would be "gradually enriched by translations of European books and by the original compositions of men whose minds had been imbued with the spirit of European advancement."[17]

It was thought, however, that a knowledge of English must 'always be essential to those natives of India, who aspired to a high order of education.' And in view of the creditable attainments in it of some of them and of the readiness in certain quarters to overcome the difficulties of a foreign language as also of the success of the Medical College and the need of providing suitable training for other learned professions, sanction was accorded to the creation of universities at the principal seats of culture Their establishment, it was hoped, would materially encourage the cultivation of the higher branches of learning and the pursuit of certain important avocations, while the examinations conducted by them would lead affiliated institutions to maintain a fairly high standard of efficiency The necessary organisations were found in the Council of Education at Calcutta and the Board of Education at Bombay to each of which it was proposed that a few members should be added to represent the different systems of education over which they might be called upon to preside But the catholicity of these governing bodies was sought to be guaranteed at the same time by a clause which forbade the inclusion of subjects connected with religious belief within the scope of their examinations.

The despatches left the framing of detailed rules for the examinations to the proposed senates But the following broad principles were laid down for their guidance The standard for ordinary degrees was to be such as might command respect without discouraging honest effort on the part of ordinary students, while that for honours was to be exacting enough to afford a guarantee of the possession of superior ability and knowledge by those who attained it To conduct these examinations was to be an important part, of course, of the work of the contemplated universities But another equally important function was assigned to them in the despatches, *viz.* that of establishing professorships for the delivery of lectures in certain branches of learning Chief among them were law and civil engineering; but the claims of the vernaculars and of the classical languages of India were not ignored On the contrary, a strong plea was put in for the latter on the ground that a knowledge of Sanskrit, 'the root of the vernaculars of the greater part of India' was necessary for successful composition in them, while 'Arabic, through Persian, was one of the component parts of the Urdu language, which extended over so large a part of Hindustan and was capable of considerable development.'

The control of schools and colleges in Bengal had been entrusted so far to the Council of Education. But it was felt that the senate in which the Council was to be absorbed might not prove a suitable agency for exercising that thorough surveillance which was necessary for efficiency and progress Hence the despatches recommended the transfer of this important duty to a department of Government, presided over by an expert educationist and composed of an adequate staff of inspectors But as public revenues would have to be drawn upon in order to meet the cost of this machinery of supervision and of certain improvements in the system of diffusing useful information, Government was also advised to rely largely and increasingly on private enterprise and local resources for the extension of higher education in the country Such a reliance, it was held, would not be detrimental to its cause if a grant-in-aid system similar to that of England was introduced to foster and develop the appreciative spirit in which western knowledge had been received by the people.

Such were the principal recommendations of the despatch of 1854 In breadth of outlook as well as in that practical logic which defines the goal and sets the pace instead of indulging in vague suggestions it surpassed previous minutes and despatches on the subject The policy that it outlined was no doubt an amplification in various respects of old familiar principles rather than a deviation from them But the decision and coherence with which they were expressed prevented the administration from groping in a maze of unconnected recommendations Its observations specially on the utility of the vernaculars as media of instruction and on the need of cultivating them and the parent languages had all ***MISSING

TEXT****** the assumption that higher education could continue to develop on the right lines without an increasing attention and support from the State.

Steps were taken almost immediately after the publication of the despatch to relieve the Council of Education of the superintendence and control of educational institutions, and before a couple of years were out a new department of Government was created with a Director of Public instruction as its head and a number of inspecting officers of different grades to assist him But for many a year very little was done for the diffusion of useful knowledge among the masses, which had been placed in the forefront of the recommendations Bengal had not to wait long, however, for a university The Government of India appointed a committee to work out the details on the lines laid down by the despatch. But an important part of its programme, viz., the foundation of university chairs, was left out of the terms of reference on the ground that the establishment of the Presidency College in Calcutta had rendered them unnecessary for Bengal Thus the scope of the proposed university was cut down at the outset with the object of converting it into an apparatus for testing the value of the education obtained elsewhere And no effort was made at any subsequent stage of the proceedings to restore to it a wider field of useful activity. Hence the bill of incorporation which was passed as Act II of 1857 limited its function to "ascertaining by examination the persons who had acquired proficiency in different branches of literature, science and art, and rewarding them by academical degrees as evidence of their respective attainments."

Public men and administrators were selected to form its senate and syndicate There was also a sprinkling of teachers, but the determining voice did not rest with them So the university was in no sense a corporation for the advancement and diffusion of learning But the limited purpose which it was designed to fulfil had a peculiar importance in the circumstances of the time, and that purpose was better served by a board composed of men not directly connected with the work of teaching For the divergent ideals of the Government and the mission colleges might have prevented the representatives of these institutions from holding out their hands to one another in a spirit of comradeship and helpfulness, while a mutual understanding among them and a common standard were necessary for the progress of higher education in the land.[18] Such a standard could, however, be authoritatively laid down only by a body of administrators whose official duties gave them every opportunity of studying the needs and aspirations of the people And it was able as a matter of fact to work colleges of different types into a general scheme of instruction by determining the nature and degree of proficiency which were to be labelled with the hall-mark of degrees The profession suffered, no doubt, in independence and intiative by such an arrangement, but it prevented education from being haphazard at a critical stage in its history.

The stress however, that was laid on external examinations as the sole tests of ability and attainment and the failure to provide scholarship with opportunities and inducements for critical study and research led to a narrowness of outlook which arrested intellectual activity and growth beyond a certain stage And a pronounced utilitarian bias was given to the education itself by the facilities which then existed for its recipients of obtaining posts under Government as the reward of their labours The university came, therefore to be looked upon as the gateway to a narrow world of official responsibilities and privileges, especially as there was very little in its activity to foster the conviction that it might lead its alumni through the threshold of life to a fuller and wider view of its meaning and scope Nor was the nature of the education calculated to develop a passion for the intellectual life for while it trained those aptitudes that find their scope in the routine of official work it did not create the special interests which dominate the mind of the scholar and steel it against distractions The predominance of administrators in the ruling bodies of the university was in this respect a defect, for the steps which they took within it and outside gave currency to the opinion that the examinations were valuable mainly because they enabled the State to pick out suitable candidates for the public service In short, everything conspired to encourage narrow and selfish aspirations in the students and to obscure the truth that moral and intellectual virtue might be its own reward It is not strange, therefore, that the desire to shine in the world in the ordinary sense lay at the root of their efforts and that with such an impulse the level of those efforts was not high.

The requirements of the 'services' were kept prominently in view by those who took in hand the organisation of the university because they happened to be high officials of Government An association of scholars would have emphasised the needs of the speculative intellect, while if the work had been entrusted to the leaders of the community, greater attention might have been paid to social ideals and aspirations It appears, therefore, that owing to the circumstances in which the university originated and to the peculiar composition of its governing body, a particular and narrow principle of organisation was ridden too hard to the neglect of other interests Nothing could be more unfortunate as there was very little in the traditions of western learning in the land that could correct the deflection due to such a bias. The university degree became the recognised goal of ambition, not because it testified to a genuine intellectual stamp, but because it furnished the pass-

*****************MISSING PAGE 148*****************

of the new university, and it has been often made, is that it intensified the demand for western knowledge, but failed to stimulate research or to develop a genuine passion for learning But the conclusion which has been sometimes drawn from it about the sterility and superficiality of the Bengali intellect is an unmerited slur on the community and its traditions For those who cultivated the new lore were 'more sinned against than sinning' in this seed-time of modern progress If they were generally content with a 'shallow and fluent omniscience,' it was because such a showy accomplishment answered, and there was no effective demand from any quarter for more substantial qualifications Their detractors found fault with their disinclination to go beyond the surface of subjects, but in doing so forgot to make due allowance for the cramping effect of the educational arrangements which were in no way conducive to intensive study Nor is it true that the great literature to which they were introduced left them entirely spiritless and unimproved. For it quickened their faculties and increased the flexibility of their minds, while on the best its influence was much more striking and profound, as the creative impulse which appeared among them was due in no small measure to the impact of new ideas The modern Bengali language which has become 'the vehicle of as great things as any speech of men' was to a great extent the work of this highly cultured class So also was the literature which grew up rapidly in it and which was remarkable as much for its new way of looking at our old problems as for its earnest effort to comprehend the rhythm and beauty of our ancient life[19] Probably more might have been achieved in this direction, and classical dignity and repose might have been added to the vigour and freshness of the new literature if the culture which gave birth to it had been based on the broad foundation of what was great in our ancient faith and tradition But the achievement such as it was was enough to refute the charge of superficiality and sterility which ignorance or malice delighted in bringing against the Bengali intellect.

Still it remains true that the vast majority of the students looked upon the pursuit of knowledge as a competitive struggle for a limited good which was not enough for all And if the noblest among them went beyond gainful aims they found the master impulse not in the system but in the thoughts and sentiments that they picked up while engaged in what was virtually a contest for place and power The education which they received was in many ways valuable but its ideal was narrow What was sought and made much of was not the light of speculation nor the fire of creative energy but the ability to appropriate within a limited time a certain amount and variety of 'pre-digested knowledge' Probably in other countries as well higher education was no more than a preparation for careers for the majority of the students But their universities provided for the attainment of a high level of culture by a considerable minority, and on the work of this minority did the intellectual life of the communities in a large measure depend. In Bengal, however, the system stopped short of such a consummation and the inevitable consequence of the halting measure was her failure to contribute to the sum total of theoretical knowledge and to give to the scattered forces in the practical field the unity and vigour of life.

It has been said that the creation of the University 'fired the ambition of the literate classes' in Bengal But the ambition was of a low order and had very little in common with the insatiable longing for new truths and for their application to life which had been specially nurtured in the universities of the West Nor was it akin to the passion for thoroughness which had distinguished the votaries of oriental learning even in the most discouraging circumstances It disappeared, therefore, as soon as the examinations were over, leaving behind not the true academic spirit, but a thin veneer of general culture and a stolid sense of superiority But the defect remained long unperceived, because the literate classes among the Hindus were composed mainly of people who had always valued a secular learning as a marketable possession The best traditions of scholarship were not indeed unknown to the land But they were confined to a limited section which was too self centred and too unresponsive to the social passion to be interested in a movement that affected other classes And so their ideal of devotion to study and indifference to objects of transient importance was never seriously taken up by others especially as it was suspected and not without reason that there was a pharisaic spirit lurking in its shadow.

The facts that strike the eye in following the development of education under the new system were the multiplication of high schools and the rapid increase in the number of students in colleges Of the new institutions some owed their existence to the offer of grant in aid by Government but others relied almost entirely for their maintenance on the great and growing demand for secondary education Indigenous enterprise hesitated however for a time to cater for those who aspired to higher studies So the call for them had to be met by Government and the Christian missionaries And Government acted wisely in shouldering the responsibility for the instruction of increasing numbers of undergraduates and starting new institutions for the purpose Such a development was no doubt in violation of the principles laid down by the despatch of 1854 which had contemplated the retirement of Government from the field of higher education But it was nevertheless on the right lines as local effort could not be trusted at this stage to provide adeguate facilities for the training of those who wanted to proceed beyond the secondary stage.

But the departure was no more than a temporary concession to an insistent demand It did not involve a deliberate revision of the programme chalked out in the despatch of 1854 and emphasised by the despatch of the 25th of April, 1864, which advised the Government to look after the wants of those who could not be expected to help themselves and "to gradually induce the richer classes to provide for their own education" Prominence was to be given to the educational needs of the masses, and since the resources of the State were limited, higher education was to be left more and more to its own devices Such was the settled opinion of the rulers, and it received a special value from the decision of Lord Ripon to give to the people a certain measure of self-government For it seemed that the only feasible method of enabling them to realise their new privileges and responsibilities was to give them some measure of education The Government of India appointed, therefore, a commission on the 3rd of February, 1882, to report on the progress which had been already made in it and to suggest measures for the diffusion of knowledge among those to whom circumstances had denied every facility for making an articulate demand for it.

The commission presented a fair and comprehensive survey of the progress of learning under British rule But the terms of reference did not permit it to discuss in detail the relative importance of the two types of education and the shortcomings and possibilities of the University For a sort of finality had been claimed for the design of instruction as sketched in the despatch of 1854 and the scope of enquiry had been limited to the extent of correspondence between this design and the superstructure which had been raised by a generation of administrators Moreover the enquiry had to be undertaken mainly for the purpose of suggesting the best means of relieving Government of a portion at least of its financial responsibility for higher education so that funds might be available for the promotion of education among the masses Thus a discussion of the merits of the accepted scheme of higher education did not fall exactly within its purview Yet two questions of vital importance relating to it were mooted *viz.,* its influence on the morale of the students and its adequacy as a preparation for the life of the scholar and the scientific investigator.

While generously maintaining that those who best knew the educated Indian had the most to urge in his favour the commission was constrained to admit that certain unlovely traits had developed in him with the spread of western learning But in trying to account for these disagreeable concomitants of the new knowledge it did not go far enough when it fastened the blame on his environment which was supposed to be quite out of keeping with the dignity and refinement of his intellectual pursuits. The difference between the learned and the illiterate was not confined to India, nor was it such as to give a decided superiority to the former in every respect. Hence if his self-love degenerated into barren conceit in the atmosphere in which he passed his days, the fault lay with his training which precluded a simple and effective relation of his attainments to the needs and potentialities of the world to which he belonged, while it filled his mind with an extravagant notion of his own worth and ability. He could have little interest in the work and the recreation of the people about him so long as the knowledge which he had acquired after years of arduous toil was not directly and easily applicable to them And yet he was able to carry his head high because his showy accomplishment was a rare possession and had a concrete value in the market for employments.

The pretentious self-assertion of the Indian graduate had its roots in the one-sidedness of his education, and the commission was not right in assuming that it was due to the meanness of his surroundings Nor was it more successful in its quest of adequate causes and convincing explanations when it associated his spirit of irreverence with the conflict between the revelations of modern science and the outworn dogmas which still claimed his attention[20] The apparent contradiction between the shadowy conceptions of religion and the verities of experience is as old as man and quite as ubiquitous as he But it has led elsewhere to occasional reconstruction of the entire basis of thought and belief Such a happy result might well have been expected among the Hindus especially as their eclectic temper and the exalted character of their theology were favourable to a reconciliation of faith and knowledge But the educated among them turned away from religion as from a useless encumbrance in the economy of life it seemed, indeed to some a craziness in the human make up which had to be corrected by a course of mental discipline along prescribed lines The commission was of opinion that they were disgusted with its grosser forms and dissatisfied with the narrow principles of the traditional morality The grosser forms however, were the creation and the delight of uninstructed minds and it is significant that only a few among the educated went beyond them Grandeur and purity were certainly not lacking in the indigenous systems of thought and belief, but the equipment required for their appreciation had been left out of the accepted scheme of training for the majority of our undergraduates They threw away their priceless inheritance because they did not possess the knowledge and reflective spirit which were necessary for appraising it Thus vanity and ignorance circumscribed their outlook, and both of them were the direct consequences of the almost exclusive importance which was attached to an alien culture as enshrined in a foreign tongue.

It is noteworthy that several of the witnesses in the Punjab advocated the inclusion of religious training in the curriculum of the colleges. They proposed that equal facility should be offered in Government institutions to Professors of the prevalent creeds to look after the spiritual needs of their coreligionists "The argument adduced in favour of such a policy was that the minds of the students were so filled with their secular studies that religion dropt out of view and ceased to influence them, and that home influence had been found in practice too weak to counteract the anti-religious, or rather non-religious, influence which exclusive attention to the subjects studied at college was exerting" But the scheme was summarily brushed aside as impracticable in the existing state of Indian society.[21] There were, indeed, serious difficulties in the way of its adoption, but nothing could be easier than an improvement in the standard of proficiency in Sanskrit and Arabic to one or the other of which the Indian student must turn for a discovery of the principles that should determine his relations to his fellow-creatures and his obligations to himself As a result of the bias which had been given to his education he was leaving the university in the majority of instances not with a sense of easy mastery over these languages which might induce him to seek in their literatures for resources of faith and aspiration but with the feeling that they had been prescribed as subjects of study to give to the curriculum an appearance of comprehensiveness and to add to the difficulty of the examinations which he had to pass.

It is possible, however, to magnify the short-comings of the education which our young men received in the colleges Even ethically it was an immense power for good, and the commission was justified in referring to the many virtues which it had implanted and nourished and the eagerness of social feeling which it had called forth Petty class-interests did, indeed, expand into the catholicity of national aspirations under the stress of the new ideas and sentiments which it gave the students[22] But for obvious reasons its influence on their character could not be far-reaching and thorough If moral life consists not in the mere possession of a number of uncoordinated virtues but in the maintenance of a proper and fruitful relation with the environment, then it must be evident that in a community with traditions dating back to the childhood of civilisation, the relating principles could not be found in an alien culture alone. It achieved much in creating a craving for such an adjustment, but it could not possibly supply all the factors needed for the satisfaction of that craving The missing elements might have been found and a more harmonious development might have followed if the second languages' had been duly cultivated But instruction in them was so defective and the test of proficiency was so inadequate as to create the impression in the majority of students that the superficial knowledge which satisfied it was only an added burden to them if not quite a mockery.

The commission deplored that even among the highly educated morality was based to a large extent upon considerations of prudent self-interest rather than upon any higher principles of action And it suggested that a text-book embodying rules of good conduct derived from natural religion should be taught in every college Such a suggestion however ignored the fact that morality when thus inculcated tends to become flat and unprofitable unless the teacher is an extraordinary man capable of investing the dry bones of familiar precepts and maxims with a soul compelling power by the fervour of his imagination and the spiritual grandeur of his character Besides it was based on an imperfect knowledge of the nature and genesis of the moral evil which it sought to cure The Indian graduate was by no means more immoral in the ordinary sense than are graduates in other lands But high resolves that transcend ordinary ambitions and cares were comparatively rare even among the best of them. And they still showed sometimes a disposition to imitate the externals of Western civilisation and to scoff at or disregard the healthy restraints of the traditional morality, which certainly did not beautify their nature These shortcomings, however, were directly traceable to the one-sidedness of their education, which loosened the hold on them of the conventions and decencies of Indian society while it did not or rather could not provide regulating principles of equal authority and usefulness At the same time the circumstance of its being dominated by an external and inadequate test of attainments within certain narrow limits served to obscure the view that growth in mental stature and expansion of outlook were its best and ultimate rewards No systematic effort was made, in fact, at any of its stages to foster and train intellectual curiosity and the capacity for idealism in which the Indian character had never been deficient Thus the responsibility for the unsatisfactory equipment of the Indian graduate was due in no small measure to radical defects in his education, which inspite of its intensely secular character might have achieved better results if it had not been fettered also by a narrow utilitarian outlook and an undue stress on an alien culture.

There was pointed reference in the report of the commission to the fact that "with a few brilliant exceptions no eminent scholars were to be found in the long list of university graduates." And the explanation which it offered of this dearth of research and scholarship was correct so far as it went The education which was imparted was general in all but the final stage and even in that specialisation was not on lines that might lead to independent thought and enquiry.[23] Besides, the students were in the vast majority of instances compelled by poverty to earn their livelihood as soon as they went out into the world, and when once fixed in the routine of professional or official life, they found little leisure or inclination for continuing their studies The commission expressed the opinion that private liberality should come to the assistance of the most promising among them and pointed out that while it had done much for education in other directions, it had exhibited a stolid indifference to the claims of independent investigation But individual initiative was bound to be weak and unfruitful in the matter so long as its advantages were not clearly demonstrated It should have been the prerogative, therefore, of the university to make a beginning by endowing research and creating an atmosphere favourable to it But the university was content with prescribing text-books and taking examinations and holding an annual convocation for conferring degrees and honours.

When one passes from the pious wishes of the commission to definite recommendations of a practical nature, one finds that the most important were those which tried to limit the financial obligation of Government with regard to higher education Government had, indeed, decided already to rely increasingly on local effort for the maintenance of colleges in Bengal and to stimulate private enterprise in this sphere by suitable grants from the public revenue So a full enquiry into the question in all its bearings could not be undertaken, and the commission limited its attention to matters of detail with a view to suggest rules for the effective application of the policy to which the rulers had committed themselves It found that among the colleges there were some which supplied more than a local need and were in other ways so important as to justify their maintenance by the State There were others which, it thought, might be transferred with advantage to local bodies on their undertaking to maintain them permanently and in full efficiency Others however, were being run at a cost that appeared disproportionate to their utility, and these, the commission recommended, should be closed unless local efforts were made to finance them.[24]

The new policy appears at first sight to have been justified by events For in the last quarter of the nineteenth century there was a considerable increase in the number of private colleges, some of which rapidly developed into important and popular institutions[25] But there are reasons for thinking that it was a premature if not a retrograde step. Western education had no great traditions in the land, and under the auspices of the university, even Government colleges had sunk to the low level of coaching institutions. So instead of seeking pecuniary relief by cutting down its expenses on higher education, Government should have augmented its allotment to provide for intellectual activities that were not bounded by the narrow horizon of university examinations As it was, the new ventures had no worthy ideals to work up to, no comprehensive programme of education to be guided by They aimed, therefore, at simply preparing increasing numbers for the tests of the university, and as success in these tests did not depend exclusively or even largely on the excellence of the teaching, competition among them came to be shifted from the quality of the work to the lowness of the fees charged for it.

But whatever might have been the defects of this development it led to a rapid increase in the number of graduates And as their ranks swelled the value of their academic distinctions declined in the market for employments The depreciation was indeed so rapid and marked as to attract early notice even in the highest quarters Sir Courtney Ilbert observed in his convocation address of 1885 that as collegiate education has become more common the value of the symbol which denotes it has proportionately fallen And a few years later Lord Lansdowne expressed the same view more pointedly when he said—I am afraid that we must not disguise from ourselves that if our schools and colleges continue to educate the youth of India at the present rate we are likely to hear even more than we do at present of the complaint that we are turning out every year an increasing number of young men whom we have provided with an intellectual equipment admirable in itself but practically useless to them on account of the small number of openings which the professions afford for gentlemen who have received this kind of education Such an estimate of the spread of higher education was in fact inevitable so long as it was taken to be but a preparation for a career within certain narrow and more or less inelastic limits And there was very little in the scope and nature of that education to justify the view that it was a preparation for life in a higher or a more comprehensive sense.

To the complaint of overproduction, there was soon added another, *viz.*, that of deterioration in the quality of the output.[26] And yet the excess of supply went on increasing while no serious effort was made to remove the defects which gave occasion for adverse criticism Thus the feeling gained ground that the existing university system had almost broken down under the pressure of the additional work imposed on it by the rapid multiplication of colleges and schools And it found authoritative and practical expression at last in a resolution of the Government of India of the 27th of January, 1902, which announced that the Governor-General in Council had decided to appoint a Commission "to enquire into the conditions and prospects of the universities established in British India, to consider and report upon any proposals which had been, or might be, made for improving their constitution and working and to recommend to the Governor General in Council such measures as might tend to elevate the standard of university teaching and to promote the advancement of learning."

The circumstances did indeed, call for a searching enquiry into the constitution and working of the universities, and such an enquiry was undertaken by the commission of 1902 in a practical spirit of reform It examined the type which had eventuated under the stress of peculiar conditions and instead of endeavouring to complicate the pattern by the application of untried principles, suggested measures for underpinning the structure on its old foundations The scheme outlined in the despatch of 1854 was not subjected therefore, to a close scrutiny in the light of the riper experience of more advanced nations, nor was the need definitely recognised of a wider outlook to get rid of the ugly facts and unpleasant symptoms' which the Commission of 1882 had associated with the system On the other hand, it was taken as the standard, and the results obtained by its operation were compared with the optimistic forecast of its authors with a view to recommend minor improvements and modifications Such an empirical point of view had, however, its advantages, as it concentrated attention on what was immediately possible and thus enabled the commission to furnish the logical sequel to the original scheme.

The limits of the present treatise will not permit an examination of the proposals for reorganising the administrative bodies of the university or of those which were calculated to secure an effective control over affiliated institutions But there were other proposals which have to be noticed here because they aimed at modifying the scheme of studies and providing suitable facilities for them in the light of ascertained needs and drawbacks The commission recommended the formation of large and well-arranged reference libraries in universities and colleges on the ground that the habit of independent and intelligent reading could not be formed where they did not exist. It laid stress on the need of improvement in the methods of scientific instruction and in the equipment of laboratories. It found the course in English for the M. A. examination of the Calcutta University too easy and suggested that it should be combined with a course in the vernacular or in a classical language. It recommended, moreover, that the vernaculars should be independent subjects for the M. A. degree and that the examinations in them should be exacting enough to ensure their thorough and scholarly cultivation It went further and proposed that composition in the vernacular should figure in every test of attainments up to the examination for the first degree in arts It denounced also the practice which was unfortunately too common in the schools of relegating to incompetent teachers the task of imparting instruction in it and in English and expressed the opinion that every boy who aspired to a collegiate education should be able to express himself with ease and propriety in these languages At the same time it emphasised the educational value of the classical literatures of India, the cultivation of which, it thought, should prove a mental discipline of no mean order and pave the way for the right appreciation of the indigenous cultures and for the improvement of those dialects which bid fair to develop into media of literary expression.

These proposals were conceived in a spirit of compromise which sought to introduce necessary reforms without necessitating an abrupt transition to new lines of development The entire report was, in fact, inspired by the desire to complete the scheme which had been outlined in 1854 and to adjust it to the difficult conditions which had been created by the multiplication of schools and colleges This rapid growth, it was thought, had obscured the importance of a good broad training as the foundation of university study and added to the difficulty of offering suitable conditions of specialised study to the increasing number of graduates The commission dwelt with evident dissatisfaction on the fact that the majority of educated Indians were deficient in general information and did not possess a proper command of the English language It felt also the need of making systematic arrangements for postgraduate education which had been left till then to the care of affiliated colleges And it realised the desirability of opening out new avenues to useful and attractive employment by providing facilities for thorough instruction in mining and electrical engineering, in the science and art of agriculture and in those subjects which should be studied by young men preparing for a commercial career.[27]

The scheme of reform, as chalked out by the commission, was adopted with certain modifications in an Act to amend the law relating to the universities in

British India It received the assent of the Governor General on the 24th of March, 1904 and came into operation on 1st September of the same year Among other things it empowered the universities to appoint Professors and Lecturers for undertaking post graduate instruction and to equip and maintain laboratories, libraries and museums They were also authorised to determine the conditions of affiliation, to insist on adequate residential accommodation for undergraduates and to improve the curricula as well as the standards of the various examinations There were misgivings in certain quarters that the restraints sought to be imposed on schools and colleges might cause a set-back in the course of education while in others it was assumed that harder conditions would acclimatise sounder views about the requirements of efficient teaching and the factors of a complete education So the measure was warmly debated in the Legislative Council and outside it, and in certain parts of the country there was an outburst of criticism which amounted almost to a popular outcry But Lord Curzon was convinced that a thing of vital importance like education could not be left to the haphazard of casual enterprise and that to place it under the direct control of Government and of the best intellects in the land was the most effective way of freeing it from 'the miserable gyyes and manacles that had stunted the growth of the youths of India, crippled their faculties and tied them down.'

There were many in the newly constituted senate and syndicate of the Calcutta University who shared the Viceroy's optimism and looked forward to an era of progress in which the dominant influence would he with their new educational standards. It did not occur to them that supervision and guidance could not effect much in the way of a satisfactory advance so long as the necessary driving force was not supplied by a general conviction of the propriety or utility of the improvements which they had in view.[28] Or indeed they might not have realised how much there was in the hard realities of Indian life that stood in the way of such a conviction They expected for instance, that teachers and students would recognise at once the importance of a higher proficiency in English than had been usually attained But where was the inducement for a more thorough command of this difficult language? The blankness of the prospect that opened before the majority of our graduates was certainly not favourable to a passion for excellence People who were nothing if not critical might laugh at their slovenly incorrectness and set it down as a sure mark of superficial training But they were not prepared on that account to revise their own estimate of the acquisition as they knew full well that in the weary round of duties of the toil worn drudge there was not much scope for the appreciation of greater elegance and accuracy Their lack of general information was another theme for depreciatory comment But much of what they learnt at school and college had only the remotest relation to their environment and no obvious bearing on their life[29] And no special discernment was required on their part to find out that the only useful purpose which it could serve was to make a show at examinations So they dropt it by the way or retained it in the form of half-understood propositions to disguise their ignorance from others and, if possible, from themselves The case would have been very different if they had been taught something of the world into which they were to fling themselves to sink or swim. But the stuff which they received in place of such knowledge had no life and growth in it for the simple reason that it could not be converted into practical efficiency They felt oppressed by the weight of this unnecessary encumbrance and were naturally disinclined to add to it by a more intensive study of the subjects prescribed for their examinations.

The strength of the educational system lay in the fact that it introduced to the Indian mind the great ideas in Western literature and the principles of physical science But in endeavouring to appropriate these priceless treasures our undergraduates had to overcome the difficulty of a foreign tongue, the obscurity of the setting as well as the unfamiliarity in many instances of the illustrations And if while handicapped in this fashion they failed to undertake a thorough study of idioms and accents with a view to attain faultless accuracy in composition and speech surely their shortcomings should have been excused by critics who had seldom shown an equal facility in acquiring languages other than their own Besides from a cultural point of view the thing of supreme importance was that the new thoughts and sentiments should kindle into living fires in their minds and not that their form of expression in English should be beyond cavil Both form and substance had been mastered indeed by an earlier generation of Indian graduates But they had been sustained in their arduous effort by the encouragement given to them as interpreters of modern culture to their benighted countrymen The situation however had greatly altered since then and it is not strange that Indian students in the closing years of the nineteenth century were unmindful of form and finish while their hearts recoiled at the thought that they might have to drift through existence like leaves blown before the wind.

It has been said that the longing for a degree was never the main cause of the spread of western education in Bengal but that behind this selfish-motive there was always a vague and obscure feeling that the new knowledge might provide the law and impulse required for social regeneration, political unity and economic progress. There was very little, however, in the scheme of this education or in the opportunities that it secured for its recipients which might justify this uncritical faith in its possibilities. The first Indian graduates had postured, indeed, as reformers in various departments of life, and they had reasons for being proud of their responsibilities if not of their achievements But no such proud distinction could be claimed by the thousands of students who had since then left the university with the hall-mark of a degree And if there was sometimes a passing ebullition of a wider interest than a narrow self-regard in the minds of the ordinary graduates, it was immediately set down as sentimental nonsense in the light of the realities of their existence It was obviously not given to them to transform and fashion their environment which they were told was responsible for their weakness and poverty But while any comprehensive effort at reconstruction was clearly beyond their opportunities and powers, there was ample scope in their humble sphere for social service and local patriotism. Here, however, their education was at fault They learnt too little of the life around them, of its material interests and spiritual aspirations, of its difficulties and distinguishing features to be able to work to some purpose among their neighbours.

The equipment with which they left the university appeared therefore inadequate from every point of view It was not a fine capital to start [******* * **] business with on their own account nor was it such as might enable them to hold out their hands in a spirit of comradeship and helpfulness to their ignorant countrymen And yet it was sought as conferring some sort of distinction and furnishing the passport to employment under Government or in the learned professions The distinction was not indeed striking and the prospects were not very bright in the dingy office and in the crowded ranks of teachers and lawyers But economic pressure and the desire of rising in the social scale impelled increasing numbers to qualify for these avocations by devoting long years to the study of subjects which had no obvious bearing on their life They did so because the extreme simplicity of the educational arrangements provided no other outlet for their ambition There were however no illusions in the matter the literary training prescribed and tested by the university was recognised as the orthodox course only because it gave them just a chance of being independent of charity or accident To men whose expectations had thus shrunk to modest dimensions a scheme of educational reform which aimed at a higher standard of proficiency could not be very welcome They did not want more of light unless it could help them to find better food and clothes and lodgings for them selves It was no doubt an erroneous and degrading view of what university education ought to achieve But the true academic spirit had never been properly cultivated, while a number of circumstances had combined to associate a narrow practical object with the theoretical knowledge that formed the stock-in-trade of the educated.

Besides, instead of a variety of educational courses with more or less divergent ideals, there was a uniform mental drill for men who differed widely from one another in their aptitudes and their outlook on life. Hence reforms which might have been beneficial to one set of students were likely to dishearten others as imposing needless restraints in the pursuit of their ends or as ignoring factors of education which had a special significance in their eyes There were among them some who were hardly cut out for the rough and tumble of ordinary life and who wanted to ripen in learned leisure apart from the unsympathetic world of practical affairs. They needed above all a many-sided theoretical training and freedom from the cramping influence of too frequent examinations to prevent their intellectual life from disintegrating into a very limited number of special interests But they were vastly outnumbered by men who regarded education as a competitive struggle of which their after-life was to be an exaggerated continuation. They were naturally solicitous about acquitting themselves at the earliest opportunity, but the motives that prompted them were not far removed from the hard materialism of the jostling crowds in an overgrown modern city. Among them again some looked for quick and conspicuous success in service or profession while others felt or feared that they were venturing beyond their power and yet decided to take their chance at the examinations in preference to the uninviting certainties of a career outside the recognised avenues to employment These formed the bulk of the student community and they required more than anything else a good working knowledge of English and of those subjects which were not altogether unrelated to the kind of service that they might be called upon to render to their employers and to their countrymen So any system of education in which the practical necessities did not take precedence of the intellectual could not be much to their taste They had measured and mapped out their commonplace life and its possibilities and frankly recognised that there was no scope in it for high hopes and important responsibilities They looked askance, therefore at the attempts that were being made to raise the standard of proficiency in theoretical studies.

There was also within this class a growing consciousness of the fact that the public services and the learned professions could not continue to absorb all who were leaving the portals of the university with the necessary passports So many of them would have been glad to learn how to stand on their own feet and to do good and valuable work in the way of industry and commerce for which society might thank and pay them. But the training could not be very attractive unless it bore the orthodox academic stamp, for university education had made its way into the social structure and established there a warrant of precedence which those who cared to get into good society could not afford to ignore Thus a diversity of courses under the auspices of the university could alone suit the needs and potentialities of a community which was still in the rapids of transition. And no educational reform could be thorough or widely popular which did not accept this necessity as the fundamental principle of organisation The reformers hoped to spread abroad by their measures a true conception of the value and uses of knowledge. But they do not seem to have sufficiently stressed the fact that for the ordinary student the only real knowledge was that which he could convert into practical power.

A choice of courses was provided, indeed, at the intermediate stage by the new regulations of the Calcutta University But it was still entirely in the theoretic field and was designed to enable students who aimed at degrees in science to specialise early in scientific subjects. The bifurcation was justified by a reference to the example of the University of London; but probably it was not in accordance with the principles of modern education to allow any class of students to proceed to the highest degrees without an elementary knowledge of physical science.[30] Save for a little mechanics which again was to be an optional subject, no provision was made for instruction in it at the secondary stage, and it was quite possible for Arts students to avoid it altogether in their subsequent academic career Moreover, this possibility became a disconcerting reality in the case of many of them owing to the circumstance that scientific instruction was so costly that few colleges could provide it for their arts as well as science students Another feature of the new scheme was that history could be eschewed even by the former at every stage of their education. Yet it was a study of history and of English literature that had stirred the still waters of oriental self-complacence and led people to realise that excellence consisted not in resting and being but in growing and becoming, in a perpetual advance, that is, in intelligence and power.

The exclusion of the classical languages of India from the list of compulsory subjects for the Intermediate Examination in Arts was also unfortunate. It is difficult to overrate their importance from a cultural point of view for those who aimed at a purely literary training For while history and the gems of English literature wėre valuable as furnishing the impulse to change and movement, equally valuable were Sanskrit and Arabic owing to their conservative influence without which change could not be progress And there was no reason for assuming that the lessons which they could teach might be learnt equally well elsewhere for in the higher realms of literature, language is not merely the dress of thought but serves also to control its physiognomy and organisation The multiplicity of options was, indeed, an advantage and was appreciated as such by the generality of students But it should not have been extended so far as to enable them to eschew subjects which could not be neglected without prejudice to the mental and moral discipline which they needed as Indian students.

Freedom of choice was allowed, of course, as a necessary condition of thoroughness. But it was carried to unwarrantable lengths in certain directions with the result that it defeated the very object which it was expected to attain Such, for example, was the liberty given to Arts students to take up two out of a number of subjects with no other restriction than that only one of them could be a natural science. For it was often exercised in grouping for the purposes of their examination absolutely unrelated subjects like Sanskrit and Political Economy or History and Botany It was, indeed, only natural that inexperienced youths should be guided in their choice not by the desire to secure an organic unity in their studies but by their estimate of the relative difficulty of the different courses But none the less was the frequency of this unsound principle of selection among them a thing to be deplored in so far as it tended to break up their intellectual life into a number of uncoordinated and transitory interests.

While commenting on the defects of the Regulations it would be unfair however not to admit at once that they formed the first comprehensive attempt to define the conditions which should govern the extension of higher education in the land Nor is there much reason for doubting that the lines along which it has proceeded under their operation have led to important results Among these are the remarkable development of post graduate education in the various branches of Arts and Science the interest aroused for the first time in research and the advancement of knowledge the recognition of the legitimate place of the vernacular in education in all its stages and the general acceptance of the principle that the study of natural science cannot be fruitful and thorough unless it is supplemented by experimental work But as already observed many difficult problems arising out of the economic situation were not tackled in these Regulations and their authors seem to have assumed that a healthy moral tone and atmosphere could be created without a direct and powerful appeal to the spiritual instincts and aspirations of the students.[31]

Just at this stage the control of higher education passed into the hands of the late Sir Asutosh Mookerjee He had been for some time the dominant figure in the Senate and the Syndicate, and so all eyes were naturally turned towards him at the commencement of what appeared to be a new phase in the history of the university But the hold which he retained over its affairs for long years and even after he had ceased to be its Vice Chancellor is less easily explained Careless onlookers were inclined to attribute it to the glamour of his splendid academic and professional career and of the high position which he held as a judge of the Calcutta High Court But there were others on the controlling bodies of the university who could boast of similar distinctions and had won them by virtue of talents quite as striking as his Yet his was without doubt the dominant mind there and he was able in no small measure to indoctrinate his colleagues with his views The secret of this remarkable success lay probably in the fact that the cause of higher education was the one commanding interest of his life He had lived in an age of religious social and political experiments and observed how his countrymen had set up new idols then shattered them in petulance and then grovelled again to pick up the broken fragments for fresh attempts at reconstruction The sight must have filled his heart with dismay for it was a spectacle of intolerable futility But it did more as it gave him the conviction that if efficiency was to be the keynote of their efforts the wastes of ignorance on every side must first be reclaimed This was his religion and he devoted all the powers of his extraordinary mind to the type of social service which it indicated Hence he could afford to be firm and hopeful in the centre of a changing world of a world which was strewn with the wrecks of petty political schemes and the mournful vestiges of piecemeal social and religious reforms It was the triumph of a powerful and disciplined imagination over narrow creeds and shibboleths that 'had indeed their day, but soon ceased to be.'

To such a man was virtually entrusted the difficult task of putting in motion the machinery of educational reform which had been provided by the Regulations and of determining the speed at which it should be worked He decided that its operation should be slow so far as improvement in the standard of proficiency and elimination of defective methods of teaching were concerned And such a decision was quite in keeping with his zeal for the spread of education and his estimate of the difficulties that stood in its way But about the fitness of that education for the thousands of students who flocked to the university, there was assuredly room enough for a difference of opinion And since he was responsible in no small measure for the new rules which defined its scope and character, it may very well be asked why he ignored the signs of the times and formulated a scheme which was already out of date in important respects.

Did it not occur to him while standing on the threshold of what appeared to be a new era that a wide variety of more or less specialised courses was needed to offer adequate scope to differences in aptitude of the students and thus to secure a many-sided development of the life of the community? Or was he unmindful of the fact that for the majority of them the only real knowledge was that which they could turn to account after entering the world? Or again could it have escaped his observant eye that not a few were accepting a purely literary training with important mental reservations which robbed it of half its interest and formative influence? These things which are patent to ordinary men today must have been matters of clear vision to him even then And yet the fact remains that he could not achieve much in the direction of providing a variety of courses to meet the legitimate aspirations of the clear sighted among the rising generation and to place new and definite goals before those who were still proceeding along the orthodox lines on the old unthinking assurance that they might be led thus to some desired or desirable end The educational tide was on the turn at the commencement of the present century and a great and comprehensive effort was needed to direct it into healthy and profitable channels But there was little beyond tentative and inadequate attempts to cut new courses for its reception.

The explanation that is readily offered is that the University of Calcutta could not arrange for direct vocational training on an extensive scale without overriding its scope as an institution for the advancement of theoretical knowledge But such an extension of the purview had been recognised in some of the universities of the West as quite in keeping with

*****************MISSING PAGE 189*****************

study for the benefit of those who were prevented by natural inclination or external conditions from entertaining any but utilitarian motives.

A more satisfactory explanation of this serious defect may be found in the circumstances which shaped the educational policy of the time Sir Asutosh Mookerjee's coadjutors were not, indeed, opposed to an enrichment of the pattern, but they were probably not ripe enough for a material alteration of the outline A better knowledge of English, a more thorough acquaintance with certain subjects and a new interest in branches of learning till then neglected, these were the minor improvements to which they had pinned their faith, while others looked askance at every proposal of reform out of an excessive solicitude for the backward student Thus the stupendous task of combining in a single system the training of the speculative intellect and of those powers that find their scope in practical life was clearly outside their narrow horizon And public opinion was not sufficiently explicit about the expediency of such a departure, for while there was discontent with the literary type of education, there was no clear idea of and much less an articulate demand for what should take its place An attempt to give a pronounced vocational tendency to the courses for ordinary students was fraught, therefore, with complications and difficulties of a peculiar kind And Sir Asutosh Mookerjee may be held responsible for the omission only because he had that glorious personality which could impose itself even on a hostile environment and triumph over obstacles that were insurmountable by others.

It is, indeed, unfair to judge him by any ordinary standard of effort and achievement But we must bear in mind that death overtook him in the midst of his labours and that we have only the segment of an unfinished circle from his hands The short-comings of his educational arrangements may be the inevitable defects of a system that remained incomplete, though as having more than a limited objective it stood in obvious need of readjustment and elaboration One hesitates, therefore to regard it as the final embodiment of his deliberate convictions about the scope and nature of undergraduate training But no such doubt or hesitation crosses the mind in estimating his services to the cause of advanced study and research And here it is not enough to say that he powerfully stimulated research, he recreated in this country the spirit that must always underlie it and consecrated it far above any effort of ours to add to or detract from its value by giving currency to the view that the well-being of a people depends as much on the advance of knowledge as on its mere dissemination and that for the individual as well as for the race the discovery of new truths and their application are even more important than the broadcasting of borrowed ideas The Government of India had it is true, expressed the opinion that the promotion of research should be one of the objects of the university, and the Regulations had provided for its encouragement by the award of degrees But pious wishes and even regulations could not have accomplished much without his unremitting personal interest in the advancement of knowledge Research may have to face in future defects of organisation and the stolid indifference of practical men to its claims But these are obstacles which it has successfully overcome in other countries, and if experience is a reliable guide, it will not languish here on account of their presence This was the greatest achievement of Sir Asutosh Mookerjee, as it raised the institution in Calcutta from the low level of an examining board with a coaching establishment by way of a new appendage to the rank of a true university and paved the way for the removal of the prejudice that the Bengali intellect could hunt old trails with facility but lacked the virility required for venturing into the hazy world of independent thought.[32]

The significance of this new departure has been imperfectly appreciated in certain quarters The present craze for research as the critics of Sir Asutosh Mookerjee would designate it, threatens in their opinion to disintegrate the intellectual life of the educated into a congeries of special investigations They point also to the undoubted fact that the results which have been obtained so far are not particularly striking But important discoveries are not made to order, and what is wanted and can be provided for is the presence of the spirit that leads to them Besides, attempts to collate information derived from various sources and to marshal the ideas of others in a new order and for a new purpose, though they are not research of a high order, are often the necessary steps towards it So whatever may be thought of the intrinsic excellence of the output, it cannot be said to disagree flatly with the sanguine expectations of the promoter of this new temper among scholars Nor is there any reason for assuming that it is less desirable than that wise receptivity which dresses itself in a borrowed glory and sets an extravagant value on the mere acquisition of knowledge For even knowledge lives by renewal and rejection of whatever is effete or out of date or out of place Sir Asutosh Mookerjee was proud of our ancient and priceless heritage, but he knew also how to prize the spirit of ceaseless enquiry that dominated the centres of culture in the West And so he was no mere champion of traditionalism or even of scholarship, but wanted that the best among his countrymen should be able to offer the old and the new learning in a happy and fruitful union Such an ambition is to be judged, of course, not by its immediate results but by its far-reaching consequences But in the meantime we must not grudge the price that is being paid for the experiment which it has dictated, for it is an experiment with a view to provide better for the morrow of the race than the earlier educational system had done A cool, calculating spirit may be ruinous in a matter like this; for as in nature so even in the highest departments of human endeavour, all excellence depends on apparent waste, while careful precautions against it can only lead to mediocrity.

It may be doubted, however, if those who engage at present in research are always properly equipped for it by previous training. One feels that its foundation should be broad enough to comprise a wide variety of related subjects in order that the light of other knowledge may be brought to bear on the special study and the special interest may be viewed in its true proportions But here we encounter once more the weakness underlying the delusive assumption of the sufficiency of a uniform standard of attainments for students who differ widely from one another in tastes and aspirations and of whom some have a genuine passion for learned pursuits while others acquire with irksome toil and ill-disguised repugnance just so much as would enable them to pass muster It is, indeed, generally supposed that a remedy for this weakness exists in the encouragement which is offered to intensive study by means of examinations for honours But there is all the difference in the world between the outlook and methods of students who want to show off at the ordeals prescribed for them and of those who are anxious to lay in a stock of information that may serve as a basis of life long study and research We arrive thus by another path at the conclusion that differentiated courses are needed for the growth of the true academic spirit as well as of the practical capacity which finds its scope in the ordinary affairs of the world.

The students who join the Arts Colleges may be roughly divided into three classes There are some among them who hope to rise above ordinary desires and purposes and to develop their passion for knowledge into the master-impulse of their lives Others seek in education the mental outfit required for success in trade and industry, while a much larger number want to be properly equipped for the manifold requirements in the way of service of the State and of other important corporations The university may cater of course for all these classes, but it must recognise that purely academic courses cannot suit all of them This important truth, however, has never been sufficiently stressed, and it seems to have been obscured in the early years of the century by the rapid increase in the demand for collegiate education that synchronised with the adoption of the revised scheme of studies Hence the opinion gained ground that all that was necessary was that the University should spray out its light in every direction and for all classes of students without pausing to enquire if that light could warm as well as illumine those who received it But an ominous comment on this view of the educational situation was furnished during the non-co-operation movement in the attitude of the students and of some of the teachers, who stoutly demed the fitness of their training for practical purposes as well as for the development of their inner life in accordance with the best traditions of their race They had, indeed, striven hard to secure the fruits of the tree of Western knowledge; but these had turned to dust and ashes in their hands So they repudiated the idea of encumbering themselves any further with these costly but useless possessions This wholesale rejection of the new light was, of course, irrational and short-lived And a reaction set in earlier than might have been expected owing to its association with a political scheme that was predestined to failure. But though students have since returned in increasing numbers to schools and colleges and the educational machinery is once more in full working order, there is still except among the very best a disconcerting lack of seriousness and stability of purpose, the root cause of which must be sought in the narrowness and mechanical rigidity of the system which claims to shape their future.

Whether we regard the magnitude of the end or the difficulties to be encountered on the way the task at present before the educationist appears to be almost unique in character Pointed reference was made to the difficulties by the Calcutta University Commission of 1917 when it observed that the problem was not merely academic or intellectual but involved also social political and economic issues of far reaching significance And it was equally explicit on the urgency of a satisfactory solution in its remark that steady progress was out of the question for the community so long as the great mass of its intelligent manhood was driven in ever increasing numbers along the same often unfruitful course of study which created expectations that could not be fulfilled and actually unfitted those who pursued it from undertaking many useful occupations.

Notes

1 It was conveniently assumed that learned Hindus would object to the introduction of useful knowledge into the regular course of their instruction But the enquiry of William Adam on the subject showed the absolute baselessness of such an assumption See his *Third Report on the State of Education in Bengal,* 1838, from which the following sentences are taken as embodying the result of his enquiry.

"I put a case in writing before the Pandits of the Sanskrit College and subsequently before such Pandits as I met in South Behar and Tirhoot, a translation of which with their answer and the signatures attached to it I subjoin.

'Case.' To the Learned—'I have observed that the teachers of Hindu learning in this country in their respective schools instruct their pupils in Hindu learning only There are however many English books of learning, in which Arithmetic, Mechanics, Astronomy, Medicine, Ethics, Agriculture and Commerce are treated at length I beg to be informed whether if such works, exclusive of those which relate to religion were prepared in Sanskrit, there is or is not any objection to employing them as text-books in your schools.'—W. Adam.

'Opinion—English books of learning, exclusive of those which are explanators of the religion of the English nation, containing information on Astronomy Ethics Mechanics, etc. and translated into the Sanskrit language are of great use in the conduct of worldly affairs In the same manner as the *Rekha Ganita,* the *Nilakanthya Tajaka* and other works translated into Sanskrit from Arabic astronomical books, were found to be of much use and were employed by former teachers without blame So there is not the least objection on the part of the professors and students of learning of the present day in this country to teach and study books of learning translated from English into the language of the gods—Ram Chandra Vidyavagisa, Sambhu Chandra Vachaspati, Haranath Tarkabhusana, Nimai Chandra Siromani, Hari Prasad Tarkapanchanana, Premchandra Tarkavagisa, Jay Gopal Sarmana, Gangadhara Tarkivagisa (Professors of the Sanskrit College), Kamalakanta Vidyalankara (Private Professor, Calcutta) Harachandra Nyayavagisa Gurucharan Tarkapanchana (Private Professors Burdwan District), Panchanana Siromani, Bancharam Nyayaratna, Girvananath Nyayaratna (Private Professors, Jessore District) Chalrapani Sarmana Chintamani Sarmana, Hari-sahaya Sarmana, Hari Lal Sarmana, Bhawani Din Sarmana (Private Professors South Behar), Parmananda Sarmana, Kalanath Sarmana, Thakur Datta Sarmana (Private Professors, Tirhoot District).

2 C. E. Trevelyan one of the prominent Anglicists characterised the Vaids and Hakims as quacks who unacquainted with anatomy or the simplest principles of chemical action prey on the people and hesitate not to use the most dangerous drugs and poisons See his *Education of the People of India 1838* A fuller knowledge has taught moderation to the champions of the western system of treatment It is unnecessary to quote here the opinions of mere students of the history of medicine and surgery But the verdict of a man like Sir Pardey Lukis late Director General of the Indian Medical Service has a special value because his reputation was based not only on a profound knowledge of the medical science but also on extensive and successful practice under Indian conditions In one of his public lectures he said—I wish to impress upon you most strongly that you should not run away with the idea that everything that is good in the way of medicine is contained within the ringed fence of allopathy or western medicine The longer I remain in India the more convinced I am that many of the empirical methods of treatment adopted by the Vaids and Hakims are of the greatest value and there is no doubt whatever that their ancestors knew ages ago many things which are nowadays being brought forward as new discoveries.

3 W. Adam reported in 1838 that there were 2087 Hindus to 1409 Muhammadans who were learning Persian in the districts of Moorshedabad Birbhum Burdwan South Behar and Tirhoot.

4 See *Petition of the Students of the Government Sanskrit College to the Right Hon'ble Lord George Auckland dated 9th August, 1836,* which is given in the *Educational Records* compiled by H. Sharp.

5 The Educational Policy of the Committee at this time is explained by J. Kerr in his *Review of Public Instruction in the Bengal Presidency from 1835 to 1851* from which the following sentences are taken.

We endeavour in the first place to give a good elementars instruction in the common subjects of Reading, Writing, Arithmetic, Grammar, Geography and the Elements of History At this point the instruction imparted in the provincial schools stops In the colleges, the pupils pass on to higher studies, embracing such subjects as General Literature, Composition Moral Philosophy and the higher branches of Science The General Committee desire rather to give a thorough education in a few central colleges than to multiply means of inferior instruction in a great number of small schools Lord Auckland held this to be the wisest course and advocated it strongly, pointing out to the Educational Committee that the enlargement of schools into colleges, when practicable, deserved 'a decided priority of attention' in all their plans for the improvement and extension of native education."

6 The controversy was bitter and the combatants on either side had much to say in support of their respective positions The attitude of the Government institutions on the subject may be seen from the following observations of J. Kerr Principal of Hooghly College.

It is said that the Bible is not a class book that the word of God is not honoured in the Government Colleges It has been usual to represent them as Nurseries of Infidelity and those engaged in the useful office of instruction as doing the work of Satan The efforts of the educational authorities are systematically directed towards the object of communicating truth in historical philosophical and scientific subjects Are the opponents of the Government system prepared to say that the communication of true know ledge on these subjects has a tendency unfavourable to belief in true religion? Secondly it is stated that we take from the Hindus their own belief and give them nothing in its place It is true that the knowledge we communicate clears the Hindu mind of much that is frivolous and false in their own religious system But it cannot be admitted that it shakes in the least their belief in those principles which form the foundation of all religion such as the existence of God the the greatness and goodness of God the Providence of God the probability of a future state of rewards and punishments. . . . Thirdly, if we look at actual results, it will be found that of the well-educated converts to Christianity, nearly as many have come from the Hindu College and other Government institutions as from the Missionary seminaries The fact is perhaps not so strange as may at first appear In the Missionary institutions, the youths acquire a habit of listening with apparent attention of admitting everything that the teacher requires, of answering questions on religion by rote without any exercise of the understanding In some cases a habit of dissimulation is formed and the youth in whom this habit of dissimulation is formed is most unlikely ever to act with manliness or to do anything that demands a sacrifice such as a conversion to Christianity very often does.

7 There was complaint from various quarters that secular knowledge was not proving an unerring guide See H. C. Tucker's *Memorandum of the Past and Present State of Government Education in the Bengal and Agra Presidencies, 1843,* in which after deploring that Government education was not only destitute of religion but even of morality and that the instruction given was merely intellectual without any bearing on the improvement of the heart and character, he observed that "there was a wide field of morality common to all people, of religious feeling common to all creeds, which the Government was bound to cultivate." The Christian missionary's estimate of the influence of this secular training was given once more a few years later in William Keane's *Present State and Results of Government Public Instruction in India, 1850* "I am satisfied," he observed, "that when the present race of 'Young Bengal' are grown up, you will find the moral and social condition of the country such as to require an 'ecclesiastical law' or something of the kind to enforce religious rights and duties My own experience of the subsequent conduct of those educated at Government colleges has chiefly led me to this opinion Many a time have I been reminded by their course of the Parable in Matthew XII 43–45 At first it would seem as if the evil spirit had gone out of them, through the influence of the college teaching Their condition is clean, as of one walking in 'dry places;' but finding nothing in intellectual philosophy which affords rest to the seeking soul or supplies a principle of sufficient strength to control lust and selfishness, they presently throw off all restraint; and taking to themselves multiplied additional vices of pride, discontent, drunkenness, they defile the flesh, despise dominion, speak evil of dignities and sometimes succeed in casting from them for a time the naturally implanted fear of a Supreme Being."

8 The Resolution was as follows:—

"The Governor-General having taken into his consideration the existing state of education in Bengal, and being of opinion that it is highly desirable to afford it every reasonable encouragement by holding out to those who have taken advantage of the opportunity of instruction afforded to them, a fair prospect of employment in the public service, and thereby not only to reward individual merit, but to enable the State to profit as largely and as early as possible by the result of the measures adopted of late years for the instruction of the people as well by Government as by private individuals and societies, has resolved that in every possible case a preference shall be given in the selection of candidates for public employment to those who have been educated in the institutions thus established, and especially to those who have distinguished themselves therein by a more than ordinary degree of merit and attainment.

"The Governor-General is accordingly pleased to direct that it be an instruction to the Council of Education and to the several local committees and other authorities charged with the duty of superintending public instruction throughout the provinces subject to the Government of Bengal to submit to that Government at an early date and subsequently on the 1st of January in each year returns of students who may be fitted, according to their several degrees of merit and capacity for such of the various public offices as, with reference to their age, abilities and circumstances, they may be deemed qualified to fill.

The Governor-General is further pleased to direct that the Council of Education be requested to receive from the governors or managers of all scholastic establishments other than those supported out of the public funds similar returns of meritorious students and to incorporate them after due and sufficient enquiry with those of Government institutions and also that managers of such establishments be publicly invited to furnish returns of that description periodically to the Council of Education.

The Returns when received will be printed and circulated to the heads of all Government offices both in and out of Calcutta with instructions to omit no opportunity of providing for and advancing the candidates thus presented to their notice and in filling up every situation of whatever grade in their gift to show them an invariable preference over others not possessed of superior qualifications The appointment of all such candidates to situations under the Government will be immediately communicated by the appointing officer to the Council of Education and will by them be brought to the notice of Government and then published in their annual reports It will be the duty of controlling officers with whom rests the confirmation of appointments made by their subordinates to see that a sufficient explanation is afforded in every case in which the selection may not have fallen upon an educated candidate whose name is borne on the printed returns.

With a view still further to promote and encourage the diffusion of knowledge among the humbler classes of the people the Governor-General is also pleased to direct that even in the selection of persons to fill the lowest offices under the Government respect be had to the relative acquirements of the candidates and that in every instance a man who can read and write be preferred to one who cannot.

9 For a fuller account of the scheme see Howell's *Education in British India prior to 1854* and Kerr's *Review of Public Instruction in the Bengal Presidency from 1835 to 1851* It was drawn up by Dr. Mouat Secretary of the Council of Education and submitted to Government in 1845 The object which he had in view was not so much the creation of facilities for higher attainments in the branches of learning that were being already cultivated as the provision of a variety of courses some of which might enable the students to find careers outside the narrow circle of the public services.

10 See *Minute by the Hon'ble Mr. Bethune dated 23-1-1851* from which the following sentence is taken.

"I have never neglected any opportunity of inculcating the importance of inducing the students of our colleges to cultivate also their native language, but I have addressed those exhortations to our English scholars, firmly believing that it is through them only that we can expect to produce any marked improvement in the customs and ways of thinking of the inhabitants of India."

11 Was it due to imperfect assimilation, to the difficulty that Indians are said to experience in mastering the English language and the thoughts that are enshrined in it? The testimony of two competent observers is offered below by way of an answer.

William Keane, Canon of St. Paul's Cathedral, Calcutta, who was deputed by Bethune in 1850 to inspect and report on the Government colleges and schools in Bengal summed up his estimate of the work done in them in the following words.—"To say that in science, history, geography, thorough grammar, general knowledge and English literature, they equalled the run of grammar schools in England, would by no means do justice to my impression Though something must be deducted for the more showy intellect of the Bengali, still there is nothing superficial, but as far as the subjects admit, and the native minds attain, there appears a solid proficiency and good grounding in the instruction given."

In 1852 Principal Woodrow of the Martinere observed that "though under his care there were many whose parents loved to tell them of a home in 'dear old England' he had none who knew the language of that home so correctly, or were so familiar with its stores of learning as these Hindu youths."

It may be thought at this distance of time that a certain degree of excellence was secured at the cost of comprehensiveness But a reference to the curriculum of the Hindu College and other Government institutions and to the list of text books read in them will convince the reader that the course for the highest classes was at least four times as long as that for the B.A. examination in these days It included English Literature History and Political Economy Mathematics Mental and Moral Philosophy Science Logic and Philology and Vernacular Composition and Essay Writing And some of the books which were prescribed would be considered now too stiff or too advanced for undergraduates (For some account of the course in 1848 see Rev. James Long's *Handbook of Bengal Missions*).

12 His hopes however were frustrated by the indifference of the public to the type of education which he sought to impart at the Sanskrit College and by the failure of Government to provide suitable openings for its alumni The Council of Education resolved in 1854 that the students of the Sanskrit College should be so trained that they might form a most efficient class of vernacular teachers as well as a most efficient class of contributors to an enlightened Bengali literature A number of them were accordingly provided with berths in the model vernacular schools established by Lord Hardinge These schools however were shortlived and when they disappeared, the opportunities of earning a livelihood by serving as Pandit necessarily declined At a later time (in 1881) Principal Mahesh Chandra Nyayaratna departed from the educational policy of Vidyasagara by opening title classes, which are even now managed on rigidly orthodox lines and in which bona fide hereditary Pondits of the old type impart to their pupils the traditional interpretations' of Sanskrit work The institution conteins today a tôl or Sanskrit department besides the Anglo-Sanskrit College and School which are connected with the university, and so there is a juxtaposition in it of the two kinds of training instead of a systematic effort to harmonise and combine them.

The Calcutta University Commission of 1917-19 remarked that there could be no question that scholars, steeped in eastern learning counted among them men of unquestioned ability whose usefulness to society might be enhanced if they could be brought into touch with the methods and aims of Western learning, especially in their own departments It did not offer, however any suggestion about the way in which this might be done, because the problem was difficult and the materials at its disposal appeared inadequate for a definitive solution But when one takes account of all that depends on it, one cannot help feeling that a solution ought to be attempted, whatever may be the difficulties in its way.

13 The record of the Madrassah had been one of continued failure up to 1853 when the Council of Education submitted the scheme of reform on which Lord Dalhousie acted An English department had been constituted in fact so far back as 1829 But it had not succeded and the attempt of the Governing Body to render it attractive by increasing the value of the stipends had only filled it with unwilling pupils In 1842 the discipline of the college had been reported once more as loose and unsatisfactory In 1847 Anglo Arabic classes had been started for the exclusive benefit of the Maulvis

but the measure had proved quite inadequate So the Council decided to give up the attempt to combine instruction in Arabic and in English and in consideration of the vast changes in the nature and requirements of the public service and in the temper and habits of the people to provide means for combining a fair knowledge of English with such a degree of education in Muhammadan popular literature (Persian) as might be considered indispensable But this concession to the seeming needs of the hour does not seem to have been more successful than previous experiments "In 1867 the Anglo-Persian department was affiliated to the university as a second-grade college, but the number of students was small and showed a tendency to decline." So the classes were closed at the instance of a committee appointed in 1869 to report on the work of the institution.

The failure of the Madrassah was due not to any lack of interest on the part of the rulers Government had in fact been very liberal towards it and had always endeavoured to place it on a sound footing In its infancy it had been maintained by Warren Hastings for some time at his own expense In 1785 lands yielding Rs. 29,142 had been assigned for its support In 1819 Government had enhanced the annual allotment to Rs. 30,000 and guaranteed it from the public treasury In 1821 a suitable grant had been made for the formation of a respectable library and two years later a larger sum had been voted for the erection of a splendid building in a central position Moreover, the Committee of Management had been busy in noting defects and formulating schemes of reform But every measure had proved abortive owing to the languid interest of the Muhammadan population in knowledge and intellectual progress And matters could not be improved by shifting the emphasis from Arabic to Persian so long as this apathy lasted In any case there could be no justification for the comparative neglect of Arabic within the walls of the Madrassah, which had been designed to be a great centre for its special study The Bengali Muhammadan's interest in Persian was adventitious as is his present interest in Urdu But to Arabic literature he must always turn for inspiration and guidance in the same way as the Bengali Hindu turns or ought to turn to Sanskrit lore (For a fuller account of the Madrassah the reader should consult the *Memoir of Thomas Fisher* Howell's *Education in British India* and the chapters in the *Report of the Calcutta University Commission* dealing with oriental studies).

14 Specially noteworthy in this connection was the evidence of Sir Charles Trevelyan and Halliday The following is an extract from the evidence of the latter:—

"It is not the opinion of those who are interested in education in India that enough money is spent upon it, the reason being of course that there has not been hitherto generally much money to spend The desire is, that as fast as means can be found those means should be applied to the extension of education; it being a matter in the opinion of persons in authority in India of the very last importance, superior perhaps to all others, towards the improvement of our administration.

I should desire to treat the subject liberally and to consider it a very important branch of the Government expenditure and to be ready to lay out upon it at all times as much money as could possibly be afforded."

15 The two despatches are taken together though Act II of 1857 which created the University of Calcutta was the outcome of the earlier of the two which was sent out to the Indian Government in 1854 by Sir Charles Wood (Viscount Halifax) who was then President of the Board of Control The despatch of 1859 of Lord Stanley (afterwards Earl of Derby) ratified the policy outlined in it and probably went a step further in declaring that if Government shall have undertaken the responsibility of placing within the reach of the general population the means of simple elementary instruction those individuals who require more than this may as a general rule be left to exert themselves to procure it with or without the assistance of Government.

16 The trade interests of England had been kept steadily in view at the beginning, and even a missionary like William Ward had not lost sight of them while enumerating the

manifold benefits of a dissemination of knowledge See his *Letter to the Rt. Hon'ble J. C. Villiers on the Education of the Natives of India, dated 6th January, 1820,* from which the following sentence is taken as descriptive of a state of things that education was expected to improve—"At present the Hindus of the middle ranks, not to speak of the lower, want nothing which can be supplied from England,—sixty millions of subjects requiring not one article from the governing country."

The advantage to the public service from a spread of education was realised and stressed at a later time See C. E. Trevelyan's *On the Education of the People of India, 1838,* which describes the administrative change that prepared the way for it in the following words—"The system established by Lord Cornwallis was based upon the principle of doing everything by European agency Europeans are no doubt superior to the natives in some of the most important qualities of administrators, but the public revenue did not admit of the employment of a sufficient number of them The wheels of Government thus soon became clogged More than half of the business of the country remained unperformed and at last it became necessary to abandon a plan which after a fair trial had completely broken down The plan which Lord William Bentinck substituted for this was to transact the public business by native agency under European superintendence.

17 These clauses sound like echoes of the reiterated observations of Bethune on the subject In the course of an address to the students of Krishnagar College he said—The English language can never become familiar to the millions of Bengal The ideas which you gain through English will by your help be gradually diffused by a vernacular literature through the masses of your countrymen But though his view influenced a number of talented and educated Bengalis and Madhusudan Dutt in particular, yet the fact remains that no great attempt was made under the auspices of the Council of Education to improve the standard and method of instruction in the vernacular J. Kerr maintained, indeed that students in colleges 'did not cultivate English to the neglect of their own tongue and that though they could not attain proficiency in that high style which consisted in a superfluous infusion of Sanskrit words, they learnt to speak and write correctly and as far as was needful elegantly the language of business and of daily life among the more intelligent classes of the community.' (See his '*Review of Public Instruction in the Bengal Presidency from 1835 to 1851*) But what their proficiency could have been may be guessed from the statement of one of his best pupils, the late Raj Natam Bose, that Bengali was taught for a time at the Hindu College by a man who had been a cook in an opulent family and had no sort of previous training which might justify his appointment to a lecturership.

18 The divergence was great indeed as may be seen from the following statements of two leading ministers of the Christian religion in Calcutta "The Government schools," wrote Dr Duff restrict pupils to secular English literature and science while the others (Missionary colleges) superadd a large portion of purely Christian literature and the latter is by far the most comprehensive course including many subjects which constitute the most massive and important portions of genuine English literature The Government schools cannot be conducted on other principles than those on which they now stand, and hence all Government direct interference with education should be withdrawn and the funds devoted to its encouragement, distributed among 'private institutions.' " The attitude of William Keane was even more definite on this question, as will appear from the following extract from his letter to Bethune dated 12-6-1850.

"I would express my deliberate opinion that learning without religion is an unmixed evil The tree of knowledge without the tree of life can only tend to sin and misery The living branches of Christian truth have intertwined themselves amid the dictates of wisdom, the researches of reason and the discoveries of science, so that it is impossible very seriously to separate them, and I think it by far the greatest blot on the Government system, that in a few instances the sacrilegious attempt has been made (see Richardson's Selections and other standard books at the Government schools and colleges in Bengal and Bombay) I think it becomes every Christian man to denounce a system which professes to teach English sciences, ethics and history without subverting Hinduism or teaching Christianity I would be the last to wish for, way I would *Illegible Text* the favour on the *Illegible Text* of the State being used to enforce Christianity But I also humbly protest against the immense influence of our Christian Government being pledged to a system, professing to educate the human mind and yet avowedly withholding from the ignorant the only wisdom worthy of the name—true religion."

19 The spade work was done indeed by Sanskrit scholars like Pandit Ishwar Chandra Vidyasagara Madan Mohan Tarkalankar and Dwarka Nath Vidyabhusana But the rich crop which followed we owe to Michael Madhusudan Dutt Bankim Chandra Chatterjee Dinabandhu Mittra Hem Chandra Banerjee and Nabin Chandra Sen all of whom had mastered English literature and fully profited by it.

20 Sir H. S. Maine made much of this conflict when he observed in a convocation address that happily for the human race some fragment of physical speculat on had been built into every false religious and ethical system that here was its weak point for here it was that the study of physical science formed the inevitable breach which led to the overthrow of the whole fabric He had in mind the Hindu cosmogony as given in the *Puranas* and other works But he might have paused to reflect that other religions continue to flourish inspite of the onslaughts of science for the simple reason that the vulnerable points do not constitute the citadel.

21 The question of religious education is once more coming to the front Sir Valentine Chirol has made out a very strong case in favour of teaching the principles of the Hindu religion to Hindu students in his admirable book *Indian Unrest* The late Sir Gooroodass Banerjee considered that it might be beneficial if it was introduced with proper safeguards in our schools and colleges But he took care to observe that no salutary effect could be expected from education in dogmas and in the observance of a few forms and he was fully alive to the difficulties in the way of introducing religious training of the right type These difficulties again are emphasized and probably over emphasized by Mr. H. R. James when he observes that in India there are many and various cults and that there is at all events the danger of reviving religious cults in favour of evil morals rather than good. The subject deserves a separate treatment on account of its importance and so can not be discussed here in all its details But the reader is advised to consult Sir Valentine Chirol's *Indian Unrest* and *India Old and New,* Sir Gooroodas Banerjee's *Education Problem in India* H. R. James's *Education and Statesmanship in India* and Prarnatha Nath Basu's *Illusions of New India.*

22 Sir Verney Lovett felicitously describes the change as the triumph of a sense of national unity over the old idea of ordained separation Political conditions have been no doubt a contributory cause of this change, but the prejudices associated with the over-organisation of Hindu society could not have been so easily overcome were it not for the liberalising influence of western education and the circumstance that it was imparted to all classes of men.

23 The course has become less and less comprehensive with the lapse of years and so the facilities for specialisation are much greater today than they were at the outset The subjects for the examination for the first degree were in 1858 Languages (English Sanskrit or Arabic and the Vernacular) History Mathematics Natural History and the Physical Sciences and the Mental and Moral Sciences Any candidate who passed it and was placed in the first division could if he had not lost a year anywhere in his academic career proceed to the Examination for Honours in one or more of the following subjects—Languages History; Mathematics Natural History and Philosophy The

Vernacular ceased to be a compulsory subject after 1870 A and B courses were probably instituted in 1873 but the bifurcation of studies was not sufficiently marked and the number of subjects to be offered continued to be large Later on their number was reduced to three in either case English and Philosophy were made compulsory subjects in the A course and English and Mathematics in the B while the choice of the third subject was allowed from among History including Political Economy Mathematics and the Classical Languages in the former and from among the various Physical Sciences in the latter Honours courses were introduced at the B. A. stage in March 1882 though the result of the development appeared for the first time in the examination in 1885 Thus the kind of specialisation which the commission had in view was provided before the publication of its report Subsequent reform has been in the direction of simplifying the course for the M.A. examination in certain subjects.

24 The recommendations of the commission were only partially adapted The Midnapore College was transferred to the control of the local Municipality and the College at Bethampore to that of the Maharaja of Kasimbazar in 1887 but the Rajshahi and Chittagong Colleges remained Government institutions.

25 In 1884 were founded the Ripon and Jagannath Colleges, in 1886 the Victoria College at Narail, in 1887 the Uttarpara and Bangabasi Colleges in 1888 the Victoria College at Cooch Behar, in 1889 the Braja Mohan College at Barisal, in 1896 the Central College in Calcutta, in 1897 the Krishna Chandra College at Hetampur, in 1898 the Edward College at Pabna, in 1899 the Victoria College at Comilla and the St. Paul's Cathedral Mission College in Calcutta, and in 1901 a branch of the Calcutta City College at Mymensingh.

26 One of the causes of this deterioration was said to be a plentiful lack of competent teachers Another was the undue importance which came to be attached to the University examinations and their requirements and which degraded both teachers and students The late Raj Narain Basu refers with no small measure of indignation to this second cause in his *Autobiography,* and probably no one was better qualified to form an opinion on the subject than he, for he had a first-hand knowledge of the system of instruction that existed before the birth of the University and of the system that came into vogue after it had begun to dominate completely educational standards and ideals.

27 The need of providing a variety of courses to suit the varied needs of the community has been repeatedly stressed, but our educated people have always taken it as a mere counsel of perfection "However large," said the *Despatch of 1854,* the number of appointments under Government may be, the views of the natives of India should be directed to the far wider and more important sphere of usefulness and advantage which a liberal education lays open to them." The terms of reference of the Education Commission of 1882 precluded it from discussing the question in detail But it too expressed the hope that "the habit of looking for employment elsewhere than to Government will help people to form the habit of looking elsewhere than to Government for the means of becoming qualified for such employment for what men feel to possess a natural and intrinsic as distinct from an artificial value they will always make efforts to obtain for themselves and for those whose interests they have at heart." The hope, however, was not realised And then the Indian Universities Commission of 1902 pointed out that "the teaching of the special subjects which ought to be studied by young men preparing for a commercial career had received very little attention in Indian Colleges and schools and that in Europe and America and during the last few years in England in particular, increasing attention had been paid to the training even up to the highest standards of those who sought employment in houses of business." But our schools and colleges still thought that they must not deviate from the beaten track unless the example was set by the University.

28 Among them was Mr. H. R. James, whose forecast has not been justified by events because he attached undue importance to regulations and external improvements See his *Education and Statesmanship in India* from which the following sentences are taken.

"A definite impetus has been given to the improvement of both schools and colleges under the pressure of the new regulations, more money, much more money, is being spent on them There is improvement in buildings, in staff, in equipment Government has voluntarily set the example in its own colleges, but everywhere pressure has been exercised by the Syndicate to induce colleges to raise their staffs in accordance with more exacting views of the requirements of efficient teaching Unless the conditions laid down are conformed with, affiliation is refused, and this applies equally when the college asking affiliation is a Government college."

29 An extreme case will serve to illustrate this statement It is taken from the Right Reverend Henry Whitehead's *Indian Problems in Religion Education and Politics* While commenting on Macaulay's cheap fling at the Hindu poet's conception of the universe the Bishop says A visitor greatly interested in education when he arrived in India two years ago was astonished and amused to find that in the first school he visited Indian boys were being taught the names of English railways And he was more astonished still to find that the managers and teachers of the school saw nothing fanny in it It was all very well for Macaulay to heap scorn on the old indigenous schools of learning for teaching their students about seas of treacle and seas of butter', but after all it is not much improvement to substitute for that The London Chatham & South Eastern." A case similar though not equally bad is the prescription of Greek and Roman History for the Intermediate Examination in Arts. An option surely ought to be allowed for the benefit of ordinary students, but this is probably not done because it will add to the work and therefore to the expense of affiliated colleges.

30 The course at the Intermediate stage had included English, a classical language Mathematics, Physics Chemistry, History and Logic before the Regulations came into force But it had not been absolutely necessary to pass the examination in some of them The framers of the Regulations seem to have thought that instruction must be useless unless it was followed by a searching test, but this was an error, for even the ordinary student had profited by his introduction to Logic and Physical Science.

31 Mr. H. R. James ably defends the present system "The thing to be done," says he, "is so to tram boys that they may grow up to be manly, courageous, law-abiding, with just notions of self-respect and of what is due to others." He admits, however, that "it is by no means easy anywhere to bring this to pass through the daily routine of school and college" and that in India there are hindrances of a very baffling nature Sir Valentine Chirol's attitude on the question is more decided He says that "even if the attempt had been made or were in the future made to instil ethical notions into the minds of the Indian youth, independently of all religious teaching, it could only result in failure." But he too is of the opinion that it is impossible for the State to provide the religious training that will be acceptable to Indian parents The late Sir Gooroo Dass Banerjee thought that "the text-books of students required careful regulation to make them helpful for moral education." (The student will find the question discussed with remarkable freedom and freshness in H. R. James's *Education and Statesmanship in India 1797 to 1910.* Sir Valentine Chirol's *Indian Unrest* and Sir Gooroo Dass Banerjee's *Education Problem in India.*

32 It is not implied that research was unknown in Bengal before the days of Sir Asutosh Mookerjee But the view that scholarship finds its highest vocation in research had its origin in the principles on which he organised the Post Graduate department of the University and in the encouragement which he gave to individual researchers.

3

LOKMANYA TILAK, 'NATIONAL EDUCATION', IN *BAL GANGADHAR TILAK: HIS WRITINGS AND SPEECHES* (MADRAS: GANESH AND CO., 1922, 3RD EDN), 81–88

(Extract from the Speech delivered in 1908, Barsi, (Original in Marathi)):—

I shall speak here this evening on national education. We are not accustomed to this term, hence it needs a little explanation. To be able to read and write alone is no education. These are simply the means of its attainment. That which gives us a knowledge of the experiences of our ancestors is called education. It may, however, be through books or through anything else. Every business needs education and every man has thus to give it to his children. There is no business indeed which does not require education. Our industries have been taken away by other people, but we do not know it. A potter knows how to shape a pot of China-clay but does not know what this clay is made of; hence his industry is lost. Similarly is the necessity of religious education, How can a person be proud of his religion if he is ignorant of it? The want of religious education is one of the causes that have brought the missionary influence all over our country. We did not think of it until very lately, whether we get the right sort of education or not. The tradesmen who are present here this evening send their sons very reluctantly to school and some of them do not send at all; because they do not get their education which they need. Besides their sons educated in the present-day system turn out fashionable. They wish to become clerks. They feel ashamed to sit on the *gaddi* where their forefathers earned the whole of their estate. The reason of this is that the education which they receive is onesided. The Government wanted Engineers, Doctors and clerks. It therefore started such schools which could supply its need. The students therefore who came out of these schools at first were bent upon services. It was the state of things sometime back that after passing three or four classes in school one could easily get on in life, but it has now become absolutely difficult, even to live from hand to mouth. We have therefore become conscious. It has become now almost clear that it is not the fault on our part that even after getting so much education we remain unable to satisfy our bare necessities; but the fault goes direct to the education that we receive. Naturally therefore the question as to how to reform the present system of education stood before us. If the Educational Department had been under our control we could have effected in it any necessary changes immediately. At first we asked the Government to transfer it to our control—the selection of the text-books for schools, for example. We feel now the necessity of such education which will prepare us to be good citizens. His Excellency the Governor of Bombay also admits the necessity of reforms in the present system of education. But he says that the Government is short of funds. I do not think this excuse reasonable, it may be true or otherwise. It is, however, true that the Government cannot think of this matter. The Government cannot give us religious education; and it is well that they are not doing it; because they are not our co-religionists. We are not given such education as may inspire patriotic sentiments amongst us. In America the Proclamation of Independence is taught in V or VI classes. In this way they train their children in politics. Some eighty or ninety years ago the industries of Germany declined on account of the rivalry between England and that country. But the German Government at once started scientific and mechanical education in that country. In this way Germany became so powerful in commerce that she has now become an object of dread to other countries. Properly speaking these things ought to be done by the Government itself. We pay taxes to the Government only that it may look after our welfare. But the Government wants to keep us lame. There is conflict between the commercial interests of England and India. The Government therefore cannot do anything in this matter.

There being no convenient schools in the villages, our villagers cannot train their children. We must therefore begin this work. There has been a good deal of discussion over this matter. And in the end we have come to the conclusion that for proper education national schools must be started on all sides. There are some of our private schools but owing to the fear of losing the grant-in-aid, the necessary education cannot be given there. We must start our own schools for this education. We must begin our work selflessly. Such efforts are being made all over the country. The Gurukul of Hardwar stands on this footing. Berar and Madras have also begun to move in this direction. Our *Maharashtra* is a little backward. A few efforts are being made here also; but they need encouragement from you. Money is greatly needed for this work. I am sure, if you realise the necessity and importance of this subject, you would encourage the organisers generously. So far I have told you about the subject, now I turn to tell you what we shall do in these schools of national education.

Of the many things that we will do there *religious education will first and foremost engage our attention*. Secular education only is not enough to build up character. Religious education is necessary because the study of high principles keeps us away from evil pursuits. Religion reveals to us the form of the Almighty. Says our religion that a man by virtue of his action can become even a god. When we can become gods even by virtue of our action, why may we not become wise and active by means of our action like the Europeans? Some say that religion begets quarrel. But I ask, "Where is it written in religion to pick up quarrels?" If there be any religion in the world which advocates toleration of other religious beliefs and instructs one to stick to one's own religion, it is the religion of the Hindus alone. Hinduism to the Hindus, Islamism to the Musalmans will be taught in these schools, And it will also be taught there to forgive and forget the differences of other religions.

The second thing that we will do, will be to lighten the load of the study of the foreign languages. In spite of a long stay in India no European can speak for a couple of hours fluent Marathi, while our graduates are required as a rule to obtain proficiency in the English language. One who speaks and writes good English is said, in these days, to have been educated. But a mere knowledge of the language is no true education. Such a compulsion for the study of foreign languages does not exist anywhere except in India. We spend twenty or twent-five years for the education which we can easily obtain in seven or eight years if we get it through the medium of our vernaculars. We cannot help learning English; but there is no reason why its study should be made compulsory. Under the Mahomedan rule we were required to learn Persian but we were not compelled to study it. To save unnecessary waste of time we have proposed to give education through our own vernaculars.

Industrial education will be the third factor. In no school this education is given. It will be given in these schools. It is an important thing. During the whole of this century we have not known how a match is prepared. In Sholapur matches are manufactured from straw; and straw is found abundantly in our country. If therefore this industry is taken into our hands the importation of matches will largely decrease in India. It is the same with the sugar industry. We can procure here as good sugarcane as is found in Mauritius. It is seen by scientific experiments that the sugarcane found in the suburbs of Poona can produce as much sugar as is found in the sugarcane of Mauritius. Six crores of rupees are drained out every year from this country only for sugar. Why should this be? Well, can we not get here sugarcane? or the machinery necessary for its manufacture? The reason is that we do not get here the education in this industry. It is not so in Germany. The Department of Industry investigates there as to which industry is decaying, and if perchance there be any, in a decaying state, substantial support at once comes forth from the Government for reviving it. The British Government, too, does the same thing in England. But our Government does not do it here. It may be a mistake or the Government may be doing it knowingly, but it is clear that we must not sit silent if the Government is not doing it. We are intending to start a large mechanical and scientific laboratory for this purpose. Sugar produces *Rab* and from *Rab* is extracted liquor, but the Government does not permit us this extraction; hence we cannot get here cheap sugar. Mauritius imports to this country twenty thousand tons of sugar every year. All this is due to the policy of the Government, but we do not know it. The Government will be obliged to change it if we put pressure upon it. We have come to learn these things not earlier than twenty-five years after leaving the college. Our young men should know them in their prime of life.

Education in politics will be the fourth factor. We are not taught this subject in the Government schools. The student must understand that the Queen's Proclamation is the foundation of our rights. The Government is trying to shut our young men from these things. What has been proved by our revered Grand Old man—Dadabhoy Naoroji, after a ceaseless exertion for over fifty years, should be understood by our students in their youth. Every year some thirty or forty crores of rupees are drained out of India without any return. We have, therefore, fallen to a wretched state of poverty. These things, if understood in the prime of life, canmake such a lasting impression over the hearts of our young men, as it would be impossible in an advanced age. Therefore this education should be given in school. Educated men of the type of Prof. Vijapurkar, have come forth to devote their lives in the cause of this education. The educationists are helping with their learning and experience, and it now remains with the well-to-do to help them with money. It is a matter of common benefit, if the future generation come out good, able to earn their bread and be true citizens. We should have been glad if the Government had done it. If the Government cannot do it, we must do. The Government will not interfere with us and if at all it does so, we should not mind it. As the dawn of the Sun cannot be stopped so it is with this. Our poverty-has not yet reached its zenith. In America such work is done by a single man. But if no one man can venture to do it here, let us do it unitedly, for we are thirty crores of people. A sum of five lacs of rupees goes out every year for liquor alone from Sholapur. Can you not therefore help us in this work? The will is wanted. Let the Government be displeased—we hope the Government will never deter us—we must do our duty. If the Government prohibits us from marriages, do we obey it? The same is the case with education. As men do not give up building houses for fear that rats would dig holes, so we should not give up our work for fear of Government displeasure. If perchance any difficulty arises our young men are to face it. To fear difficulties is to lose manliness. Difficulties do us immense good. They inspire in us courage and prepare us. to bear them manly. A nation cannot progress if it meets no difficulties in the way. We do not get this sort of education for want of self-Government. We should not therefore await the coming of these rights, but we must get up and begin the work.

4

HINDUSTANI TALIMI SANGH, EXTRACTS FROM *BASIC NATIONAL EDUCATION* (WARDHA: HINDUSTANI TALIMI SANGH, 1939), IX–X, 3–5, 14–22, 25–28, 57–70, 75–76, 79–89

(B) The Stages of Nai Talim:

This New Education has been described as "Education for Life". The usually accepted educational procedure is that the educational process begins with the earliest years of childhood and in the case of the majority of children, ends with the primary stage. For a fortunate few, it extends through the secondary, high and university stages. In *Nai Talim,* however, the educational process is approached from a different angle. It seems clear that if this New Education is to be effective, its foundation must go deeper; it must begin not with the children but with the parents and the community. The first stage in the educational programme is therefore adult education, that is the education of the community as a whole, and of every individual member, for a happy, healthy, clean and self-reliant life.

The second stage is that of pre-basic education or the education of children under seven, As soon as the child is independent of the mother and is able to walk to the school, the sphere of the educational process is extended from the home to the school. Pre-basic education, therefore, in the fullest sense, is the education of children under seven for a development of all their faculties, conducted by the school teachers in co-operation with the parents and the community in schools, in the home and in the village.

The programme of pre-basic education includes physical nurture, medical care, personal and community cleanliness and health, self-help, social training, creative activities (both in work and play), speech training, the development of the mathematical sense, nature-study, art and music.

The third stage is the eight years' programme of basic education for boys and girls between the seventh and the fifteenth year. The objectives, programme and detailed syllabuses recommended for this stage of education are the subject matter of this book.

The fourth stage is that of post-basic education, experiments in which are now in progress in Sevagram and Bihar. This is to be conceived as the educational nurture of adolescent youth from the fifteenth to the eighteenth year of life. While basic education may be described as "education for self-sufficiency", post-basic education should be planned as "education *through* self-sufficiency." The educational community which at this stage should be residential, possibly taking the form of a "school-village", should provide opportunity for a great range of productive activities which will both support the community and afford the basis of sound and well-organised knowledge. The post-basic school should lead on naturally either to the responsibilities of adult family life in one or other of the normal productive occupations of humanity, or (in the case of those with strong natural bent and aptitude) to some form of professional training *in* a University.

The fifth or university stage of *Nai Talim* will demand much careful thought in the near future; in order that the principles of education for life and through life may permeate the work of the Universities, and so that these may effectively serve the real needs of mankind, without losing any of the distinctive and valuable university tradition of sound and accurate scholarship or the zest for knowledge for its own sake. The chapter on Rural Universities in the University Commission Report referred to above is a stimulating contribution to practical thought on these lines.

CHAPTER I

The Objectives of Basic Education

The objectives of basic education can be summarised as a two-fold aim, each part of which is integrally bound up with the other.

1. All boys and girls in India should grow up as citizens of a new social order, based on co-operative work as envisaged by *Nai Talim,* and with an understanding of their rights, responsibilities and obligations in such a society.
2. Every individual child should have full opportunity for the balanced and harmonious development of all his faculties, and should acquire the capacity for self-reliance in every aspect of a clean, healthy and cultured life, together with an understanding of the social and moral implications of such a life.

A few brief comments on this statement of objectives may be of help to the teacher in maintaining the true atmosphere and healthy balance of activities in the daily work of the school.

The social aspect of education has been put first in the statement of objectives because of the intimate connection between the practice of education and the social philosophy on which it is based. In *Nai Talim,* there is no room for the merely selfish pursuit of the good of the individual. The development of the individual and of the society in which he moves are the two sides of one coin; the good of the individual is not an end in itself, it is an integral part of the common good.

It follows from this that Basic Education does seek to develop in the individual certain qualities of mind and character which have been recognised in every civilised country as the finest fruits of true culture. These qualities are not included in the standard of attainment laid down in Chapter II, because they cannot be 'taught' directly or measured objectively. They can only be 'caught' from the spirit and atmosphere of the school, and from the personal example of the teachers. Yet no statement of the objectives of *Nai Talim* would be complete without some mention of them, and they are more important to society than any specific attainment however valuable in itself.

If the phrase "a scientific attitude of mind" is rightly understood, it expresses a great deal of the quality of personality which Basic Education should develop. A scientific *attitude* of mind is sometime quite different from the possession of scientific *information.* It means (1) a keen intellectual curiosity to know the 'how' and 'why' of things, (2) patience and detachment to test all phenomena, all ideas and all traditions by the standards of truth, (3) the courage and power to think for oneself, (4) the intellectual and moral honesty to abide by *all* the facts, and to 'cook' no results either in the laboratory or outside.

A truly scientific integrity involves the frank recognition that there are vast areas of life and experience of which our knowledge is limited and partial; it is closely allied to personal humility, to a reverence for Truth beyond our grasp, and therefore to the charity which respects other men's sincerely held religious beliefs whether we share them or not. It connotes mutual forbearance and the desire to understand the other point of view, between Hindus and Christians, Muslims and Sikhs, and also between the man of faith and the agnostic or atheist.

The true scientist's disinterested pursuit of truth is also closely allied to simplicity of life. Such a man understands the urge to get rid of encumbering paraphernalia in order to be free to work for what one most values. He understands a scale of worth, in which honest dealing, trustworthiness and neighborliness hold a higher place than wealth.

It is not suggested that every child who leaves a Basic School at the age of 15 will be consciously imbued with such an ideal. What *is* suggested is that an ideal of this sort is implicit in the philosophy of *Nai Talim,* and that those who accept it for themselves and attempt however imperfectly, to put it into practice, are best fitted to understand and carry out the ultimate objectives of Basic Education.

CHAPTER III

DETAILED SYLLABUS

A. Capacity for Clean and Healthy Living

The importance of training in personal and collective cleanliness, and the reasons for placing it first among the objectives of a good general education, have been, explained in Chapter II.

Practical work comes first and must be carried on right through the school. It is only by regular daily practice that habits of cleanliness can be thoroughly established and a right attitude of mind formed.

Children who have previously attended a pre-basic school or class should already have begun to form correct habits when they enter Grade J, and these must be carried on and developed. If there is no pre-basic foundation, these activities should occupy the chief place in the daily programme for the first two or three years of school life.

It will be noticed that this programme cannot be carried out fully except by co-operation between the school and the homes of the children, and it is of the greatest importance that the teacher should win the support of the parents from the very beginning. Nearly all parents, if properly approached, will be glad to co-operate for the physical well-being of their children.

There are two factors which, if they can be introduced, will greatly facilitate the success of this syllabus of work, and also of the syllabus in Social Training and Citizenship. These are:—

1. *A School Meal:*

Basic schools are normally non-residential schools serving a small area, and the children take their food at home, There are however various possibilities, A "lunch" or "snack" of some kind, calculated to supply the commonest deficiencies of the home diet, may be provided. If the children themselves can prepare it from the produce of their class and school gardens, so much the better. Children may occasionally bring their own food to school and to be trained to eat it cleanly and with good manners. Class and school "feasts" and "picnics" may be arranged on special occasions; the children may plan to supply the raw food materials from their homes and prepare, serve and eat the meal as a community project.

2. *A School or Village Dispensary:*

In places where there is no medical aid of any kind the teachers and children of a basic school can perform a great service by running a simple dispensary open to their neighbours. Where a dispensary or child welfare centre already exists, they may co-operate in the work to the benefit of all concerned. Wherever possible they should be on friendly terms with local doctors and constitute themselves a volunteer squad to render general assistance whenever it is needed.

The practical programme for cleanliness and health may be divided into four sections:—

1. How to keep oneself clean.
2. How to keep one's surroundings clean.
3. How to keep oneself healthy.
4. What to do in illnesses and accidents.

Knowledge of the underlying scientific principles of hygiene, physiology, nutrition etc. may be correlated with the programme as suggested below.

Grades I, II and III (age 6 to 9 years).

In grades I, II and III the syllabus under this head is entirely practical, and information about "why" we should do this or that should be given, in a very simple way, only when the children ask for it.

Section 1. How to keep oneself clean.

This will include training in:—

(a) How to answer calls of nature—the proper time, the proper place, the proper use of water, earth, etc.
(b) How to clean the eyes and ears, hands, feet and nails.
(c) How to clean the nose and mouth, gums and teeth. Materials for cleaning teeth. Gargling, spitting, and cleaning the nose in a proper way.
(d) How to clean the hair and scalp. What to do about lice.
(e) How to bathe—keeping the body and skin clean.
(f) How to wash clothes and arrange them properly.
(g) How to keep bedding clean.
(h) How to eat and drink in a clean way—clean room, utensils and hands; keeping flies away.
(j) How to keep one's personal possessions (utensils, toys etc.) clean and tidy.

Note:—This will involve a gradually increasing familiarity with the cleaning agents locally in use—earth, ash, dal-powder, *imli,* tamarind, soap, etc. The children should learn how to keep these neatly.

Section 2. How to keep one's surroundings clean.

(a) Cleaning of class rooms, verandahs and compound.
(b) Cleaning of almirahs and proper arrangement of books and papers.
(c) Keeping all school equipment clean and tidy—i.e. the tools for all crafts including gardening, sanitation equipment and play things.
(d) Disposing of refuse, waste material and dirty water in a proper way.
(e) Helping to make, store and repair all equipment for cleanliness.

Note:—This programme will not be complete unless the standards of cleanliness insisted on in school are gradually extended to the homes also. The best proof that right attitudes are being acquired is that children should spontaneously take the initiative in cleaning up their home surround-tags with the friendly support of the teacher.

Section 3. How to keep oneself healthy.

(a) Eating: When, how and how much we should eat. Why no rice or *roti* during illness.
(b) Drinking-water: When, how and how much. How to keep the drinking-water clean at home and at school.
(c) Elimination: (See Section 1 a). Why it is necessary for health.
(d) Breathing: How we should breathe; why through the nose and not through the mouth.
(e) Sleeping and resting: When, how and how long. Why we should not sleep in a closed or crowded room, or cover our faces.

(f) Growing: Monthly records of weight should be kept. The children should discuss them freely—why weight should increase.

Section 4. What to do in illnesses or accidents.

In these grades the work should be based on actual occurrences among the children in the class. Cases of fever, cold, indigestion, sore eyes, running nose, skin disease, boils, etc. are sure to occur. Cuts and scratches, burns and blisters etc. will happen during gardening, kitchen work or play. The children should watch and help the teacher as he treats these cases, and should be told very simply how they are caused and how they can be prevented.

The foundations of the all-round programme should be laid in Grade I. In Grade II the children should be able to take a greater share of responsibility for the cleanliness of their persons and their class room. In Grade III their habits and attitudes should be so developed that they can help with the care of younger brothers and sisters, and can carry out the ordinary routine of class room and compound cleanliness without the help of the teacher. Children in Grade III will usually be old enough to take responsibility for the cleanliness of their homes and courtyards, and to share in programmes of collective cleanliness in school and village.

Grade IV (age 9 to 10 years).

Section 1. How to keep oneself clean.

Continue and develop the work of previous grades. The connection between uncleanly habits and the illnesses that occur in the village should be clearly understood.

Section 2. How to keep one's surroundings clean.

The syllabus of the previous grades should be continued, but the children should be trained to plan the work for themselves, and to assess and report on the results.

In addition, special attention should be given to the following:—

(a) How to clean roads and paths.
(b) How to keep wells and tanks clean.
(c) How to clean water-channels and drains, and make a soak-pit.
(d) How to keep the kitchen and eating-place clean.
(e) How to prevent the breeding of mosquitoes and flies.

Children of this grade should help Grades V and VI in the care of latrines and urinals and the making of compost manure.

Section 3. How to keep oneself healthy.

Elementary principles of healthy living:—

(a) Food: What kind of diet do we need? The "Basic Seven"—cereals, dal or nuts (for non-vegetarians meat, fish or eggs), green leafy vegetables, raw fruit, root vegetables, milk or curds, fat or oil. Scientific terms like protein, vitamin etc. should not be introduced at this stage The children should understand their needs in terms of the locally available food-stuffs.

(b) Drinking-water: Provision of clean drinking-water for the class. Sources of water—sources of unclean water—methods for making and keeping it clean.

(c) Fresh pure air: Ventilation of home and school, fresh air during sleep, breathing exercises.
(d) Work (exercise) and rest: Proper times for work, rest and physical exercise. Making a daily programme for healthy living.
(e) Happiness: Mental contentment is necessary for health.

Health Records:—

The children should themselves maintain, individual and class records of height and weight, of illness in the class and their treatment.

(See Section 4).

Section 4. What to do in illnesses and accidents.

(a) A more systematic study of some common illnesses, their causes, treatment and prevention (in connection with illness among the children). These may be: indigestion and constipation; coughs, colds and malarial fever; itches.
(b) Treatment of simple cuts, grazes and cracked feet, insect and scorpion stings.
(c) Use of saline gargle, saline and boric lotion, sulphur, iodine etc.
(d) Very simple dressings and bandages.

Grade V (age 10 to 11 years).

Section 1. How to keep oneself clean.

The work of Grade IV should be continued, with emphasis on personal cleanliness as a social duty.

Section 2. How to keep one's surroundings clean.

In addition to the routine of cleanliness in the class room and at home, Grade V children should undertake the following:—

(a) Organisation of general cleaning-up programmes for the whole school—preliminary survey, planning, distribution of work, selection of equipment, assessment of results, preparation of report.
(b) Responsibility for school latrines and urinals and the disposal of waste and refuse of all kinds. Preparing and maintaining soak-pits at school and at home.
(c) Cleanliness in cattle sheds and in the housing of all domestic animals and birds.
(d) A study of the types of brooms, baskets, dustbins, etc., in common use—collecting materials, making them, placing dustbins in proper places. Responsibility for storing, numbering, distributing and stocktaking of cleaning equipment for the whole school.

Section 3. How to keep oneself healthy.

Children of this grade should begin to understand the scientific basis of physical well-being.

(a) A *general* knowledge of the human body, its parts and their functions. Toning-up the body by exercise.

(b) A *general* knowledge of the types of food needed for the health of bones, blood, skin, eyes, nerves, etc., using (as in grade IV) common names and not scientific terminology.
(c) A *general* knowledge of the characteristics of healthy clothing and housing.
(d) Maintenance and study of *school* health records as well as those for the individual and the class.

Section 4. What to do in illnesses and accidents.

(a) A more systematic study of the common infectious and contagious diseases affecting children, on the occasion of local infection or epidemics—small-pox, chicken-pox, influenza, measles and whooping-cough. Their causes, treatment and prevention.
(b) Treatment of simple burns and scalds, sprains and bruises, boils and sore eyes. The necessary dressings and fomentations.
(c) Use of common disinfectants in connection with the sick-room, sanitation and the prevention of epidemics.
(d) The preparation of simple invalid diets.

Grade VI (age 11 to 12 years).

Sections 1 and 3. How to keep oneself clean and healthy.

(a) The daily practical hygiene programme should be maintained, and each activity of the morning routine, school programme and evening routine should be reviewed to bring out the scientific principles of health and hygiene upon which correct habits of living are based.
(For detailed suggestions see Chapter IV).
(b) A special study of health-giving morning exercises, and of healthy postures in work and rest. Beginnings of sex-hygiene.
(See note below).
(c) Beginnings of a scientific study of food values: Food for energy—calories and their sources, starches, sugar and fats.
Food for building and repairing the body—proteins and their sources—complete and incomplete proteins.
Food for strengthening and regulating the body—minerals (calcium, phosphorus, iron) and their sources.
Food for smooth and healthy functioning—Vitamins A B C D and their sources.

(d) Study of the functions of the human body and how they are performed:
The skeleton and muscular systems.
The digestive and excretory systems.
The respiratory and circulatory systems.
The nervous system.
The reproductive system.
(See note below).

Note:—It is desirable that the subject of sex and the elementary facts of reproduction should be presented to children in a simple, objective but reverent manner *before* the physical and emotional developments of adolescence take place. Questions about the origin of babies are commonly asked by much younger children, and if these are frankly and naturally dealt with as they arise, children of Grade VI age are ready to be given sufficient knowledge and (what is at least equally important) the reverent attitude of mind for clean living during adolescence. No rules can be laid down, for it is imperative that each teacher should approach the subject in the way most natural to him (or her) and most suited to the circumstances of the children. Questions arising from births at home, or from the observation of plants and animals at school and in the village, often make a natural starting-point. Two principles however should be kept in mind:

1. Sexual information should not be given an artificial or morbid interest by being treated as different *in kind* from any other piece of biological knowledge. A matter-of-fact, natural attitude is helpful; the children should take this biological knowledge as much "for granted" as their knowledge of (say) the processes of digestion and excretion.
2. On the other hand, children must not be given the impression that man is *merely* an animal and may behave like one with impunity. The functions of sex make possible the privilege of home and family life; they must be treated with reverence and a sense of responsibility in preparation for one's place in society.

Section 2. How to keep our surroundings clean.

(a) Study of various types of latrines and urinals, their advantages and disadvantages in various soils and seasons.
(b) The preparation of compost manure, scientifically carried out—where and how to dig the compost pit, the correct mixture, the action of bacteria, temperature and moisture, the value of animal and human excreta—the chemical composition of urine and its action as a "starter".
(c) The cleanliness of places of public resort—wells and tanks, open-air meeting places, dharmasalas, places of worship.
(d) Cleaning bushy growths and destroying the breeding-places and haunts of flies, mosquitoes, snakes and scorpions within the village.
(e) Constructing good pathways for the village where they are needed.

B. Capacity for self-reliance in food, clothing and the repair and maintenance of ordinary buildings and tools.

1. Food:

In all schools, whatever the basic craft chosen, the syllabus in Gardening and Agriculture (See Section C, p. 26) should be followed up to Grade V. In schools where a different basic craft is chosen, the pupils of Grades VI to VIII should continue to maintain an all-the-year-round vegetable garden as a subsidiary, activity; arrangements should be made in co-operation with parents for them to observe and assist in agricultural operations in the village and the care of field crops.

Simple cookery, including the care and arrangement of the kitchen, the cleaning of grains, and the serving of the meal, should be practised in Grades IV and V in connection with the syllabus in Cleanliness and Health, In Grade VI special attention should be paid to the proper storage of food articles and to the processes of husking, grinding etc., in relation to the preservation of food values; and in Grade VII the whole syllabus in Health (food values) should be based on actual practice in preparing and serving food by scientific methods. In Grade VIII special attention should be paid to well-planned menus, family food-budgets and household accounts.

2. Clothing:

In all schools, whatever the basic crafts chosen, the syllabus in spinning, weaving and needlework (Section C, p. 40) should be followed up to Grade V. Where this is not the basic craft the school should provide time and facilities for the children of Grades VI to VIII to maintain and improve their skill in the different processes (including weaving). After Grade V children should not need regular classes in spinning, ginning or carding, but half an hour every day should be set apart during school hours for work for cloth self-sufficiency, and pupils should be encouraged to spin and weave outside school hours and to maintain records of the work done at home by themselves and the members of their families.

Besides the regular practice of all the processes of cloth-making as taught up to Grade V, children of Grades VI, VII and VIII should be trained to plan a complete year's programme of work for self-sufficiency in clothing, to prepare the budget and keep all necessary records and accounts. In Grade VI they may concentrate on their individual needs, in Grade VII on those of their families, and in Grade VIII on the cloth self-sufficiency programme of the village as a whole.

An elementary knowledge of the mechanism of the different pieces of apparatus used in the processes, ability to fit them up, carry out simple repairs and keep them in good order should be included in the training.

3. Household Tools and Repairs:

Training in the use and care of common household tools should begin from Grade IV in connection with the syllabus for cleanliness of the environment. In Grade V it may be carried out in connection with the study of healthy housing (p. 20) and in Grade VI with the making and repair of equipment for storing food and the making and repair of fences. Seasonal and other repairs to school and home buildings, protection of structures against rain, whitewashing, oiling, painting, and other methods for preserving woodwork, may be practised in Grades VII and VIII. If possible the school should possess a cycle, which the pupils of Grades VII and, VIII should be trained to ride and care for, and keep ready for immediate use for community business or emergency. (See e.g. First Aid for Grades VII and VIII in Section A pp. 23 and 24).

C. Self-sufficiency through a selected basic craft

Any craft which fulfils the following conditions may be accepted as the basic craft of the school.

1. It must be sufficiently rich and varied in educational possibilities for the necessary knowledge of subject matter, habits and attitudes (particularly in language, general science and mathematics) to be developed with reference to it.

2. It must be of such economic value that the boy or girl who completes the full basic course can if need be earn sufficient for a balanced diet and other minimum necessities by its practice as a vocation.

The crafts of (a) gardening and agriculture (b) spinning and weaving have been found in practice to fulfil these conditions extremely well, and are practicable in some form in every part of India. There is no objection however to the adoption of any other suitable basic craft where local conditions favour its introduction (e.g. carpentry in forest areas).

Out of the total work-hours available for craft-work, two-thirds may be devoted to the basic craft, and the rest to the subsidiary craft or crafts practised in the school.

I. Syllabus in Gardening and Agriculture as a basic craft.

Introduction:

A syllabus in gardening and agriculture cannot, for obvious reasons, be laid down in detail on an all-India basis. The following syllabus is confined to indicating general principles for the guidance of teachers and workers.

Gardening is a compulsory subject in the first five grades of all basic schools. Where it becomes the basic craft for Grades VI—VIII, the pupils who complete the course must have the necessary knowledge and skill to earn their living by agriculture. Children in the last three grades should be physically sufficiently developed and mentally sufficiently responsible to make their school economically self-sufficient by their co-operative efforts.

Where this is the basic craft, the school should possess sufficient wet, dry, and garden lands for balanced cultivation (see below). The extent of acreage will vary from place to place, and must be determined according to locality.

In normal conditions, a child attends school in his own village, and so his home life and activities should also be included in the educational programme. The school should not only permit but encourage him to assist his parents whenever there is pressure of work in the home-farm. Proper records of such work should be maintained by the pupil concerned and assessed by the teacher.

The following types of crops are suggested for balanced cultivation. Local varieties of all these types should be cultivated, subject to natural limitations of soil, climate and irrigation.

1. Vegetables for daily family use; brinjals, bendai, tomato etc.; roots and tubers; legumes; pumpkins and gourds; green leafy vegetables (*sag, keerai*); some spices.
2. As many common local fruits as possible.
3. Cereals—wheat, rice, ragi, maize, jowar and other millets.
4. Pulses in common use.
5. Oilseeds in common use.
6. Some sugar-cane.
7. Cotton sufficient for school needs.
8. Fodder for cattle.
9. Timber and firewood in fences, bunds etc.
10. Flowers along hedges and near living quarters.

E. Citizenship and Social Studies.

1. Fundamental aims:

It is the fundamental aim of basic education, to fit the individual for the responsibilities of citizenship. (See Chapter I). His habits and attitudes are of far more importance to the success of this aim than the extent of his factual information, and it follows that there is no branch of school activity which may not form part of this training. Personal cleanliness and health is not merely a duty to oneself, it is a duty to society. The whole syllabus in cleanliness of the environment, and in the elements of public health and medicine, is an important part of practical training in citizenship. Knowledge of scientific principles and skill in basic crafts are not imparted for the benefit of the individual alone, but are meant to be applied consciously and deliberately, as the relevant syllabuses show, for the benefit of one's family and of local society, especially by the pupils of the higher grades, Even the recreative pursuits, and the appreciation of art and beauty, are essentially social in their nature, and are closely linked with the cultural achievements of mankind. All these are in a sense "social studies". But the sense of social responsibility with regard to them is best learned not so much by formal teaching as by spontaneous imitation of the attitude and example of the teacher. Given teachers whose own sense of social responsibility is keen, the children should have learned by the end of the course what the social and moral ideals of *Nai Talim* are and how their own school activities are related to them.

2. Specific objectives and methods of work:

The objectives are set out under Section 5 of the Standards of Attainment described in Chapter II ("capacity for the responsibility of citizenship;" p. 11). The detailed syllabus indicates the type of work which should be planned to attain this standard. Essentially, it is *the practice and study of human relationships*—how men supply their physical, social and spiritual needs through various economic, governmental and cultural activities, how and why they co-operate or compete with one another, and how the conditions of human life have been determined and modified during history. Human geography and history must therefore be taught as the story of mankind, not as a mere chronicle of physical facts, past events, and the names of cities and kings. The emphasis, both in Indian and world history, should be on the motives that shape events and the great personalities who have influenced the life and thought of mankind. The biographies of saints, thinkers, artists, scientists, and explorers, as well as political leaders and the heroes of great social reforms, should form an important aspect of social studies.

3. *Practical Activities:*

(i) Class and School Assemblies. Training to responsibility, individual and collective, can best be given. through the organisation of a children's assembly and the election of ministers to take responsibility for various tasks. The foundation should be laid from the very beginning. Children of Grades I and II can, with the help of the teacher, take responsibility for such things as:

(a) Daily cleanliness programme.
(b) Neat and orderly arrangement of material for spinning, gardening and games.
(c) Serving meals and cleaning the eating-place.
(d) Seating arrangements for school prayers.
(e) Care of drinking water.
(f) Helping new pupils.
(g) Helping in entertainments and festivals at school.

Each class should be organised in this way as a democratic family community, with the teacher as an elder brother or sister, and should plan the distribution of work and responsibilities according to its own needs. The "family" feeling should secure consideration for weaker members and the equal status of boys and girls. As the children grow older the class assembly should shoulder more and more responsibility, and should be the starting point for study of other self-governing bodies, local and national.

The school assembly should take similar responsibility to matters affecting the school as a whole, in relationships between class and class, and with other schools in the neighbourhood. Its constitution and rules of procedure, the functions of its cabinet of ministers, their tenure of office, the provision for the maintenance of discipline, can be educational materials of the greatest value, The proper conduct of meetings, the discussion of plans, the reception of ministerial reports, the exercise of the vote, the record of proceedings, will all help to form good civic habits of fair play, the patient appraisal and adjustment of differing points of view, and loyalty to majority decisions.

(ii) The school assembly may organise a School Co-operative Store. Just as class and school assemblies will educate in the basic principles of democracy, so a properly run School Co-operative Store can educate them in the basic principles of co-operation. Besides giving useful practice in record keeping and accounting, it can demonstrate the vital need of moral integrity and personal reliability in all forms of public service.

(iii) Newspaper reading and the discussion of current events.

This may be begun in its simplest form in Grade IV and should be continued and developed in all subsequent grades. A map of India and a large map or globe of the world should be kept ready for reference. For the younger children the teacher should select suitable items of news; the older pupils should be trained to read for themselves and to select items for class discussion in consultation with the teacher. Daily readings and weekly discussions will normally be satisfactory.

Newspaper reading should be the starting-point for study of current social, economic, political and cultural problems in India and the world. Discussions must supply the necessary back-ground for understanding day-to-day happenings, and must be varied in interest. Here are a few illustrations of what may be done:—

Social: Prohibition news—why men drink—local conditions—scientific, social and political aspects of the drink problem.

Economic: An international trade pact—background in the countries concerned.

Political: Local or national elections—programmes of different parties, securing fair play.

Cultural: A well-known leader visits a foreign country—study of its culture.

The presentation must be objective, and the essentials of each problem and situation must be given in their simplest form. In Grades VII and VIII special attention should be paid to forces and organisations working to eradicate exploitation and secure international justice and peace. Children should come to regard themselves as world citizens as well as citizens of a particular village, town, state and nation.

(iv) Celebration of festivals may also be planned by the *school* assembly. These may include regional, national and social festivals, representative holidays of the great world religions, commemorations of great men or special undertakings such as an Animal Day, Tree-planting Day or World Peace Day. Much of the material in the programme of studies can be introduced in preparation for these festivals, The children of each grade should contribute to the celebration in a way suitable for their age-level as indicated in the detailed syllabus.

4. Programme of Studies.

Grades I and II. (6—8 years).

The syllabus in these grades is almost entirely practical in its emphasis. It is a training in acceptable social behaviour.

Grades I and II (6—8 years).

I. *Practical training in social behaviour.*

(i) General:

(a) Methods of greeting older people, younger people, and casual visitors and guests.

(b) How to treat younger brothers and sisters at home and younger children at school

(c) How to stand, sit and talk in a meeting, in a crowd.

(d) Not to interrupt when others are speaking.

(e) Not to pass between two people when they are talking to one another.
(f) Not to block the way.
(g) Not to shout when talking.
(h) Not to use bad language,
(i) Asking and answering questions politely.
(j) Waiting for one's turn in speaking.
(k) Making use of the queue system.
(l) Not to take other people's things without asking.

(ii) In eating: If there is provision for a meal in the basic school, all the processes connected with cooking and serving of the food, cleanliness of the place of eating, cooking etc., can be used for giving social training:
(a) Sitting in an orderly and peaceful manner for eating.
(b) Waiting for one's turn.
(c) Taking only as much food as is required.
(d) If there is only a little, sharing it fairly.
(e) Eating nicely.
(f) Cleaning and putting away eating and serving utensils.

(iii) In craft:
(a) Proper use of craft materials and equipment.
(b) Sharing material and equipment with others.
(c) Waiting for one's turn.
(d) Working in groups.
(e) Leaving the class-room clean and replacing the material and equipment in proper order after work.

(iv) In Play:
(a) Fair play. Not to take advantage of another's weakness.
(b) Inviting other children to come and play.

(v) In the Home:
(a) Helping parents.
(b) Looking after younger brothers and sisters.
(c) Helping to keep house and environment clean.
(d) Helping to look after family cattle and poultry.
(e) Helping to look after and guard fields.
(f) Looking after guests.

II. *Observation of local social life:*

Food, clothing, housing, occupations, water-supply, bazaar, post-office, places of worship, fairs, festivals and entertainment. (cf syllabus in General-Science).

III. *Stories of other regions and customs:*

Children who live in a way different from ours—e. g., nomads (desert or steppe), hunters (forest), fishers (coast and island), farmers in other (colder) climates etc.

Grade III. (8—9 years).

Social Training.

The general social training outlined for Grades I and II will be continued to this and higher grades until good habits are formed.

Social Studies.

1. The locality. Other villages within easy reach, their direction and how to get there; the nearest market town. The local bus routes, the destination of railway trains from the local station. Where things in the local bazaar come from. Historical sites, if any, in the immediate-vicinity and stories connected with them.
2. The idea of a map—reproducing the same shape in a smaller size. Very simple idea of scale drawing—diagrams of class-room, school local roads and villages etc.
3. The world—shaped like a ball. The globe, land and water on the globe, position and shape of India. General description of India—mountain, river, plateau, desert and coastal areas (with a relief map if possible). Position of our own village in India.
4. Social organisations. The Post office and how letters are sent all over the world by various means. The village officers and the village *panchayat.* Doctors and medical aid. Care of animals and kindness to animals.
5. Stories. Stories of life in different countries, (continued) and of children long ago (beginnings of history). Stories from the Epics, Puranas, Bible and Quran in connection with the celebration of festivals etc.

Grade IV. (9—10 years).

1. The map and globe. Continued practice in reading maps and simple drawing to scale (correlated with mathematics), Orientation of maps. Colour conventions—meaning of shades of brown, green and blue.
2. Local knowledge. Extend from the immediate vicinity to the District. Its produce, industries, handicrafts (starting from cotton and cloth industry), rivers, roads, railways, centres of pilgrimage, history and historical sites.

   An introduction (correlated with spinning and gardening) to the economic geography of the State and of India.

   Extent of self-sufficiency in food and clothing in the village, district, state and India.

   Elementary knowledge of how district, state and India are governed. Function of the police.
3. Stories from history, planned round local sites of interest and local and national festivals. Emphasize:
   (a) Social and cultural history, beginning from the Cave men and the Stone Age.
   (b) Rulers who made *positive* contributions to Indian life and culture.

(c) Dealings of the Indian people with other countries as traders, explorers, settlers, pilgrims etc., and visits from other countries.

4. The study of current events (see p. 60) will begin in this grade.

Grade V. (10—11 years),

1. The map and globe. Idea of contour and of latitude and longitude, the equator and the tropics. Simple idea of the effect of geography on industry and communications—why cities, towns and villages group up at certain sites and roads follow certain routes.
2. (Closely connected with the above). Simple outline of the economic geography of the world starting from cotton and agriculture and including the main trade routes, present and past.
3. The food, mineral wealth, crafts and industries, population and communications of India. Famine and its prevention. Local self-sufficiency and world resources—mankind as one family.
4. Stories from Indian history continued, building up a simple chronological picture by means of (e. g.) a time-line. Include (also on time-line):
   (a) Major ancient and modern civilisations influencing India (Chinese, Greek, Islamic, Western European etc.).
   (b) The chief religions of India and how they arose here. Some stories of founders, teachers and sacred places, and of saints who worked for brotherhood and charity in religion.

Note: From this grade onwards children should be encouraged to read for themselves and the library should contain as much Interesting and suitable historical and geographical material as possible.

Grades VI, VII and VIII.

During these three grades the subject-matter of study should be so planned as to cover the following:

1. The main outlines of the history of India—social, cultural, religious, political and economic.
   This should include:—
   (a) India's relationship with other countries from early times.
   (b) The chief countries with which India has economic relationships today (beginning from the wares in the local market).
   (c) One's own locality and its relationship with other regions of India and the world.
2. An outline of the story of mankind:
   (a) How man has obtained his physical necessities at different times and places—food, clothing, shelter, tools, amenities.
   (b) How man has satisfied his social, cultural and spiritual needs:
      His social organisations.
      His religious traditions.
      His music, drama and other cultural activities and amusements.

(c) How the human race has been drawn together into one family by the development of trade, communications and travel. The contributions made by the various groups, societies and communities to the welfare of the human family. The part played by science in the development of one world.

(d) An outline of the political and economic geography and the international organisations of the world today.

The syllabus given below shows *one possible* way of dividing the subject-matter between the three grades. It is not by any means the only way; it is not necessarily the best way in every case, and teachers should feel free to re-allocate topics according to circumstances, interest and convenience.

Grade VI. (11—12 years).

A. Man and his environment.

(The work of Grade V and previously acquired information will be reviewed and consolidated to show how man supplies his physical needs in various regions and from various natural resources).

1. Life in forest areas, (a) Tropical forests, in India, Africa, South America and Malaya. (b) Temperate forests in Canada and Russia.
2. Life in deserts: (a) Hot deserts—Rajputana, Arabia, the Sahara. (b) Cold deserts,—the Tundras.
3. Life by the sea. The West Coast of India, the Pacific Islands.
4. Life in river basins. India, Burma, China, Mesopotamia.
5. Life in Grasslands (steppes). South Russia, North and South America, South Africa.
6. Food-crop areas in India and world. Millet areas (*jawar, bazra, ragi* etc.), maize, barley, rice, wheat, and sugarcane areas in India and the world.
7. Fibre for clothing etc. Cotton, wool, silk, flax, hemp and jute areas in India and the world.
8. Coal and iron areas in India and the world.
9. Mineral Oil areas in India and the world.
10. Water-power areas in India and the world.

Note: The part played by scientific inventions and discoveries in agricultural and industrial production and manufacture should be noted.

B. Man and communications.

1. Paths and tracks, rivers, canals and the sea. Roads for wheeled traffic and motors. Railways and air-routes. Discoveries and inventions which help man to find his way.
2. Vehicles used by men through the ages on land, water and air. Science and the speed of travel.
3. Travellers through the ages.
   (a) Merchants: The Arabs, the merchants of Gujarat, Malabar and the Coromandel Coast, the Portuguese, Dutch, French and English.

(b) Religious teachers and pilgrims, Hindu, Buddhist, Christian and Muslim. (Stories of selected examples).

(c) Fighters and adventurers by land and sea. e.g. Alexander, Timurlane, M.d. Ghazni, the pirates of the Arabian Sea, the Spaniards in the New World, Drake).

(d) Observers and explorers, (e. g. Ibn Batuta, Marcopolo, Vasco da Gama, Cook, Livingstone etc.).

4. Inventions for the communication of ideas—languages, signalling, writing, the story of books, the printing press, telegraph, telephones, radio, television.

Note: In connection with the story of books children of this grade may be introduced to great passages in the scriptures of the world religions, through translations in their own language. (See also practical work (iv) the celebration of festivals).

Grade VII. (12—13 years).

A. The Growth of Civilisations.

A study of the development of various types of civilisation with special reference to Indian history. Cultural achievements should be emphasized throughout.

1. Growth of the earliest civilisations in the most favourable environment, the river valleys. Some examples of river civilisations:
   Egyptian in the Nile Valley.
   Babylonian in Mesopotamia.
   Chinese on the Yellow River.

2. Study of Indian river civilisations and the early history of India connected with them.
   Mohenjodaro-Harappa in the Indus basin.
   Aryan civilisation on the Indo-Gangetic plain.
   Dravidian civilisation on the Kaveri.

3. Maritime—Mercantile civilisations.
   The Phoenicians, the Arabs.
   Mercantile communities of Buddhist and mediaeval India, and of Islam.

4. Empires, a synthesis of cultures
   The Persian Empire and Alexander.
   The Roman Empire.
   The Muslim Empire in India.

5. Mercantile—industrial civilisations.
   Mercantile communities of West Europe, their impact on India.
   The "British Period" in Indian history.
   The Industrial Revolution and its consequences in (a) West Europe, (b) Japan, (c) India.
   Industrial imperialism.

6. The future of civilisation. Possible trends.
   The ideal of *Sarvodaya Samskriti*.

B. The contribution of Religion to World Culture.

The great religions of the world and their founders studied in their historical setting, with emphasis on the contribution they have made to the ethical and cultural advancement of the people who adopted them. The study may be closely related to the study of the various civilisations e. g. as follows:

Egyptian civilisation—Moses and the Jews.
Babylonian civilisation—Zarathustra.
Aryan civilisation—the Vedic religion, Gautama the Buddha and Mahavira.
Roman Empire—Jesus the Christ.
The Arabs—Mahommed the Prophet.

Grade VIII. (13—14 years).

Social and Political Organisations.

A study of the social and political institutions of mankind with special reference to India.

Note: Throughout this study, the following mutually related themes will constantly recur if the subject is properly handled:

(a) The tension between centralizing and decentralizing tendencies in society.
(b) The tension between democratic and totalitarian forms of government.
(c) The tension between ideals of liberty and various forms of slavery and exploitation.
(d) The rule of law and the rule of force.

These must of course be treated in the simplest possible way, largely through biographies of those who fought injustice.

1. The most primitive societies, the family, clan and tribe. Patriarchy, matriarchy, and primitive communism.
2. Early kingdoms and republics in India and abroad. Hindu, Chinese and Egyptian kingdoms: the Sakyas, Luchavis, Mallas, and the Greek republics.
3. Early empires, their growth and administration—the Persian, Mauryan, Roman, Gupta and Moghul empires.
4. Feudal society and trade guilds. Examples in Buddhist and mediaeval India and in mediaeval Europe.
5. Nationalism and democracy in the West—the evolution of democratic nation-states in England, the United States, France (the Revolution), China, etc. Influence of democratic ideals on struggles for the abolition of slavery, prison reform, the rights of women etc., and on Indian political development.
6. Capitalist Industrial Society—the struggle for raw materials and markets—industrial imperialism and the exploitation of Asia and Africa. Industrial imperialism and the first world war (1914—1918).
7. Socialism as a world force—the demand for economic justice—experiments in Christian socialism—the Soviet social revolution and industrial socialism.
8. Fascism, communism and the planned "welfare-state". The Second World War (1930—1945) and its aftermath. National and world

government. The power of modern scientific knowledge for the service for the destruction of humanity.

F. Mastery of Language and Number.

I. Use of the mother-tongue or regional language.

(Whichever is the medium of instruction).

Notes: (i) Special methods may be needed during the first two or three years of school life tor the minority of children whose mother-tongue is not the medium of instruction, or is a non-literary dialect of the regional language.

(ii) Language is the essential medium of communication in every activity. Its study is therefore closely correlated with every side of school life.

(iii) The use of language for literature, and the appreciation of literature, are dealt with in Section G.

II. Use of the National Language.

(Where this is not the mother-tongue or regional language).

1. It is recommended that the study of Hindustani as a second language should not be begun normally till Grade VI.
2. The study should be based on any series of *good* text-books written specially for non-Hindustani speaking learners.
3. Pupils of Grades VII and VIII may practise keeping simple school records and writing necessary business letters in Hindustani as well as in the mother-tongue.

It is recommended that the detailed syllabus in Hindustani should be drawn up for each region to suit local conditions.

G. The Creative and Recreative Arts.

This section includes:

I. *Literature.*

II. *Music, Dance and Drama.*

III. *Drawing, Painting and the Decorative Arts.*

IV. *Recreative Games.*

All these are closely inter-related and the production of a good drama—a project which should be undertaken at least once a year—will involve all, or almost all of them, besides giving most valuable training in co-operative team-work.

I. Literature:

The foundations of good taste in literature should be laid in Grades I and II, where all poems and stories selected for reading to the children should be of a good literary standard.

Grades III and IV. (8—10 years).

1. The teacher should read to the children specimens of good literature in the mother-tongue suited to their age and understanding. Good simple poetry, well read or recited, should be included.

2. The children should begin to read for themselves in the class or school library.
3. The choice of items for an entertainment gives training in appreciation.

Grades V and VI. (10—12 years).

1. Beginnings of the study of the literature of the mother-tongue, through suitable representative selections.
2. Free library reading. Stories from the great epics, romances and dramas of world literature should be chosen for the library.

Grades VII and VIII. (12—14 years).

1. A more advanced selection from the best writers in the child's mother-tongue, arranged chronologically and with a *simple presentation* of the history of the literature of the mother-tongue.
2. Selections from the masterpieces of various Indian and world literatures, in the best available translations, including extracts from the scriptures and religious writings of the principal world religions.

II. Music, Dance and Drama:

A. *For Grades I—V.*

Music: The main objective for the teaching of music at this stage is to give the children joy in good music and rhythmic movement and to lay the foundation for the promotion of good taste and appreciation of the cultural heritage of India in music.

Every basic school may not possess a trained music teacher. In that case the headmaster or headmistress should try to make use of local talent in music and invite local singers to the school to give demonstrations and if possible teach simple songs to the children. The songs should however be selected by the headmaster.

Equipment: 'Only simple locally available musical instruments (like the dholak, flute, cymbals, or in South India mridangam, tambura or sruti box) should be provided at the school.

Every training school for teachers should make a careful graded selection of songs suited to children in grades I to V for the use of the teachers in its own linguistic area. The songs should include:

(i) Simple bhajans and religious songs.
(ii) Simple 'dhuns' set to music.*
(iv) Folk songs, including songs relating to the life of nature.
(v) Marching songs and action songs.
(vi) Popular songs.

Children should be taught to sing together with full voice and with clear articulation, keeping time with their hands. Habits of correct posture and voice production should be formed from the very beginning. The following mistakes should be avoided:

(i) Singing through the nose.
(ii) Singing in too high pitch.

Individual singing should be encouraged from Grade III onwards. Formal training in music should however begin only from Grade VI onwards.

Dance and Drama: Group dancing and the performance of simple dramas should form an important part of the educational programme of children in Grades I to V.

Group dancing with simple steps based on the tradition of local folk dancing should be taught. Children should also be encouraged to improvise dancing and musical games of their own. Many old rural games with singing may be adopted as group dancing. Acting of simple dramas should form a regular part of the school programme. The decoration of stage and children should be simple but artistic. A selection of such simple dramas should be prepared at every training school and every teacher should be provided with a copy before leaving. A few subjects are suggested:

(i) Dramas and dances based on agricultural operations in school or village, e.g. sowing and harvesting.
(ii) Incidents from mythology and legend, and from the lives of saints and religious teachers.
(iii) Incidents from history
(iv) Dramas illustrating the life of children in other lands.

B. Hindustani Music for Grades VI, VII and VIII.

Introduction: The syllabus of music for Grades VI, VII and VIII is partly a continuation of the syllabus of Grades I to V and partly an introduction to classical music.

Group staging of religious songs, dhuns, national songs, and folk songs will be continued; at the same time children with a musical gift will begin formal training in classical music. The system recommended is that of Bhatkhande which has been accepted at the Bhatkhande university of Music and most of the universities of North India. Tambura and Tabala should be used as accompaniments to singing and the use of the harmonium should be disallowed.

Grade VI.

1. Knowledge of the twelve notes of Hindustani music.
2. Alankaras in Shuddha notes.
3. Sargam and songs in the following Ragas:—

   (i) Yaman Kalyan. (ii) Bilawal. (iii) Bhupali (iv) Kafi.

4. Tal—Trital.
5. At least two songs each from the following:—Guru Nanak, Kabir.
6. Shabads from Granth Sahib.
7. National songs.
8. Folk songs and popular songs.

Grade VII.

1. Revision of the syllabus prescribed for Grade VI.
2. Sargam and songs in the following Ragas:—
   (i) Bhairavi, (ii) Asavari, (iii) Khamaj, (iv) Des.

3. Tal—Dadara and Kaharwa.
4. Bhajans—at least 2 each from the following saints.: Surdas, Mirabai.
5. Shabads from Granth Sahib.
6. National songs.
7. Folk songs and popular songs.

Grade VIII.

1. Revision of the syllabus prescribed for Grades VI and VII.
2. Sargam, Lakshan geets and songs in the following Ragas:—
   (i) Bhairavi, (ii) Bihag, (iii) Bhimpalasi, (iv) Hamir, (v) Sarang.
3. Talas—Knowledge of Ektal and Jhaptal.
4. Definition of Saptak, Thata, Raga, Alankar, Swara, Shuddha, Komal and Talas.
5. Knowledge of the ten Thatas of Indian music.
6. Bhajans from the following saints in addition to those mentioned in the syllabus of Grades VI and VII.
   (i) Tulsidas, Raidas, Dadu.
   (ii) At least one Bhajan each from the following saints from the other provinces of India:—Tukaram (Maharashtra), Vidyapati (Bihar), Chandidas, Tagore (Bengal), Narasingh Mehta (Gujarat), Thyagaraya (S. India).
7. National songs.
8. Folk songs and popular songs.

N. B. Tests in music will be only practical for classes VI and VII and both theoretical and practical for class VIII.

C. Karnatic Music for Grades VI, VII and VIII.

It is recommended that Basic School in South India should follow the syllabus published by the Government of Madras for the Reorganised Secondary School Course, Forms, I, II and III. For this purpose Grade VI of a Basic School may be regarded as equivalent to Form I. For ready reference the syllabus of the Madras Government is given below. A few songs by famous composers in other parts of India should also be learned, as suggested under Hindustani Music, Grade VIII Section 6 (ii).

Syllabus in Karnatic Music for 'the Reorganised Secondary School Course (Madras) Forms I—III.

In each year the pupils may be taught about 15 to 20 songs and also made familiar with at least ten technical terms, five ragas and four composers so that at the end of the II form, a pupil would have learnt about 50 songs and become familiar with 30 technical terms, 15 ragas and 12 composers. In addition to Abhyasagana (technical course), songs taught in the three forms shall include graded selections from art music, sacred music, opera music and folk music. National songs, marches in South Indian ragas and some ballads shall also be taught. Songs taught shall be in the regional language.

Form I: Sruti svara exercises; Svaravali; Higher and Lower octave svara exercises; Kala pramana svara exercises; Janta svara exercises; Simple songs in Adi and Rupaka talas in sama eduppu.

Form II: Datu svara exercises; practice of the Svaravali and Janta svara exercises in trikalam; Sapta tala Alankaras; The four gitas in Malahari raga. Simple songs with a few sangatis in Adi and Rupaka talas.

Form III: Practice of the Sapta tala alankaras in trikala; six gitas; one svarajati and one Adi tala varna. Easy songs in Chapu tala and kritis with a simple gamakas.

III. Drawing, Painting and Decorative Arts.

Grades I and II. (6—8 years).

Self-expression should be the main object of art teaching at this stage. Children will paint from their daily experience and imagination, and draw pictures connected with their activities and the things refund them. They should be provided with *large* surfaces (paper, blackboard etc.) for their work and free, bold arm-movements should be encouraged. Care should be taken to secure correct posture, a correct way of holding the pencil, and habits of cleanliness and orderliness in handling material and equipment. Slate and pencil, pen and colours, crayon, water-colours may be used.

Colour and form (to be treated as it arises naturally from the children's activities).

Correct names of colours. Colour contrasts, e. g. black and white, red and green, yellow and black. Seeking clolours in nature. Comparison of different forms, e.g. the leaves of mango, peepul, banana. Arranging coloured seeds on the traced outline of leaves. Making pictures on the floor with coloured seeds.

Grade III. (8—9 years).

1. The chief objective should be free self-expression as before. Children will draw freely from their imagination or experience in school life and at home.
2. Illustrations of stories.
3. Blending of colours—red and blue, blue and yellow.
4. Further study of form and colour.
5. Design and decoration—of the class-room or school with flowers, leaves and floor designs (*rangoli, alpona, kolam*).

Grade IV. (9—10 years).

1. Drawing of memory pictures with colours.
2. Colour—different shades of the same colour, e. g. of green in various leaves.
3. Form—study in greater detail.
4. Design and decoration—development of Grade III work.
5. Mounting drawings on a harmonising background.
6. Designing borders with colours.

Grade V. (10—11 years).

1. Continuation of work of previous grades.
2. Beginnings of perspective.
3. Colours—mutual relationships. Warm and cool colours, matching and contrasting colours.
4. Landscape sketches for book covers etc.
5. Illustrations for social studies or general science.
6. Design and decoration for festivals or school celebrations.

Note:—Children at this stage should start *making* their own colours and brushes with locally available material.

Grade VI. (11—12 years).

1. Continuation of the activities of Grade V in original painting, class-room and school decoration, study of perspective etc.
2. Colour—naming shades according to natural and other familiar objects (Sadrishyam), e.g. parrot green, sky blue.
3. Model drawing—fruits, vegetables, flowers, class equipment.
4. Nature study. Study of an animal, a bird and a tree, with pencil, pastel, or chalk on blackboard.
5. Design. Study of basic forms in ornamental art. Collection of traditional and other designs by tracing or copying. Making original textile designs.
6. Decorative crafts. Decorating earthen pots. Papier machi work, embroidery, toy-making, mat and basket making may be encouraged. Local crafts, stitches and designs should be studied.
7. Ideas of proportion and picture composition. Posters, and picture albums for children of lower classes.

Grade VII. (12—13 years).

1. Design. Finding the ornamental form in nature and utilising it for decorative art.
2. Decorative craft continued.
3. Original painting—composition and colour scheme, detection of obvious flaws.
4. Studying and copying of old paintings in pencil and colours, together with a brief outline of the history and main centres of art in India, (A map of these may be made).
5. Posters, wall-paintings and illustrations on village health, social and cultural work.
6. Preparing, illustrating and binding a book on a subject of the pupil's own choice.
7. Elementary anatomy in connection with nature-study work.
8. Black board drawing (The *Rupavali* of Shri Nandalal Bose is recommended as a guide).

Grade VIII. (13—14 years).

1. Sketching from nature in water-colour, pastel and pencil.
2. Plan drawing, elevations, and section drawing.

3. Colour and composition—designing costumes and stage arrangements for school dramas.
4. Design and decoration. Ability to take responsibility for decoration for any festival or function in class, school or village.
5. Further study of art in India.
6. Revision and continuation of work of the previous grades.

Note: Throughout the course, as many different techniques as possible should be introduced, e.g. paper-cutting, stencilling, lino-cut, crayon, pastel, clay-modelling. This may be done in all eight grades according to circumstances.

IV. Recreative Games (and Physical Training):

A large part of what is usually included in Physical Education has already been dealt with in this syllabus under two heads.

1. *Health.* In any well-run Basic School a great deal of physical exercise is obtained through normal life activities, such as sweeping, digging and drawing water. The value of these for the development of the body should be stressed in the health syllabus.
   Formal drills and asans intended to exercise and develop the body, or particular organs, are also noted in the health syllabus.
2. *Dancing* is an admirable exercise and an excellent training in the control and balance of the body. Folk dancing as a recreation should be everywhere encouraged.

In addition, the following points may be noted.

Grades I, II and III. (6—9 years).

Free play activity. Wherever possible some simple equipment for climbing, jumping and skipping should be provided.

Formal exercises. Falling in, walking and running in a line, halting promptly and with balance, right and left turn.

Grades IV—VIII. (6—9 years).

Individual skills and exercises.

Children should be encouraged to practise all local and indigenous physical skills which are suited to their stage of growth. They may also be encouraged to measure and improve their skill in athletics—long and high jump, pole jump, ball throwing, running speed etc.

Team Games.

Indigenous team games, especially those that provide enjoyment without needing any equipment, and which are possible in the poorest village, should be taught and encouraged in the school.

Note

* In South India, simple namavalis, selections from Tevaram, Tiruppugazh, and Divyanama Kirtanas.

5

EXTRACTS FROM *MESSAGES TO INDIAN STUDENTS (AN ANTHOLOGY OF FAMOUS CONVOCATION ADDRESSES)* (ALLAHABAD: STUDENTS' FRIENDS, 1936), 40–80, 91–119, 120–127

[*Convocation Address delivered by Dr. Sir S. Radhakrishnan, Kt., M.A., D. Litt., Vice-chancellor, Andhra University, on November 13, 1934.]

.... In conformity with tradition, let me offer my hearty congratulations to you who have received degress to-day. You have successfully completed the prescribed courses of study and are now looking forward to your work in life for which the University training has been a preparation. Latterly, the lack of adjustment between the needs of life and studies in the University has come in for a good deal of comment and criticism that it is unnecessary for me to draw your attention to it. If I tell you, young men and women, that you will have soft jobs and great careers awaiting you, now that you have acquired University degrees, I will be rousing hopes that are destined to disappointment. Unemployment is the lot of many University men the world over. There is something wrong about a system which turns out men who are not wanted by the society which has paid for their training. It is not the function of Universities to produce an academic proletariat which is fed on idleness and so develops mental flabbiness and neurasthenia. The responsibility for this state of affairs is not merely in the educational system but also in the economic situation. You are not accountable for either. But it is a healthy sign that there is a remarkable agreement among educationists to-day that the system of education requires prastic revision from the foundation to the flagpole. It is out of date and unsuited to modern conditions and involves a colossal waste of intellect and energy.

In all its stages, Primary, Secondary and University, a reorientation is necessary. While any member of the general community is entitled to the minimum of education, at any rate, to the Primary standard if he is to function as a unit in a democratic state, the large numbers who constitute the mainstay of any society, the peasants working on the soil and the skilled workers engaged in industries require to be looked after in the Secondary schools. Secondary education is the weakest link in our system. It is dominated exclusively by the University requirements. It must provide a type of education which is complete in itself, enabling those who have benefited by it to take up a position in life. It must, therefore, be so organised as to give a general cultural standard to the bulk of the population and enable them, at the same time, to face the varied requirements of practical life. It must not be its exclusive aim to prepare candidates for University studies. The value of University education is considerably impaired by the presence in the University of men who are unfit for higher, literary or scientific education. The technical schools should train our youths not merely for urban occupations, because the country is fundamentally rural. Agriculture is the foundation of Indian life and will continue to be so for a long time to come.

To-day, with the low agricultural prices, our farmers who are the producers of wealth in our land, are unable to get enough food for themselves out of the soil they cultivate. In more favourable circumstances, they have a very small surplus to sell. So long as we continue to cultivate our fields with the tools of a past age, the bent stick and the wooden plough, the yield from the soil cannot be increased. If there is to be any improvement, agricultural training suited to our rural conditions is essential. A large number of agricultural schools, small in size and limited in scope, require to be established. Besides, our farmers are generally engaged in some subsidiary industry during the intervals of leisure which field-work involves. In former days, spinning and weaving were the subsidiary industries. Gandhi's attempt to revive them is not a madman's dream. Technical schools where training can be given in industries which can be carried on in small workshops are most urgently needed.

The Universities should be called upon to produce a higher intellectual class, not only willing subordinates but responsible leaders, who will fill important and influential positions in the liberal professions, in the great industries and in public life. They must pay special attention in technological institutes to research in subjects relating to agriculture and industries.

Besides teaching and research, the training of leaders is an essential function of the University. To-day there is no lack of moral energy or disinterestedness, but it is taking unnatural shapes on account of wrong direction. The responsibility of the intellectuals, the natural leaders of thought and life, is immense. The anxious pre-occupation of the statesmen of all countries at the present moment when competing social, economic and political views are in the field, raises questions of fundamental importance. The issues involved are vital to every interest both of the individual and of humanity. Universities which have for their function the conserving and dispensing of the best traditions of human thought and conduct are deeply affected by the great moral issues about the first principles of social organisation, which these questions raise.

Mazzini defined democracy "as the progress of all through all under the leadership of the wisest and the best." A democracy fails if the people are not sufficiently enlightened to be able to select wise and intelligent leaders. The leaders to-day are neither wise nor intelligent. Scepticism and selfishness are their chief characteristics. They are supported by the rapacity of profiteers, the apathy of the masses, the faint-hearted servility of the intellectuals who make themselves the advocates of devastating prejudices which it should be their mission to uproot. Without any clear vision of humanity's goal, our leaders set forth programmes which they value more than the lives of their fellowmen. They will not hesitate to send millions to death to prove themselves in the right. Their own particular purposes should be achieved by any means, however barbarous or inhuman.

We are witness to-day of the terrible and sinister portent that some of the progressive nations of the West whose names are synonymous with advanced civilisation are embarking with cynical deliberation on a course which is in conflict not so much with the high injunctions of the religions they profess, but with the most elementary dictates of natural justice and humanity. In a large part of Europe, democracy which was for long considered the great contribution of Europe to world's political thought is now abandoned. Parliamentary government is killed, the press is muzzled, freedom of thought, of speech and of assembly is forbidden. The ordinary decencies of public life, the conventions which raise human society above a pack of animals, the bonds of personal loyalty and friendship, are being swept away by groups who neither respect laws nor recognise the common obligations of humanity. The zeal of the dictators shrinks at nothing, not even carefully planned and cold-blooded murders of political opponents.

The obvious incompetence of governments to deal in a just and effective way with the problem of economic inequality is the cause of the discontent with democracy and this discontent has carried dictators to power. Unimpeded freedom of trade resulted in the exploitation of man by his fellows. The demand for greater economic equality was resented by the vested interests and class conflicts developed. Regulation of private industry on a large scale was undertaken by the governments but not as rapidly as one would desire. Economic effort was, therefore, put under political direction. Peaceful evolution which is the method of democracy yielded to forcible revolution.

Compulsion thus became the controlling principle of social, economic and political life. If there is a restriction of personal liberty and a denial of opportunities for a full, satisfying and noble life, it only means that economic justice and security ask for their price. The price has been paid in many countries but they are not nearer the goal. The new slavery for mankind has not resulted in economic justice and security.

Selfish and suspicious units which constitute the present politically and economically unorganised world have raised tariff walls which naturally increase personal rivalries and bitterness. It is a state of constant and continuous economic struggle. Those who believe in force for their internal affairs have no hesitation in adopting it in their foreign relations. Militarism is now in the ascendant. Might is to-day more right than ever. Our dictators are all sabrerattlers and scaremongers.

They tax the sweat and blood of innocent people in order to maintain armaments. Nations are fed on a diet of blood and iron. Italy is busy turning a people into an army. The boys of Italy are to be prepared "spiritually, physically and militarily" for the profession of arms. Germany and Austria, Russia and France, even Great Britain are piling up preparations for war, while their governments declare that they desire peace. Defending the increased Air Estimate in the House of Commons, Mr. Baldwin remarked that in future we must regard not the white cliffs of Dover but the left bank of the Rhine as our frontier. No one knows what exactly Baldwin meant and it is doubtful whether he himself knew. But the French took the words to mean that England was at last about to agree to a military alliance with France and they can always quote Baldwin.

The powers of darkness are gathering in every direction. The nations of Europe are drifting towards war with all its incalculable horrors. The next war will be fought largely from the air and it will be much more pitiless, indiscriminating and destructive than anything in the previous history of warfare. It is admitted that there is no defence against air-attack, one can only retaliate. Invasion by an army could be repelled by ranging a sufficiently strong force against it. So also with blockade by fleet. But there is no reliable defence against a raid by bombing aeroplanes. However large our flying force may be, a much smaller one could deliver a blow levelled straight against the civilian population, old and young, women and children, hospitals and nurseries. The only defence is by reprisals. The enemy can retaliate by raining from the air high explosives, poison gas and disease bacteria. If Paris cannot guard itself against German air-attack, it can bomb Berlin and the knowledge that the power exists may tame the Germans. But it is also true that air war will be decided by the power that can get its blow in first. When the next war breaks out, we will have a relapse into barbarism, if not the collapse of civilisation. The world calls itself civilised. Though it has accomplished a good deal in science and organisation, though literature and philosophy, religion and art have been going on for centuries, we find ourselves to-day as helpless and untutored children in the presence of conditions which, if not dealt with and remedied, will bring this civilisation to an end. Mankind has been defined by a cynic as an anthropoid species afflicted with megalomania. Perhaps he is right.

The present crisis is so stupid and yet so serious in its consequences that civilisation itself may be ruined. Mankind must be dragged out of the rut in which it had become wedged and compelled to make a fresh start. A society does not grow out of its own motion. It is carried forward by the efforts of a minority, a 'remnant' in the words of Matthew Arnold, and that minority owes its inspiration to individuals, the wisest and the best, of insight and wisdom, of courage and power. It is the individuals who rise above their national surroundings, who are in communion with the good, seen and unseen, who have the energy to graft their vision on to the existing social substance—it is they who will carry civilisation forward. Compared with the war cries and emotional outbursts of the political dictators to-day, the parting message of Gandhi to the last session of the Indian National Congress is like a ray of heavenly light let into a world of deep darkness. "I shall never accept self-government brought about by violence." Eagerly desirous of India's freedom, foremost among us in his power to further it, he tells us that dear to him as political freedom is, truth and nonviolence are yet more dear. He warns his fellow-workers in the Congress to develop a delicate sense of moral responsibility and respect for one's fellowmen which it would be hard to find equalled elsewhere in political struggles. He commands them to transcend the finitude and relativity which belongs to politics as a natural phenomenon and develop the capacity to apprehend absolute truth and recognise an absolute obligation, all that we include under the names of reason and conscience, truth and love. As we contemplate the stupendous movement across the pages of history, we witness the power of ideas. Here is a great idea which Gandhi is impressing on the mind and conscience of the people. He appeals to us to rise to new heights, to seek new means of endeavour to tread new paths towards national reconstruction, greatness and accomplishment, to build a new India on moral and spiritual foundations. In placing the interests of universal truth first and national politics second, he has lit a candle that will not easily be put out. The light of it will have a far penetration in time and space. It will be seen and welcomed by all honest and sincere people the world over. His appeal will be written not only by the side of the utterances of the great national leaders like Pericles and Cicero, or Washington and Lincoln, but also of great religious reformers as that of one of the immortal voices of the human race in all that relates to the highest effort of men and nations.

The problem of the great man is an intriguing one, puzzled over by thinkers everywhere in the world. The Chinese democracy of reason answered it in terms offensive to our ears by the dictum that every great man is "a public calamity." No wonder there are some who will endorse this dictum with reference to Gandhi, though their number is a steadily diminishing one.

Civilisation is the power to renounce. It is control over selfishness, individual and corporate. It is peaceful co-operation. The tense situation in the world to-day is the result of the lack of cooperation on terms of justice and equality among the nations of the world. The present international anarchy is due to no small extent to the tragedy at Versailles which created sullen and discontented peoples. We cannot keep down proud and great peoples, either in the West or in the East in perpetual humiliation and bondage and expect peace. Voltaire spoke with refreshing candour bordering on cynicism when he said "Such is the condition of human affairs that to wish for the greatness of one's own country is to wish for the harm of his neighbours." If India to-day wishes to govern herself, it cannot be said that she is out for doing someone else wrong. The Britishers to-day are in a very curious mood. The wish to have the best of both worlds, a reputation for idealism and democracy and a strong grip on realism and self-interest. Nations like individuals wield lasting influence in human affairs by their devotion to an idea greater than their own self-interest, a purpose larger than their own immediate advantage. Let it not be said that if Providence threw India on Great Britain, Britain returned the compliment by throwing

India back on Providence. For the sake of world peace and British prestige, it is to be hoped that the peace-loving, liberal-minded, section of Great Britain will realise that the days of paternalism are over and an empire is justified only because it is a partnership held together by the free consent of self-governing peoples.

When it is said that we get the government we deserve, it means that the State cannot be better than the men who compose it. There is an organic connection between the social conscience and the political arrangement. A more stable and representative government demands a juster social order. A society which tolerates the scourge of untouchability has no right to call itself civilised. There must not be any barrier to the rise of any honest, industrious and capable person to any position for which his character, his intelligence and his talents fit him. Integrity in public life should not be tampered with by caste or communal feeling. The pernicious influences at home and school which inculcate wrong notions about caste superiority and communal contempt require to be removed with a drastic hand. It is no answer to say that each one is at liberty to follow his own customs and creeds but the decencies of social life require, not passive non-interference but active sympathy and understanding. It is true that we do not shoot or guillotine people and yet we do things pretty thoroughly in our own way by means of ostracism and social boycott. Hindus and Muslims have lived together for centuries and yet we cherish the most amazing illusions about each ether's characters. By the stubborn cherishing of differences, we develop attitudes which are exploited by the self-seeking and the partisan. "Are Tories born wicked," said a child to its Whig mother in the early 19th century, "or do they get wicked as they go on?" "They are born wicked, my dear, and they get worse." In our homes, we inoculate young and defenceless childern with such poison about each other. Our education, if it is successful, should protect us against passion and prejudice, and develop in us a resistance to the power of the press and progaganda to play on our weakness.

There can be no social stability without social justice. Democracy is not only political but economic also. Workers must be liberated from grinding toil, poverty and misery so that they may have opportunies for self-development and self-expression. We are certainly more sensitive to the suffering of starving millions and so have developed many philanthropic institutions, sometimes under communal auspices such as orphanages, free boarding for the destitute, hospitals for the sick and the suffering, and maternity homes for deserving maidens. All this is excellent so far as it goes, but it is only dealing with the symptoms, not attacking the disease. If mankind cannot achieve something more satisfactory than the present order, our homes and hospitals only prolong our agony and it is better we starve and stop maternity.

Democratic states, if they are truly representative of the general will, are required to control the productive effort of individuals. The control of natural and economic resources cannot be left to the free play of individual competition. Even private enterprise clamours for state aid to prevent it from collapse. There is not, therefore, in our century much real opposition to the extension of the public ownership of monopolies except from vested interests. No society can exist without a large measure of social co-operation and control.

But, in no case is it right to surrender our central faith in the power of truth and love to break down resistance to our social endeavours. The social objective is to be gained by persuasion, not force and it should not involve any suppression of freedom of thought, speech and action, without which human life is deprived of its dignity and value. Social change must be an ordered development and not a violent and disruptive change. For this purpose, enlightened people should support policies which make for public good by educating opinion and propagating right ideas.

We live at a time when history is being remade. There is unrest in every sphere of life. There are contradictions in aim, confusion of thought in every line. In religion we preach the highest philosophy and are victims of the worst superstition. We quote Plato and Sankara and believe in charms and amulets and offer sacrifices for passing examinations and winning prizes. The growth of national consciousness is retarded by communal separatism. We proclaim the equality of the Indian and the Britisher but the clash of the caste and the out-caste is growing more and more intense and bitter. Take the economic situation. If any one visits, say the city of Calcutta in the Christmas season, and finds out the amount spent on drink and dissipation, gambling and betting, he will not consider the people of the place to be by any means poor and yet the existence of the slums and those who live in them under conditions hardly to be borne are sad commentary on the utter economic chaos and injustice. The mass of poverty, the extent of illiteracy, the social obstacles in the way of improvement, the tangled undergrowth of vested interests, religious, political and economic, reveal not one problem but an infinity of problems. Many of us have an emotional apprehension of the vastness and complexity of the situation but what is required is a scientific view. There are no short cuts to their solution. Here is work for a number of University men and women, to disentangle the confused issues, to reconcile the conflicting aims, to melt the various influences for good into one supreme social effort which is essential to make men less selfish, less aggressive, less given to frivolity. It is for the Universities to produce men who are able to stand out of the welter of common-place egoism and seek the public good, who have intellectual conscience to see the truth and the moral courage to pursue it. Man is not on earth to be happy. He is here to be honest, to be decent, to be good. Whether you get a prize post or not, it is open to you to be useful to your fellows and to work for truth, not because you hope to win but because your cause is just. Farewell!

[This address was delivered by His Highness Sikander Saulat Iftikhar-ul-Mulk Nawab Hamidullah, G. C. S. I., G. C. I. E. Ruler of Bhopal, on December 5, 1935.]

I thank you most sincerely for the honour you have bestowed on me by inviting me to deliver the Convocation Address to-day in my own university. Many years ago when, on an occasion never to be forgotten by me, I entered the portals of this great university with a large crowd of other young men, all looking equally anxious, had some good fairy whispered to me that this honour would one day be mine, I confess, I would have walked to my seat in the examination hall with a firmer step and with greater confidence. But this Age of Iron, alas! seems to have driven away all good fairies from our world, and humble mortals, such as I, are left alone and unaided to try in vain to pierce the Veil of Darkness which hides from us for all time that which is to come.

Gentlemen, I consider myself particularly fortunate to have been connected with two great seats of learning in these Provinces—for us from time immemorial the cradle of civilization. As the waters of the sacred Jamuna mingle with those of the Holy Ganges, so have the streams of two great civilizations—the Hindu and the Muslim—mingled here to produce that unique culture which has given to the world of art a new conception of beauty, and to the human soul a new philosophy. Of this culture we, the sons of India, are justly proud.

Situated as this university is in a place which has been for thousands of years a centre of devout pilgrimage, where the very earth has been hallowed by adoration and veneration, she is fortunate in possessing a background of tradition second to none in the whole world. For many years this university bore alone the heavy burden of guiding the education of the teeming millions that inhabit this part of India, and the heroic manner in which she discharged this duty has earned her of all time an honoured place in the annals of our land, To-day she is sharing this work with four other universities, but nothing can diminish the reverence in which all hold her as the first modern home of learning in these Provinces.

Gentlemen, as one who has been connected with educational work for a number of years, albeit in a modest way, the thought has often come to me that in view of the peculiar circumstances of our country, our universities have a twofold duty to perform. Not only have they to engage themselves in widening the horizon of knowledge, but they have also to adopt definite ways and means to instil in the hearts of their ***alumni*** that deep humanity which alone can be made a safe foundation for the future progress of such a country as ours.

Whereas in Europe universities have to deal mostly with one culture and one language, ours have to attempt the solution of intricate problems created by the presence within their walls of those that differ from each other in race, culture, language and religion. In other words it would not be wrong to say that our universities are in the main, though in a small way, faced with the same problems with which our country as a whole is to-day faced. This to my mind enhances for us their utility assigns to them the noblest of all tasks—that of bringing real strength through unity to displace those divisions and animosities which, unfortunately, only too often hamper the spiritual and material progress of our mother land. To be able to discharge this noble duty adequately, our universities have to concern themselves more than they have hitherto done with their immediate environment, turning away from the temptation of shutting themselves up in that serene seclusion midst sylvan glades which was the cherished dream of educationists in the Middle Ages.

Human life has now become so complex, and human relationships so intertwined, that the universities of to-day can no longer afford to ignore the storm and stress of life that goes on around them. While doing their best to advance knowledge, they have also to step out into the arena of life to compel a harassed world to listen to the voice of reason, and to point out to struggling humanity the path that leads to safety and moral grandeur. If our universities fail to prove their worth in this manner, they will soon degenerate into lifeless institutions which devote themselves only to such remote matters as the correct classification of anti-diluvian fossils.

Here I feel that I must sound a note of warning lest I be misunderstood, and at the same time perpetrate a paradox, for which I crave your indulgence. Whilst I believe earnestly in the utility of universities, I do not believe that they should themselves preach an entirely utilitarian view of life. Idealism, provided it is not extravagant, is one of the most treasured attributes of the human mind, and seems to be in these days the only brake we possess with which to make the attempt to stop the onward rush of humanity towards brutality and mutual destruction. Thus I hold that our universities have not only to develop the intellect of their pupils, but also to do whatever is possible to form their character. Too often have we seen how dangerous to society an intellect uncontrolled by high moral principles can be.

In an age when one half of the world seems to be ranged in battle array against the other half, the development of character assumes the importance of a sacred duty for universities. If they send out into the world young men possessing balanced minds and a correct perspective of life, they for their part will have done their best to serve the cause of humanity. But if, on the other hand, they continue to believe that it is only with the development of intellect that they are concerned, then instead of being a blessing, they will become yet another menace to the well-being of human society.

Gentlemen, to me it has always seemed a debatable point whether the complete secularization of education has not on the whole done more harm than good to society, and whether the time has not now-come for us to consider the desirability of openly giving to religion, in the widest sense of the term, its old honoured place in our system of education. This besides being in consonance with the highest traditions of our country would also tend to re-establish in our inner life that harmony which is to-day so woefully absent from it.

Our universities have to be something more than mere imitations of similar institutions in other lands, and so long as they remain, as I am afraid they are at present, shyly conscious of the fact that they are imitations, they will not be able to regain that confidence in themselves without which they cannot become for us real sources of inspiration. Let us not forget that education is so organic a part of a nation's life that systems transplanted from other countries can never be anything more than exotic creations, and that a university that does not reflect correctly the best culture of her surroundings is doomed to dwindle into insignificance and, finally, to wither away like a plant that has failed to take root in the soil in which it was planted.

We in India stand to-day on the threshold of great changes, and it is time that we made a comprehensive survey of our present system of education and took steps to effect those modifications which we consider uecessary to ensure the best results. Bigger opportunities of serving our country are to be offered to the young men of this generation and of succeeding generations than were offered to their predecessors, and in this test only those can prove successful who possess large hearts, high ideals and clear visions.

In planning the system of education hitherto followed by us, we seem to have unconsciously reversed the accepted order of things by trying to impart to our students a better knowledge of that which is far away than of that which is near them and round them. The majority of our educated young men to-day are apt to know more about the ***cromlechs*** found in England than about the ***stupas*** found in their own country; more about Chaucer and Tennyson than about Kalidas and Ghalib; and strangest of all, more about the English language than about their own mother tongue! Ours is almost the only country in the world where educated people find it easier to express themselves in a language which is neither their mother tongue nor even one of the languages of their own country! All this is unnatural, and has to be changed if the bases of our national life are to be strengthened.

Situated as we are, for no people is a careful study of their past as necessary as it is for us. Without it we can neither understand our present environment nor mould for ourselves a great future based on a sympathetic understanding of the origins and cultural contributions of the different races inhabiting our vast country. Mutual understanding alone will create mutual sympathy, and bring in its wake that healthy patriotism which, without being aggressive or offensive, will remove for all time from our path the obstacles to-day offered by narrow sectarianism and differerences of castes and creeds. Our contribution to the general happiness of mankind will be great if we can show how it is possible for human beings, differing from each other in language, race and religion, to live together as one people united in the service of their mother land.

Gentlemen, I look forward to the day when from our country, which has ever been the home of religions and philosophies, there will again go forth into a distracted world, for the second time in our long history, that gospel of love and mutual toleration which alone can heal the wounds caused by recent conflicts and bring lasting peace to suffering humanity.

Turning to another aspect of life in our universities, I have been forced to come to the conclusion that our students as a whole do not pay as much attention to their physical well being as those in other countries. This is probably due to the fact that we in the East have been inclined to look upon games and other similar pastimes as something befitting only children, and, consequently, beneath the dignity of young men in search of knowledge. Then to make matters worse, at no stage in the process of education have we made adequate arrangements for teaching to our students those principles of hygiene and those methods of protecting themselves against diseases which in other countries are known even to young boys still at school.

It is too trite a remark to make, though nevertheless true, that in all sound systems of education it is the physical well-being of the pupils that should come first. What our country needs most to-day is young men with strong nerves and broad shoulders—young men who would bear cheerfully the burden of such responsibilities as fall to the lot of all those engaged in constructive work.

I have ever held the belief that in nation-building playgrounds and gymnasiums occupy as important a place as class rooms. One has only to study those movements which are improving the health of the postwar generation in many countries of Europe to understand how much can be achieved by scientific physical culture. As time goes on, the struggle for existence is bound to become more acute throughout the world, and only those will be able to bear its strain that have strong nerves and strong bodies.

I have no hesitation in saying that personally I have learnt more on cricket fields and polo grounds how to face the difficulties of life than in class rooms, for, to keep smiling and to continue doing your best when you feel that all the odds are against you and your side is losing, is morally as great a discipline as any that can be taught by lectures.

The English, as you must have heard, have a saying that the battle of Waterloo was won on the playgrounds of Eton. All those that have had the good fortune of representing their university in different tournaments will understand what this saying is meant to convey, for they will know that in the realm of sport, where the weakness of one is apt to become the weakness of all, no great success can be achieved without team work.

To you young men, who are leaving this university to-day, I say: Carry this team work also into the life that now lies before you. Go into the bigger world outside and, if you wish to render real service to our country, preach to all this doctrine of co-operation. Tell our countrymen that nothing that is to endure can ever be built on foundations of hatred and distrust, which, as purely destructive forces, can lead us nowhere. I assure you that at no juncture in our history was this spirit of co-operation more necessary than to-day, when the whole world is watching us to see what use we make of the opportunity to shape the destiny of our land which is now beginning to be offered to us by a radical change in our system of government.

Unfortunately, here is a sharp difference of opinion in our country with regard to these constitutional reforms. This was only to be expected in such a complex situation as ours, and should not disappoint us or make us adopt the purely negative attitude of belittling the result of an earnest attempt to solve one of the most difficult problems with which statesmanship has been faced in modern times. These reforms are by no means perfect. No one has ever put forward that claim. But what I do maintain is that they are not as wholly bad as some would have us believe. No critic, however severe, who studies them dispassionately can seriously make the statement that in their sum total they do not represent a substantial advance. We wish they could have gone much further, but the undoubted difficulties that at present lie in the way cannot be ignored—difficulties for many of which, I am sorry to say, we have only ourselves to blame. To have ignored hard facts would have been of no help, for the best way to overcome them is always to face them boldly. In politics, as in many other spheres of life, one has to be prepared for com-promise to achieve great results. If one cannot get the best, one must be ready to accept the second best. In the case of these reforms I feel confident that, given the necessary sincerity of purpose, we shall succeed in effectively overcoming that which to-day seems to us insurmountable.

So far as we of the States are concerned, rest assured that, as in the past so in the future, we shall ever consider it the greatest of all privileges to give of our very best to the building up of that greater India for which we are all longing.

The whole world is just now passing through extremely difficult times, and a supreme effort is necessary if we are to save ourselves from falling into that quagmire of political and economic uncertainties from which so many other nations are to-day trying in vain to extricate themselves. It is up to you, young men, as the custodians of the future of our country, to make this effort, and in this you will succeed only if you keep before you the motto of all true sportsmen: Be fair to every one and always chivalrous to the weak.

[Convocation address delivered by Dr. Rabindranath Tagore at the 17th Convocation of the Benares Hindu University, held on February 8, 1935.]

The call of invitation that has led me on to this platform to-day, though imperative in its demand is. I must confess, foreign to my temperament. It speaks of a responsibility which I am compelled to acknowledge owing to my previous Karma that has identified me with a vocation specially belonging to that beneficent section of community which surely is not mine. Believe me, once upon a time I was young, in fact, younger than most of you; and in that early dawn of mind's first urge of expansion I instinctively chose my own true path which, I believe, was to give rhythmic expression to life on a colourful background of imagination. Pursuing the lure of dreams I spent my young days in a reckless adventure,—forcing verses through a rigid barricade of literary conventions. Such foolhardiness met with serious disapproval of the severely sober among the overripe minds of that epoch. If I had persisted exclusively in this inconsequential career of a versifier, you would not have ventured to ask such an unadulterated poet to take a conspicuous part on this solemn occasion when a great University has gathered her scholars to remind them of the high obligations associated with their success in college examinations.

However, towards the period of my declining youth, I took upon myself, for no ostensible reason whatever, the deliberate mission of the teacher. This transformation in my life helped to unlock the gates to me at those institutions where my right of entry could legitimately be challenged. While enjoying the unaccustomed honour thus acquired I should confess to you that it was not a compelling sense of duty which guided me to this field of education but some long maturing ideals in my mind that constantly troubled my imagination claiming definite shapes. I have decided to speak to you about those ideals.

Before I broach my subject to-day I shall claim your indulgence in one or two points. It is evident to you that I have grown old, but you who are young cannot fully realise the limitations of old age. That I am not in a full possession of my breath may not be of any importance to others whose lungs are strong and whose hearts render loyal service to them without murmur. It may have a salutary effect upon me in curtailing the garrulity to which an old man's tongue has the habit to glide in. But what is more significant about a man who has crossed his seventieth year is that by that time he has concluded most of his opinions and thoughts and thus is compelled to repeat himself. This is one of the reasons why the young persons bored by his reiterations become naturally excited to a violent fit of contradiction which may be courteously suppressed and, therefore, all the more outrageous. But to save my energies I am ready to take the consequence and openly to plagiarize my own store of thoughts and even words. I strongly suspect that you have missed them, for, not being in your text books, they must have remained beyond the reach of your serious attention, and I am confident that there is very little chance of your taking the trouble to explore them in obscure pages of publications generally overlooked by my countrymen.

In modern India centres of education have been established in large towns where the best part of energy and interest of the country is attracted. The constant flow of stimulation working upon our mind from its cosmic environment is denied us who are bred in towns. A great deal of the fundamental objects of knowledge with which Nature provides us free of cost is banished into printed pages and a spontaneous communication of sympathy with the great world which is intimately ours is barricaded against. I, who belong to the tribe of the born exiles, having been artificially nourished by "the stony hearted step-mother"—a modern city, keenly felt the torture of it when young and thus realised, when opportunity was given me the utmost necessity of Nature's own bounties for the proper development of children's mind. It helps me to imagine the main tragedy that I believe had overshadowed the life of the poet Kalidasa. Fortunately, for the scholars, he has left behind him no clear indication of his birthplace, and thus they have a subject that oblivious time has left amply vacant for an endless variety of disagreement. My scholarship does not pretend to go deep, but I remember having read somewhere that he was born in Kashmir. Since then I have left off reading discussions about his birthplace for the fear of meeting with some learned contradiction equally convincing. Anyhow, it was perfectly in the fitness of things that Kalidas should be born in Kashmir,—and I envy him, for I was born in Calcutta. He was compelled to suffer an honorable banishment from there to a city in the plains,—and his whole poem of ***Meghaduta*** reverberates with the music of sorrow that had its crown of suffering "in remembering happier things." Is it not significant that in this poem, the lover's errant fancy, in the quest of the beloved who dwelt in the paradise of eternal beauty, lingered with a deliberate delay of enjoyment round every hill, stream, or forest over which it passed; watched the grateful dark eyes of the peasant girls welcoming the rain-laden clouds of June; listening to some village elder reciting under the banyan tree a well-known love-legend that ever remained fresh with the tears and smiles of generations of simple hearts? Do we not feel in all this the prisoner of the giant city revelling in a vision of joy that, in his imaginary journey, followed him from hill to hill, awaited him at every turn of the path which bore the finger-posts of heaven for separated lovers banished on the earth?

I wish to impress you with the fact that one of the noble functions of education is to reconcile our human mind with the world of Nature through perfect knowledge and enjoyment. The great universe surrounding us with endless aspects of the eternal in varied rhythms of colours, sounds and movements constantly mitigates the pressure upon us of our small self along whose orbit whirl like meteors dense fragments of ephemeral interests. Education must have for its fulness an environment of a detached mind like the aerial atmosphere which envelopes the earth opening for her a path of communication with the infinite.

The ***mantram*** which I have accepted for my own purpose of life, and which carries within it in a concentrated form the true ideal of education is Infinite Peace, Infinite Well-being, the Infinite One.

Peace there is in the depth of the universe, the peace which is not of inertia, but for the constant reconciliation of contrary forces, the peace that reigns in the sphere of the stars among gigantic whirlpools of clashing flames. This spirit of a mighty peace we must win in our life through the training of self-control and balance of mind. Our individual beings are universes in a self-luminous field of consciousness; they have their instincts and desires as inflammatory elements which should be brought under control to be coerced into perfect creations. I was about to say that these were universes in miniature, but I hesitated when I realised that spiritual entity cannot be measured by a criterion which is that of spatial expansions. Also we cannot be certain about time limits of those realms just as we are doubtful about those of the suns and stars. In fact there, is a strong reason in favour of their being eternal pilgrims passing through countless cycles of renewal, but for which the whole world would have gone out of existence long before this.

The human spirit whose highest aim is to realise it-self in the supreme Spirit, in its progress towards finality is enjoined by our scriptures to choose for its initial stage ***Brahmacharyya***, the stage of self-discipline. This is in order that it can be established in the heart of ***Shantam***, in the infinity of detachment. The basis of education has to be acquired in this ***Shantam***, the harmony of the soul in its unobstructed sense of the Eternal The idea of pilgrimage that prevails in India has the same educational meaning. Its sites have been specially selected where nature reveals overwhelming magnanimity in its aspect of the beautiful and the grand. There at the touch of the ineffable our worldly-experiences lose their tenacious grip of immediacy and life's truth is rescued into the light from the density of entanglements.

There is another pilgrimage for us which is in the world of knowledge. This journey in the open road gives us emancipation not only from illusions of appearance and peremptoriness of the prevalent unreason, but also from wrong valuations of reality, from all kinds of bias that obscure our vision of truth, from the enchainment in the narrow cage of provincialism. It is a strenuous walk, every step of which has to be carefully taken with a solemn eagerness for the truth which is to be its goal. There was a time when the University had its origin in man's faith, in the ultimate value of culture which he pursued for its own sake. But, unfortunately, in the modern days greed has found its easy access into the sacred shrine dedicated to the cause of mind's fulfilment. The sordid spirit of success has allowed the educational institutions to be annexed to the busy market where ***Vidya*** is bought and sold according to the standard of worldly profit, where cheap facilities are offered for acquiring, in place of true education, its make-believe substitute.

It is fully worthwhile to emphasize the truth that the ultimate purpose of education is to enable us to live a complete life which can be realised through our complete unity with existence, a part of which consists of the physical nature and the other part that of the human community. For us the world of nature has no reciprocal path of union which may be termed as moral. Its manifestations in the predestined course of activities take no heed of our conduct or necessity, make no distinction between the good and the evil. The human relationship with the blind forces combining in an eternal game of creation, indifferent to our personal cry, can only be established through our own impersonal faculty of reason whose logic is universal. By understanding Nature's laws and modulating them to our needs we reach the ***Shantam*** in the extra-human world, the ***Shantam*** which is the fundamental principle of harmony. Such an adjustment of Nature's workings to human intelligence has been progressing from the beginning of Man's history, and according to the degree of that progress, we judge that department of our civilisation which we generalise, very often wrongly, as materialistic.

The Supreme Being, says the Upanishad, has to be realised with our heart and mind as well, as Visvakarma and as *Mahatma* ***sada jananam hrdaye sannivishtah***. His name Visvakarma implies laws that are universal through which his activities in the physical world are revealed. They would elude our reason if they were expressions of a capricious will, then we could never depend upon the inevitableness of their influences upon our destiny, the influences which can only be turned to our favour if we have perfect knowledge of them. There are individuals even to-day who believe in some happenings in nature which are arbitary and local, which ignore all the endless links of causes that keep the world in order. They imagine that the physical phenomena are liable to sudden outbreaks of catastrophic chasms which are like special ordinances orginating in isolated causes. Faith in such cosmic arbitrariness drives men to the primitive mentality of fear, to unmeaning ritualism, to imputations of special purpose upon natural events according to one's own personal tendencies of mind. We ought to know that numerous evils which in olden days were considered as punitive weapons in the arsenal of God have been tamed to innocuousness through accurate comprehension of their character.

It has been said in our scripture that ***avidya*** which means ignorance is the root cause of all evils, the ignorance which blinds us to the truth of the unity of our self with the not-self.

Man's ***sadhana*** for his union which nature depends for its success upon his faith in his reason and his dis-interested endeavour in an atmosphere of detachment. A perfect technique of such a training is largely found in the West, and there the people are fast assimilating in their own power the power that lies in ***Anna Brahma,*** the infinity manifested in matter. In fact, they are gradually extending their own physical body into the larger body of the physical world. Their senses are constantly being augmented in power, their bodily movements allied to nature's forces of speed. Every day proofs are multiplied convincing them that there is no end to such intimacy leading to the extension of their self in the realm of time and space. This is the true means of realising Visvakarma, the universal worker, by a mind divested of all doubts and by action.

Shantam, the spirit of peace, which can be attained through the realisation of truth, is not the whole object of education; it needs for its finality Shivam, Goodness, through the training of moral perfection, for the sake of the perfect harmony with the human world.

The greatness which man has reached in the expansion of the physical and intellectual possibilities in him shows no doubt, a great advancement in the course of his evolution. Yet, in its lop-sided emphasis it carries the course of ***avidya***, the mother of all sufferings and futility, ***avidya*** which obscures the warning for him that his individual self when isolated from all other selves misses its reality and, therefore, suffers unhappiness, just as his physical body is thwarted in its function when out of harmony with the physical world.

The union of our self with Brahma as ***Visvakarma*** may bring us success in the province of living, but for the peace and perfection in the realm of our being we need our union with Brahma who is Mahatma, the Infinite Spirit dwelling in the hearts of all peoples.

With the modern facilities of communication not merely a limited number of individuals but all the races of men have come close to each ether. If they fail to unite in truth then humanity will flounder in the bottom of a surging sea of mutual hatred and suspicion. Things to-day have already assumed an angry temper of a growling beastliness ready for an enormous catastrophe of suicide.

Most problems to-day have become international problems and yet the international mind has not yet been formed, the modern teachers' conscience not having taken its responsibility in helping to invoke it.

The word "international" may sound too indefinite, its meaning appearing large only because of its vagueness, like water acquiring volume by turning into vapour. I do not believe in an internationalism which is amorphous, whose features are broadened into flatness. With us it must be internationalism of India, with its own distinct character.

The true universal finds its manifestation in the individuality which is true. Beauty is universal, and a rose reveals it because, as a rose, it is individually beautiful. By making a decoction of a rose, jasmine and lotus you do not get to a realisation of some larger beauty which is interfloral. The true universalism is not in the breaking down of the walls of one's own house, but in the offering of hospitality to one's guests and neighours.

Like the position of the earth in the course of its diurnal and annual motions, man's life, at any time, must be the reconciliation of its two movements, one round the centre of its own personality, and another whose centre is in a luminous ideal comprehending the whole human world. The international endeavour of a people must carry the movement of the people's own personality round the great spirit of man. The inspiration must be its own, which is to help it in its aspiration towards fulfilment. Otherwise, mere cosmopolitanism but drifts on the waves, buffeted by wind from all quarters, in an imbecility of movement which has no progress.

As a people we must be fully conscious of what we are. It is a truism to say that the consciousness of the unity of a people implies the knowledge of its parts as well of its whole. But, most of us not only have no such knowledge of India, they do not even have an eager desire to cultivate it.

By asserting our national unity with vehemence in our political propaganda, we assure ourselves that we possess it, and thus continue to live in a make believe world of political day-dreams.

The fact is, we have a feeble human interest in our own country. We love to talk about politics and economics; we are ready to soar into the thin air of academic abstractions, or roam in the dusk of pedantic wildernesses; but we never care to cross our social boundaries and come to the door of our neighbouring communities, personally to enquire how they think and feel and express themselves, and how they fashion their lives.

The love of man has its own hunger for knowing. Even if we lack this concerning our fellow beings in India, except in our political protestations, at least love of knowledge for its own sake could have brought us close to each other. But there also we have failed and suffered. For weakness of knowledge is the foundation of weakness of power. Until India becomes fully distinct in our mind, we can never gain her in truth; and where truth is imperfect, love can never have its full sway. The best function of our Education Centres is to help us to ***know*** ourselves; and then along with it, her other mission will be fulfilled which is to inspire us to ***give*** ourselves.

What has given such enormous intellectual power to Europe is her co-ordination of minds. She has evolved a means by which all countries of that continent can think together. Such a great concert of ideas, by its own pressure of movement, naturally wears away all her individual aberrations of thought and extravagances of unreason. It keeps her flights of fancy close to the limits of reticence. All her different thought rays have been focussed in our common culture, which finds its complete expression in all the European universities.

The mind of India, on the other hand, is divided and scattered; there is no one common pathway along which we can reach it. We cannot but look with regret at the feebleness of stimulation in our academic training for the forming of our mind which in co-operation of knowledge and sympathy may comprehend the larger mind of the country. The most important object of our educational institutions is to help each student to realise his personality, as an individual representing his people, in such broad spirit, that he may know how it is the most important fact of his life for him to have been born to the great world of man.

We in India are unfortunate in not having the chance to give expression to the best in us in creating intimate relations with the powerful peoples of the world. The bond between the nations to-day is made of the links of mutual menace, its strength depending upon the force of panic, and leading to an enormous waste of resources in a competition of browbeating and bluff. Some great voice is waiting to be heard which will usher in the sacred light of truth in the dark region of the nightmare of politics. But we in India have not yet had the chance. Yet we have our own human voice which truth demands. Even in the region where we are not invited to act we have our right to judge and to guide the mind of man to a proper point of view, to the vision of ideality in the heart of the real.

The activity represented in human education is a world-wide one, it is a great movement of universal co-operation interlinked by different ages and countries. And India, though defeated in her political destiny, has her responsibility to hold up the cause of truth, even to cry in the wilderness, and offer her lessons to the world in the best gifts which she could produce. The messengers of truth have ever joined their hands across centuries, across the seas, across historical barriers, and they help to form the great continent of human brotherhood. Education in all its different forms and channels has its ultimate purpose in the evolving of a luminous sphere of human mind from the nebula that has been rushing round ages to find in itself an eternal centre of unity. We individuals, however small may be our power, and whatever corner of the world we may belong to, have the claim upon us to add to the light of the consciousness that comprehends all humanity. And for this cause I ask your co-operation, not merely because co-operation itself is the best aspect of the truth we represent, it is an end and not merely the means.

We are new converts to western ideals, in other words, the ideals belonging to the scientific view of life and the world. This is great and it is foolish to belittle its importance by wrongly describing it as materialism. For Truth is spiritual in itself, and truly materialistic is the mind of the animal which is unscientific and therefore unable to cross the dark screen of appearance, of accidents, and reach the deeper region of universal laws. Science means intellectual probity in our dealings with the material world. This conscientiousness of mind is spiritual, for it never judges its results by the standard of external profits. But in science the oft-used half truth that honesty is the best policy has proved itself to be completely true. Science being mind's honesty in its relation to the physical universe never fails to bring us the best profit for our living. And mischief finds its entry through this backdoor of utility, and Satan has had an ample chance of making use of the divine fruit of knowledge for bringing shame upon humanity. Science as the best policy is tempting the primitive in man bringing out his evil passions through the respectable cover that it has supplied him. And this is why it is all the more needed to-day that we should have faith in ideals that have been matured in the spiritual field through ages of human endeavour for perfection, the golden crops that have developed in different forms and in different soils but whose food value for man's spirit has the same composition. These are not for the local markets but for universal hospitality, for sharing life's treasure with each other and realising that human civilization is a spiritual feast the invitation to which is open to all, it is never for the ravenous orgies of carnage where the food and the feeders are being torn to pieces.

The legends of nearly all human races carry man's faith in a golden age which appeared as the introductory chapter in human civilization. It shows that man has his instinctive belief in the objectivity of spiritual ideals though this cannot be proved. It seems to him that they have already been given to him and that this gift has to be proved through his history of effort against obstacles. The idea of millenium so often laughed at by the clever is treasured as the best asset by man in his mythology as a complete truth realised for ever in some ageless time. Admitting that it isnot a scientifical fact we must at the same time know that the instinct cradled and nourished in these primitive stories has its eternal meaning. It is like the instinct of a chick which dimly feels that an infinite world of freedom is already given to it, that it is not a subjective dream but an objective reality, even truer than its life within the egg. If a chick has a rationalistic tendency of mind it ought not to believe in a freedom which is difficult to imagine and contradictory to all its experience, but all the same it cannot help pecking at its shell, and ever accepting it as ultimate. The human soul confined in its limitation has also dreamt of a millenium and striven for an emancipation which seems impossible of attainment, and it has felt its reverence for some great source of inspiration in which all its experience of the true, good and beautiful finds its reality though it cannot be proved, the reality in which our aspiration for freedom in truth, freedom in love, freedom in the unity of man is ideally realised for ever.

[Pandit Madan Mohan Malaviya, delivered the following address at the Annual Convocation of the Benares Hindu University, on December 14, 1929.]

. . . . I have said that the establishment of so many Universities in the course of a few years is a matter of national gratification. But I regret to find that there is a tendency in some quarters to look askance at the development of Universities in India. There are some who think that they are growing too fast and that more is being spent on University education in India than should be spent. This is a mistaken view. One has only to think of the large number of Universities in Great Britain, in Germany, in France, in Italy, not to speak of America, to understand that for the vast continent of India, which is equal to the whole of Europe minus Russia, 18 Universities are none too many, and I venture to think that this is the view which is taken by every scholar who is capable of taking a statesmanlike view of this question. University education has come to be regarded in every civilized country as the most important part of a national system of education, and if the expense incurred on University education in the West is compared with what we are expending on it here, it will be seen that we are far below the standard of other civilized countries and have much lee-way to make up. Our Universities are like so many power-houses, needed to scatter the darkness of ignorance, poverty and cold misery which hanging like a pall upon the country. The larger the number of well-educated scholars the Universities will send out, the greater will be the strength of the national army which is to combat ignorance and to spread knowledge. Every lover of India must therefore rejoice at the growth of Universities in India.

But it is said that we do not get sufficient value for the money which is being spent on Universities, that they are not turning out work of the right type to justify the expense, that University standards in India are low, that the standard of admission is unsatisfactory, and that, therefore, efficiency is sacrificed and much educational power is wasted.

I admit that this criticism is partly true. I unhasitatingly admit that, some brilliant exceptions apart, the Indian intellect cannot, under existing conditions, produce the best results of which it is capable. Indeed it is highly creditable to Indian graduates that, despite the discouraging conditions under which they live and work, they have rendered so good an account of themselves in competitions both in India and in England as they have done. To understand how we may get better value for the money and labour we spend on Universities, we must pass in review our whole system of Education, we must note all its defects and deficiencies, and the obstacles which lie in the path of Indian Universities.

It is an obvious truth that the standard of University education depends directly upon the standard of secondary education. If you wish to raise the former, you must raise the latter. But you can do this only when primary education has been organized on a sufficiently sound and extensive basis. Bearing this in mind, let us recall what the state of education in India is and let us compare it with the systems which obtain in other lands. Let us take the case of England. For sixty years England has sedulously promoted universal education among its people. In 1870 the Elementary Education Act made elementary education compulsory. The Act of 1891 made it free. Since that time elementary education has been both free and compulsory for all boys and girls up to the age of 14. Compulsory education is split into three grades: (1) Infant grade, 5 to 8 years; (2) elementary or primary grade, 8 to 11 years, (3) Higher primary grade, which is sometimes called secondary education, 11 to 14 years. The secondary schools prepare students for the University matriculation examination, and encourage them by special grants to continue their studies for special courses. There are 60 public schools which are regarded as of the first rank, which have a reputation for building up character and preparing young men for administrative appointments. There are over a thousand other secondary schools. Since the War a new type of schools called the Central School has come into existence. They take in boys and girls at the age of 11, on the result of a competitive examination, and impart free instruction. They are day schools. They divide their courses in groups, the commercial group, the technical group and the industrial group. The present-day tendency in England is to include technical subjects in the scope of general education and to obliterate the distinction between primary, secondary and technical schools. But there is at present a net-work of part-time, wholetime and evening schools and technical schools, and there are technical colleges for advanced technology. In these schools a variety of technical and professional courses are offered to suit the particular bent of each student. In addition to these there are polytechnics which prepare the lower middle and the working classes for various industries and trade which require skilled labour. They offer training in every industry which exists in the locality. There are also technical institutes which offer teaching in specialized subjects. Polytechnics also provide teaching in ordinary arts and sciences for university degrees. On the top of these institutions, stand the Universities of which there are 16 in number* A large number of scholarships is given in secondary schools to encourage promising pupils to prepare themselves to join the Universities. It will be evident from this how much care is taken in England to see that every child receives the education for which he is naturally fitted. In all important countries of the West similar steps have been taken, and the systems of primary and secondary education have been overhauled, enriched and put on a sound footing.

Let me give you some idea of the provisions that have been made in the last ten years in those countries to help the youth and the cause of education. Having imporved their respective systems of primary, secondary and technical education, they have introduced a system of vocational guidance, which has been defined as "the giving of information, experience and advice in regard to choosing an occupation, preparing for it, entering it, and progressing in it." They have created Committees of School masters and others, and Juvenile Employment Exchanges and Bureaus to advise boys and girls after they leave the School as to the career they should enter upon. They do not think that they have discharged their duty to the child when they have passed him through the School. In all these countries the interest in the child has been extended to preparing him for occupational life and to securing him employment which may be suitable to him. Thus in Austria, in 1922, an order of the State Education Office stated: "It is the duty of the School not only to provide suitable instruction and education for the children who attend it, but also to advise parents as to the future careers of their children and as to the choice of an occupation," A French writer, F. Buisson, quoted by Proof. Shields in his book on the "Evolution of Industrial Organisations" wrote in 1921: "The school is not made for the school, but for life. It must provide the society of the future with men. It is a cruel mockery suddenly to abandon its little pupils on the day they reach their thirteenth year, when they are flung unarmed into the battle of life. It is also the most foolish waste. What madness, having done so much for the school boy, to do nothing for the apprentice! From this has arisen the idea, which has rapidly spread, that the social functions of the school must be greatly extended. There are many new services which it must give, The first of these is the supervision of the transition from the school room to the workshop." In England and Wales, vocational guidance has been provided for since the Education (Choice of Employment) Act was passed in 1910 for giving advice to boys and girls under the age of 17 (extended to 18 by the Education Act, 1918) with respect to the choice of suitable employment. So also in the Irish Free State, in France, in Belgium, in Germany, and in the United States, where probably the first systematic attempt to provide vocational guidance was undertaken in 1908.

This will give you some idea of the amount of care which is bestowed in England and in other civilized countries on the proper education of the child. Every civilized Gorvernment reagards it its duty to educate the child, and to educate him in such a manner that he should be able to earn a suitable living. During the ten years since the War, every civilized country has endeavoured to give a more parctical bias to education. After six year of experiment Austria-Vienna in 1927 completely re-organized its school system. By 1928 Chile had reduced illiteracy to less than 30 percent, of the population of four and a half millions, and nearly one-seventh were at educational institutions of some kind. Vocational training has been introduced in the third year of the secondary school, and experimental schools and courses have been established and a system of model schools is to be created to determine the type best suited to Chile. In Hamburg schools are being turned into community centres, parents' co-operation enlisted, and self-Government employed. The aim of present Swedish Education is to fit young people for citizenship and to develop their whole personality. In 1918 a whole system of practical education for young people was created and is vigorously at work. In Turkey since the War the old system of religious schools has been discontinued, and a democratic secular, modern and national system of education has been put into practice to fit the country's new conditions. The number of schools has been largely increased, all education made free, opportunity for self-government given everywhere, and the activity plan put in operation into the first three years of elementary school. It is hardly necessary for me to remind you of the progress of education in France and Germany, America and Japan. The progress of their commerce and industries, the prosperity, power and happiness which they enjoy is in the largest measure due to the education which they have imparted to their sons and daughters during the last fifty years and more.

Let us turn now to our own country. What do we find here? As has well been pointed out by a distinguished English scholar, there is no country where the love of learning had so early an origin or has exercised so powerful an influence as India. Yet after nearly a hundred and seventy years of British rule, India is still stepped in ignorance. According to official reports the percentage of literates of both sexes and all ages was only 7.2, in 1921. In 1927 only 6.91 per cent, of the male population and only 1.46 per cent, of the female population were at school. The total attendance in all the schools and colleges in India in 1921-22 was 7½ million. Of this, about 5 million were in the first class (including the infant class) of the primary schools, and the remaining one-third was distributed among the remaining three classes of the primary schools and among all the other educational institutions including Universities and Colleges. The majority of the boys drop off in the first class and only 19 per cent, of those who join the first class of Primary Schools actually reach the fourth class. Children in the first class cannot read and write the little they learn is soon forgotten. There is loud wail in a recent official report that the wastage and stagnation which these figures reveal are appalling.

Where provision for primary education is so utterly inadequate, it would be unwise to expect any system of night schools or continuation schools for adult education.

Secondary schools also are inadequate in number and poor in the quality of education they impart. The standard of general education they provide is much below that which obtains in other countries and which is needed to give the education a practical value. They are also deficient in that they offer only a general and not vocational education. There are a few agricultural, commercial, technical and industrial schools. They are poor both in number and quality. We look in vain for alternative groups of courses in agriculture, commerce and industry such as the Central Schools in England provide. The official report, to which I have referred, says with regard to secondary schools: "The immense number of failures at matriculation and in the university examinations indicates a general waste of effort. Such attempts as have been made to provide vocational and industrial training have little contact with the educational system and are therefore largely infructuous."

Universities may be likened unto trees, the roots of which lie deep in the primary schools, and which derive their sap and strength through the secondary schools. Where both are woefully deficient and defective, where there is no diverting of students to vocational courses, where, speaking generally, every student is forced to adopt one general course which leaves him unfit for anything except clerical service of a very poor kind, it is not surprising that Universities have been hampered in their work by admitting "students who are not fitted by capacity for University education, and of whom many would be far more likely to succeed in other careers." In the circumstances that obtain at present, Universities cannot be expected to secure and maintain such a general high standard as they would naturally desire to. Indeed, it is a wonder that with all the handicaps under which they have laboured they have been able to show such good results as they have shown. It is clear, therefore, that for bringing about much-needed improvement in University standards of admission, teaching and examination, a national system of universal compulsory and free primary education and a sound system of secondary education, with attractive vocational courses must be adopted. This way lies the remedy for the present unsatisfactory state of things and not in proposals for leaving out in the cold students who are not gifted or have not been fitted by proper school instruction for University education.

Ladies and gentlemen, another complaint against our Universities and Colleges is that they are turning out large numbers of graduates who cannot find employment. This is obviously due to the fact that our Universities also do not provide a sufficient variety of courses to fit men for careers. As a rule those who take a degree in arts or in pure science are fit only for a teacher's work or for an administrative appointment. But schools and colleges and the public services can absorb only a small proportion of the graduates who are turned out year after year. The provision for medical relief in the country's administration is scanty, and medicine therefore can absorb only a few at present. Want of alternative courses for professional or vocational training compels many students to take to law, only to find that the bar is over-crowded and to chew the bitter cud of disappointment. The remedy lies in providing education on an adequate scale and of the right type in commerce, in agriculture, in technology, in engineering and in applied chemistry. It is no answer to say that agriculture and commerce do not demand the services of a large number at present. The education has to be made so practical that there shall be a demand for it and the demand has to be sedulously increased. The Government and the Universities have to co-operate to give the right kind of education to the youth of the country and to find careers for them. No one branch of national activity can absorb an unlimited number of trained men. But many branches can find work for a few each, and all together can accommodate quite a large number.

It has often been cast as a reproach against our students that too many of them take to law. But it ought to be remembered that it is not their fault but their misfortune that they do so. What is the alternative open to them?

At one time in Japan and unduly large number of young men used to take to the profession of law. The bar was soon over-crowded. Subsequently, a Faculty of Commerce was started, Commerce was encouraged. Banks were started and many of the young lawyers left the bar and took up commercial careers and thus served both themselves and their country.

It is the greatest condemnation of the present system—it is tragic—that after twenty years of school and university education, an Indian youth should not be able to earn a decent living to support himself, his wife, and children and his poor parents. The system is radically wrong and requires to be greatly altered. The whole atmosphere has to be changed. The education of the child has to begin from the time when he comes into the womb of his mother. For this young men and young women have to be educated before they become parents. Look at England again. There the mother is educated, the father is educated, the neighbours are educated. Almost every one has received the benefit of schooling. Educational institutions and activities greet one in every direction. The newspaper and the book are in everybody's hand. The desire to learn, to read, to know is stimulated in every conceivable way. It has become ingrained in the minds of the people. Education has become a necessity of life. An attempt has been made, and it has largely succeeded, to provide it for all stages from the cradle to the grave. It is in such an atmosphere that an English child is born and brought up. He is carefully looked after in the nursery school, the primary school, the secondary school and the technical school. When he leaves the school finally, he is fit for and is helped to get a suitable job. If he enters the University, he enters it well prepared to pursue higher studies at the University, buoyant with hope and ambition. Place the Indian student under similar conditions, give him a fair chance, and he will not be beaten by the youth of any country on earth.

There is no end to the difficulties which beset the path of an Indian student at present. But if I may say so, the greatest of them all is that the medium of instruction is not his mother tongue but a most difficult foreign language. In no other part of the civilized world is a foreign tongue adopted as the medium of public instruction. In our Anglo-vernacular schools and high schools the medium of instruction is generally English. Though in some provinces the use of the vernacular is permitted as the medium of instruction and examination in non-linguistic subjects, the use of English is yet quite general. A child begins to learn English when he is barely seven years old, and from that time the study of his mother tongue is neglected. It occupies a second place. It begins to be regarded as of inferior value and is not much cared for. The result is that from that time until a student leaves the school too much of his precious time is spent in acquiring familiarity with a difficult language as a mere medium of instruction, a language the spelling of which might make a foreigner go mad, as Gladstone once observed. It is difficult to calculate the amount of the loss of time and effort and money which is thus inflicted upon the people of India. The same course is pursued in the college. And yet any educationist will tell you that a very small percentage of our youngmen are able to express themselves correctly in English. If I may speak of my personal experience, I may tell you that I began to learn English when I was only seven years old. I have been learning it and using it for 61 years now. I have used it a good deal. But I frankly confess that I am not able to use it with half as much confidence as I am able to use my own mother tongue, I have had the privilege of the personal acquaintance of most of the great Indian scholars and public men of the last half a century. A good many of them won the admiration of Englishmen for speaking and writing English as they did. But I mean no disrespect to them when I say that very few of them would have claimed that they could use English with the same correctness and ease with which an average educated Englishman used his mother tongue. What then does this extensive use of English in our schools and public offices and bodies mean? It means a tremendous waste of the time and energy of our people. What is worse still is that with all the expenditure it involves, the knowledge which an average Indian youth acquires of English is poor and insufficient for his purposes. It is so poor that it often prevents him from acquiring a thorough knowledge of the subjects he studies through its medium, and from expressing in it what of such knowledge he has acquired. His knowledge of the subject cannot be as good as the knowledge which an English lad who receives education through his mother tongue acquires of the same subject. The Indian youth is hampered both in thinking and in expressing himself. He is placed at a disadvantage. National education cannot, therefore, be raised to the right level of excellence until the vernacular of the people is restored to its proper place as the medium of education and of public business.

I do not under-estimate the value of the English language. I frankly acknowledge that its knowledge has been of great use to us. It has helped the unification of public administration in all parts of India. It has also helped to strengthen national sentiment. I concede that it is or is on the road to become a world-language. I would advise every educated Indian who wishes to proceed to a University, or to go abroad for higher education, to acquire a knowledge of this language and also of German or French. But we should encourage the study of English only as a second language, as a language of commerce with men, of practical business usefulness. We should not allow it to continue to occupy the supreme position which it occupies to-day in the system of our education and our public administration and in the business world. It is impossible to calculate the full extent of the loss which the disregard of our vernaculars has inflicted upon our people. We should take early steps to check it. If there be any who think that our own vernacular should not be used as the medium of higher education and public business because it is not as highly developed to-day as English is, let me remind them that this very English language, which now possesses a literature of which every Englishman is justly proud, was neglected and contemned in England itself, until a few centuries ago. Up to the middle of the fourteenth century French was taught in England to the exclusion of English. It was only towards the end of the 14th century that the people of England began to use the English tongue in their schools, courts and public offices. Says Green in his 'Short History of the English People'.

"In the middle of the fourteenth century the great movement towards freedom and unity which had begun under the last of the Norman Kings seemed to have reached its end, and the perfect fusion of conquered and conquerors into an English people was marked by the disuse, even amongst the nobler classes, of the French tongue. In spite of the efforts of the grammar schools, and of the strength of fashion, English was winning its way throughout the reign of Edward III to its final trumph in that of his grandson. 'Children in School', says a writer of the earlier reign, 'against the usage and manner of all other nations, be compelled for to leave their own language, and for to construe their lessons and their things in French, and so they have since Normans first came into England. Also gentleman's children be taught to speak French from the time that they be rocked in their cradle, and know bow to speak and play with a child's toy: and uplandish (or country) men will liken themselves to gentlemen, and fondle (or delight) with great business for to speak French to be told of'. 'This manner,' adds a translator of Richard's time, 'was much used before the first murrain (the plague of 1349) and is since somewhat changed; for John Cornewaile, a master of grammar, changed the lore in grammar school, and construing from French into English; and Richard Penchriche learned this manner of teaching of him, as others did of Penchriche. So that now, the year of our Lord, 1385, and of the second King Richard after the conquest nine, in all the grammar schools of England, children leaveth French, and construeth and learneth in English." A more formal note of the change thus indicated is found in the Statute of 1362, which orders English to be used in the pleadings of courts of law, because "the French tongue is much unknown."

Ladies and gentlemen, the result of this simple natural change was that within about two centuries of it, Shakespeare, Milton, and a host of poets and writers built up a glorious literature, the most important monument of which is the English version of the Bible, the noblest store-house of the English tongue. Imagine what the loss of the English-speaking world would have been if English had continued to be neglected as it was till 1382. Similarly who can calculate the loss which India has suffered because Hindi and the other Indian vernaculars have not received the attention they deserved and their literatures have not been developed to the extent they could have been developed as the media of national education and communication? English can never become the *lingua franca* of India. After nearly three quarters of a century of education, only 0.89 percent, of the total population of India know English. It must therefore yield the place of honour in India to the principal Indian vernacular—to Hindi—or Hindustani—the language of Hindustan. So long as English will occupy its present prominent place in India in the courts of law, in public offices and bodies, in schools and colleges and Universities, the language of Hindustan cannot acquire its rightful position in the economy of national life, and a national system of education can not be developed.

Ladies and gentlemen, I have described to you some of the disadvantages under which University Education labours in India. I have pointed out its defects and deficiencies, and the obstacles which obstruct its progress. Let me now invite attention to the remedy. What is all this enormous difference between education in England and education in India due to? Both countries are under the same sovereign. The affairs of both have been controlled by the same Parliament. A hundred and fifty years ago the Parliament of Great Britain and Ireland assumed direct responsibility for guiding the destinies of India. It has during this period repeatedly avowed that it is responsible for the moral and material progress of the people of India. It has of course also been responsible for the welfare of the people of England. It has discharged its responsibility to the people of England by introducing a most excellent system of national education. Sixty years ago it made elementary education compulsory throughout Great Britain and Ireland. In 1891 it made that education free. During this half a century it has organized and recognized its system of education, general and technical, to meet varying national needs and requirements, and, by means thereof, it has enabled Britishers to hold their own in the keen competition with other advanced nations of the world in various directions. The prosperity and power which England enjoys to-day in the world is due in large measure to its system of education. Turn now to India. In spite of the repeated professions of solicitude for the welfare of the masses of India, Parliament has not been able to secure to them the blessing even of elementary education. The need for such education has repeatedly been pointed out and admitted. Only a few years after the Act of 1870 was passed in England, an Education Commission was appointed by the Government of India. It reported in 1883 and recommended the universal extension of elementary education. Several Commissions and Committees have since then made similar recommendations. The last to do so was the Royal Commission on Agriculture which reported only a year ago. Besides, for forty-five years we Indians have been asking that elementary education should be made universal, and that a system of technical, agricultural, industrial and commercial education should be introduced. But this has not been done. In 1910 Mr. Gokhale introduced a bill to initiate a system of permissive compulsory education, but his bill was opposed by Government and defeated. Since the reforms were introduced in 1920, the representatives of the people have tried to introduce an element of compulsion in certain areas in some provinces. But the total progress of elementary education brought about in India under the administration for which the Parliament of England has been responsible for a century and a half, is attested by the fact that only 6.91 percent of the total male population and only 1.46 of the female population was at school in 1927. This is truly appalling. The Conclusion to which we educationists in India are driven is that the difference is due to the fact that in England Parliament has been responsible to the people, but the Government in India has not been so, and that no foreign Government can serve the interests of the people over whom it has acquired sway as a Government of their own can.

The question of national education is the most vital problem in the administration of a country. It can be dealt with in all its varying phases effectively and well only by a national Government. When a national Government is established, as I hope, it will be established next year, one of the first things it will have to do is to call a Conference of eminent educationists to discuss and recommend a national educational policy to be pursued in India. Such a Conference will of course take note of the experience which has been gained by other nations in the matter of public education and will recommend a comprehensive programme of education suited to the needs of all classes of the people of the country. When such a policy and programme have been adopted by the future Government of this country, and have been put into operation, then and then only will the Universities of India be able to produce the highest results of which the Indian intellect is capable.

That the education system which is in vogue in India is unsuitable to our national and cultural needs hardly needs saying. We have been blindly imitating a system which was framed for another people and which was discarded by them long ago. Nowhere is this more forcibly illustrated than in the education of our women. We are asking our girls to pursue the same courses which are prescribed for our young men without defining to our selves the results which we desire to follow from their education.

The education of our women is a matter of even greater importance than the education of our men. They are the mothers of the future generations of India. They will be the first and most influential educators of the future statesmen, scholars, philosophers, captains of commerce and industry and other leaders of men. Their education will profoundly affect the education of the future citizen of India. The Mahabharata says: "There is no teacher like the mother" We must, therefore, define the goal of their education and take counsel together and obtain the best advice as to what courses will most suit them, how we shall secure to them a good knowledge of our ancient literature and culture and combine with it a knowledge of modern literature and science, particularly biological science, of art and painting, and of music, how we shall secure the physical, intellectual, moral and spiritual upbuilding of the womanhood of the country. Do we want to rear up women of the type of Savitri and Arundhati, Maitreyi and Gargi, Lilavati and Sulahba of old, or of the type of administrators like Ahalyabai, or of the type of the brave fighter Lakshmi Bai of Jhansi, or women who will combine the best characteristics of the women of the past and of the present, but who will be qualified by their education and training to play their full part in building up the new India of the future? These and similar questions will demand consideration before a national programme for the education of our women will be settled. Statesmen and scholars shall have to sit together to discuss and recommend such a programme.

....

Ladies and gentlemen, I have detained you long. But I hope you will bear with me just a little longer while I say a few words to the graduates who have obtained their diplomas to-day and who are going out to enter life. I will be as brief as possible.

I ask you young men and young women to remember the promises you have made to me and through me to your *alma mater* before you obtained your Diplomas, Remember those promises. Remember also the advice which our esteemed Pro-Vice-Chancellor has given to you in the words of the revered Rishis of old. Speak the truth, live truth, think truth. Continue your studies throughout your life. Be just and fear none. Fear only to do that which is ill or ignoble. Stand up for right. Love to serve your fellow-men. Love the motherland. Promote public weal. Do good wherever you get a chance for it. Love to give whatever you can spare.

Remember the great fundamental truth which you have repeatedly been taught in this University. Remember that the whole creation is one existence, regulated and upheld by one eternal, all-pervading intelligent power, or energy, one supreme life without which no life can exist. Remember that this universe is the manifestation of such a power, of the one without a second, as say the Upanishadas, the creator and sustainer of all that is visible and of a vast deal which is invisible to the human eye. Remember that such a power—call him Brahma,—call him God, is both imminent and transcendant, and has existed thoughout all stages of evolution. He constitutes the life in all living creation. Should a doubt arise in your mind about the existence of this power, turn your gaze to the heavens, wonderfully lit with stars and planet, that have been moving for unimaginable ages in majestic order. Think of the light that travels with marvellous rapidity from the far distant Sun to foster and sustain life on earth. Turn your eyes and mind to the most excellent machine—your own body—which you have been blessed with, and ponder over its wonderful mechanism and vitality. Look around you and see the beautiful beasts and birds, the lovely trees, with their charming flowers and delicious fruits. Remember that One Supreme Life which we call Brahma or God dwells in all, this living creation in the same way as it does in you and me. This is the essence of all religious instruction:

स्मर्तव्यः सततं विष्णुर्विस्मर्तव्यो न जातु चित् ।
सेर्वे विधि निषेधाः स्युरेतयोरेव किंकाः ॥

"Ever to remember God, never to forget Him" All religious injunctions and prohibitions subserve these two alone." If you will remember that God exists and that He exists in all living creatures, if you will remember these two fundamental facts, you will ever be able to stand in correct relation with God and with all your fellow creatures: From the belief that God exists in all sentient beings has flowed the fundamental teaching which sums up the entire body of moral injunctions of all religions, namely—

आत्मनः प्रतिकूलानि परेषां न समाचरेत्

That is, one should not do unto others that which he would dislike if it were done to him. And

यद्यदात्मनि चेच्छेत तत्परस्यापि चिन्तयेत्

i.e. whatever one desires for himself, that he should desire for others also.

These two ancient injunctions lay down a complete code of conduct for all mankind.

If anybody should steal your watch or any other of your possessions you would be pained. Therefore cause not such pain to another by stealing his watch or any article. When you are ill or thirsty you desire that some one should give you medicine or relieve your thirst. Therefore if there be any sister or brother who stands in need of similar relief from you, consider it your duty to render it. Remember these two grand negative and positive injunctions, they embody the Golden Rule of conduct which has been applauded by all the religions of the world. It is the very soul of religion and ethics. Christianity claims it to be its own special contribution. But in reality it is a much older teaching and found a place of honour in the Mahabharat thousands of years before the advent of Christ. I say this not in any narrow spirit, but only to impress upon you that this ancient teaching has come down to us as a noble heritage, and that it is one of the most precious possessions not only of the Hindus but of the whole human race. Treasure it in your hearts, and I am sure your relations will be right and loveable both with God and man.

You must at the same time also remember that this is the country of your birth. It is a noble country. All things considered there is no country like it in the world. You should be grateful and proud that it pleased God to cast your lot here. You owe it a special duty. You have been born in this mother's lap, It has fed you, clothed you, brought you up, It is the source of all your comfort, happiness, gain and honour. It has been your play-ground, it will be the scene of all your activities in life, the centre of all your hopes and ambitions. It has been the scene of the activities of your forefathers, of the greatest and the humblest of your nation. It should be for you the dearest and the most revered place on the surface of the earth. You must, therefore, always-be prepared to do the duty that your country may demand of you. Love your countrymen and promote unity among them. A large spirit of toleration and forbearance, and a larger spirit of loving service is demanded of you. We expect you to devote as much of your time and energy as you can spare to the uplift of your humble brethren. We expect you to work in their midst, to share their sorrows and their joys, to strive to make their lives happier and happier in every way you can. And here I have a definite advice to offer you. We all deplore that there is immense ignorance in our country. We should not wait for its removal till we get Swaraj. I call upon every one of you, young men and young women, to take a vow that you will start a crusade against illiteracy, a campaign to spread knowledge and enlightenment among the teeming millions of India. (Hear, hear and cheers.) Organize your strength. During the period of your leisure or vacation, make it a point to go to the villages and work among your countrymen. Be determined to dispel the darkness which envelopes our masses. Open schools, Instruct the masses in the three R's, *i.e.,* reading, writing and arithmetic. To which add one more, *vis.,* 'religion' the religion of which I have spoken, the religion of love and service, of toleration and mutual regard. Teach these four R's to every boy and girl, every man and woman, old or young. Do not discard religion, Properly understood and taught, it will contribute in rich measure to promote harmony and happiness among all mankind. Promote education by the simplest means. Help our people by your instruction to advance sanitation, health and hygiene in their villages by their own co-operative organizations. I exhort you all, those who are going out of the University now and those who will still be here, to form

लोक शिक्षा समिति

a People's Education League, and start betimes the campaign against illiteracy and ignorance, which to our shame has too long been delayed. Invite all the educated youth of our country to join in undertaking this grand endeavour. We have only to combine and work. Success is certain to crown our efforts.

Throughout the period of your work, take care to keep alive the sense of your duty towards God and towards your country. It will sustain you in the most dif ficult situations and help you to avoid the many obstacles which beset your path. A remembrance of what you owe to God will help you to cherish feelings of brotherliness, of kindness and compassion, not only towards men but towards all innocent creatures of God. It will save you from causing hurt to any one except in the right of private self-defence or the defence of your country. A remembrance of your duty to your country, will help you always to be prepared to offer any sacrifice which may be demanded of you for the protection of its interests or honour. You want freedom, you want self-government in your country. You must be prepared to make every sacrifice which may be needed for it. You have in the course of your education studied the inspiring history-past and present-of the struggles to establish or maintain freedom, which have taken place in our own country and in other lands You have read of the spirit of valour and self-sacrifice which breathes through the best part of Samskrit literature and of modern Indian literatures. You have read and re-read and admired many glowing passages in the glorious literature of England which sing in high strain of liberty and of daring and self-sacrifice in its cause. You have learnt how in the recent Great War, the youths of England and France voluntarily exposed themselves to death in the defence of their own freedom or the freedom of other countries; with what valour and courage and tenacity French and English lads continued to fight until victory crowned their efforts, and thus won imperishable glory for their motherland. I exhort you to cultivate the same love of freedom and the same spirit of self-sacrifice for the glory of your motherland. (Loud applause.) Thus only shall we again become a great nation.

The education you have received would have been lost upon yon if it did not plant an ardent desire in your minds to see your country free and self-governing, I wish you to cherish that desire, and to prepare yourselves to discharge every obligation which may be cast upon you for the early fulfilment of it. You know that the highest duty of a citizen is to offer the final sacrifice of his life when the honour of the motherland requires it. (Hear, hear.) I desire you at the same time to remember that that duty also demands that life shall be preserved for service and not lightly thrown away under wrong inspiration. I therefore wish you to act with a full sense of responsibility and to work in the right spirit and under proper guidance for the freedom of the country. I earnestly hope you will do so . . . .

[Convocation Address delivered on the 16th of August, 1927, at theAnnual Convocation of the University of Bombay by Sir Jadunath Sarkar, M. A., C. I. E., Honorary Member, Royal Asiatic Society of Great Britain and Ireland, Vice-Chancellor, University of Calcutta.]

. . . . If it is true that knowledge is power, then we are bound also to admit that the creators of new knowledge, the makers of original research, must become the masters of those who are mere borrowers of knowledge. So long as our Universities were content with merely importing to India and diffusing among our people knowledge of various kinds which had originated in Europe,—we were intellectually a debtor nation; our best writers were mere imitators or translators. Therefore, if we wish to be self-reliant in art and science, if we wish to be independent in things of the mind, we must qualify ourselves to be givers and not merely takers; we must create and not merely import; we must aspire to be a creditor nation and not eternal intellectual beggars.

If the ever-flowing fountain of research and invention be confined to the European countries and never brought to India, then India will always remain the slave of Europe. In every generation we shall lag behind Europe; we shall be always using the arts and the arms which Europe discarded fifty years ago and holding theories which were proved obsolete there two or three generations earlier. Not only a state of war, but even a temporary obstruction of transport, or the natural desire of foreign inventors to reserve the first fruits of their research to people who can give something in return, may stop the supply of the newest knowledge and the newest appliances of civilisation from Europe to us, and then India will remain helpless and weak.

From such a degrading, such a servile condition we can raise ourselves only if we can create an independent spring-head of knowledge and art in our midst and thus enable our countrymen to become the peers of the Europeans in research and discovery.

Research, or the original investigation of truth in any branch of art or science, is not a luxury or superfluous decoration in the educational world. It is the indispensable condition of the best type of University teaching and of the highest development of the human intellect.

I have been all my life a college teacher, and for the last thirty years I have ceaselessly tried to do my little in the investigation of Indian history. You will permit me to appeal to this two-fold experience in impressing upon you the importance of original research not only for the sake of maintaining India's self-respect in the assembly of nations, but also for ensuring the best quality of teaching to our ordinary students.

No body who has not investigated truth for himself, nobody who has not gone through the patient and arduous discipline of original research, can critically judge the information contained in the text-books and understand its real significance; still less can he become a source of inspiration and guidance to his pupils. The mere transmitter of other people's knowledge, the lecturer who simply repeats the text books, is an intellectual parasite; his mind has no discriminating power, no vitality of its own. Every printed word is to him equally authoritative. On the other hand, the research scholar is an explorer of new realm of thought. He has grappled with unknown difficulties and overcome them, He has personally handled the raw materials out of which truth is deduced. Thus his mind has acquired a higher discipline and he has gained a more intimate vision of truth than is possible for ordinary men. The secrets of science and philosophy are to him living realities, not catch-words borrowed from others and mechanically repeated. He can instinctively distinguish between the true and the false and correctly estimate the comparative value of different kinds of evidence. No University can discharge its functions properly unless it has this highest type of teachers among its agents.

In support of this view, I cite the testimony of a Lord Chancellor of England who also distinguished himself as one of her most successful military organisers. Lord Haldane, in the Final Report of the Royal Commission on the London University, truely observes:

"It is in the best interests of the University that the most distinguished of its professors should take part in the teaching of the undergraduates. . . . It is the personal influence of the man doing original work in his subject which inspires belief in it, awakens enthusiasm, gains disciples. All honest students gain inestimably from association with teachers who show them something of the working of the thought of independent and original minds. As Helmholtz says, 'Any one who has once come into contact with one or more men of the first rank, must have had his whole mental standard altered for the rest of his life'. . . University teaching aims, not so much at filling the mind of the student with facts and theories as at stimulating him to mental effort. He gains an insight into the conditions under which original research is carried out. He is able to weigh evidence, to follow and criticise argument and put his own value on authorities."

I may also point out that original research of the right type has an ennobling influence on character. He who has gained a vision of the secrets of nature and of the human mind, by his own efforts, is fearless in accepting truth; he cannot be content with popular superstitions, social conventions and political catch-words. Research workers form a brotherhood of truth-seekers all over the world, who rise above national jealousies, racial prejudices, and communal differences. The pure stream of truth discovered in her loftiest original source like the heaven-descended Ganges of Hindu mythology, washes away all impurities of the human mind.

In this quest of truth, there must be constant progress; there is no finality, no pause even. But this fact should not deter us from it. If eternal vigilance be the price of political liberty, it is no less truly the price of national efficiency, and that price we must be prepared to pay.

Such is the imperative need of original research in the modern world. And in the promotion of research a University can do what no private individual, however rich or industrious, can accomplish. The University must build up a library of the best books and most learned journals in all related branches of study, and a laboratory complete in scientific apparatus. It must assemble under its roof the master-workers in as many branches of study as it can, and ensure their frequent meeting together and co-operation, each schoolar supplying from his own branch the needs of the others, for no specialist can be the master of more than a few subjects, but requires light to be thrown on his special branch of study from all points of view. Therefore, the most fruitful and valuable research work has been done by those Universities where the professors regard themselves as a brotherhood of seekers after truth, working in concert and holding frequent consultation with one another. A place where each teacher comes only in his appointed hour, addresses his particular class of students, and then goes away, is a lecture institute and not a University in any sense of the term.

It is only a central authority like a University that can prevent waste through the overlapping of efforts by two or more private persons carrying on the same line of reserch in isolation from one another. it can supply the most expert guidance and full bibliographies so as to put the workers on the right track from the very outset, instead of leaving them to blunder on to truth. And it can put libraries and laboratories to the most economical use by a wise and far-sighted division of resources. The lack of cohesion has often nullified our private efforts in the past. The organised public pursuit of research will yield better fruit.

These are the necessary conditions of research, and though they cannot be a substitute for individual genius in the worker, they can help genius to produce the best results.

In this appeal I have drawn on my life's experience in the original investigation of history. But let me assure you that scientific research needs organisation and co-operative effort in the same degree as historical inquiry. It is even more important to us from the economic point of view. The immense natural resources of our country are running to waste for want of the scientific exploration and utilisation of them on modern lines. Scientific research, if carried on here as wisely and as strenuously as in Germany, would immensely increase the wealth of our country and amply repay the expenditure of State funds.

Research is not an impossibility in India, it need not be a sham here. There are two men still in our midst who have proved that India can give to Europe in science and philosophy truths of the highest value to mankind. What a Jagadish Chandra Bose or Rabindra Nath Tagore has done, their fellow-countrymen can do if they get the necessary opportunity.

....

The intellectual resurrection of India is the supreme ideal of the Indian nationalist. And in realizing this ideal, our Universities must play the leading part. This is a duty which they cannot any longer ignore without failing to justify their existence in the changed world of to-day. They must no longer be glorified schools, mere workshops for turning out clerks and school masters, mechanics and overseers, translators and copyists. They must in future add to the world's stock of knowledge. They must achieve intellectual Swadeshi, instead of clothing our people's minds with garments imported from Europe. Is political Swaraj possible, can Swaraj last if given by others, in a country which eternally looks up to foreign lands for all additions to human knowledge, for all new discoveries in medicine and science, for all new inventions in the mechanical arts and the accessories of civilised life, and for every leap forward of the human mind in its quest of truth?

Your beautiful city is rightly called the Gate of India. May it establish its claim to be remembered as the gate through which new light dawns on India, nay more, passes beyond our shores to illuminate and vivify the world outside! Such is the true Indian patriot's vision. Let the Bombay public make it a reality.

To the new graduates of this University, I have only a short message to deliver: never forget your rich inheritance, never be unworthy of the glorious opportunity which the teaching and traditions of this University have given to you. Remember that your names are inscribed as the latest recruits in the same golden book which enshrines the names of Telang and Ranade, Bhandarkar and Rajwade, and see that your life and conduct are worthy of such a noble brotherhood. By the education you have received, the treasuries of Eastern and Western wisdom have been freely opened to you. Consider your past life as only a preparation for further self-improvement and the achievement of a higher destiny for your individual selves and your countrymen in general. The world of action seldom gives its highest prizes to the most gifted in intellect or the purest in character. But that need not make us repine, that need not make us give up the struggle. The heroic soul seeks only opportunities for exerting itself, for daring, and for making its endeavour, and does not look for the meterial fruits of that endeavour. Let the graduates of the University arm themselves against the world with this eternal lesson of the Bhagabat Gita.

Note

* I have taken much of this information from my friend, Dr, Ziauddin Ahmad's valuable publication on Systems of Education.

6

B. R. AMBEDKAR, 'THOUGHTS ON THE REFORM OF LEGAL EDUCATION IN THE BOMBAY PRESIDENCY', IN HARI NARAKE ET AL (EDS), *WRITINGS AND SPEECHES* VOL. 17, PART 2 (NEW DELHI: DR AMBEDKAR FOUNDATION, 2014), 5–18

By
Dr. B. R. Ambedkar, M. A., Ph. D., D. Sc, Bar-at-law., Principal, Government Law College, Bombay.*

The Legal Profession in the Presidency of Bombay consists of diverse elements. There is difference of status and there is difference of training. There are six different classes of Legal Practitioners in the Presidency viz ;

1. Barrister-at-Law, 2. Advocates (O. S.), 3. Advocates (A. S.) of the Bombay University, 4. Advocates (A.S.) of the Bar Council, 5. Solicitors, and 6. Mukhtyars, who have the right to practise in the Courts in the Bombay Presidency. The extent of legal training which is required from these six classes of practitioners varies considerably. The Barrister's legal training extends over three years plus one year in Chambers. The Advocate (A.S.) of the Bombay University is a graduate of Bombay University who has had a compulsory training in Law extending over two years in a recognised Institution. Thus, in all he spends six years after his matriculation before he becomes entitled to practise. The Advocate (A.S.) of the Bar Council is, unlike the Advocate (A.S.) of the Bombay University, only a Matriculate and is not required to undergo compulsory training in Law in any recognised Institution and entitled to appear for the Bar Council Examination without any interval being allowed to pass. The Advocate (O.S.) is an LL.B. like the Advocate (A.S.) and he has had altogether five years of legal training. After an interval of two years after taking his LL.B. degree, he appears for the Examination of the Advocate (O.S.). He does not even then become entitled to practise unless, in addition, he spends one year reading in the Chambers of a senior practitioner, thus spending altogether nine years from his Matriculation. The Solicitor is required

to be either a B. A. or an L.L.B. before he signs Articles with a firm of solicitors. His examination is held three years after he has signed his Articles. His previous training, therefore, is either seven years if he joins the firm as a B. A. or nine years if he joins it as an LL.B. At the lowest rung of the ladder is the Mukhtyar. He need have no training in Law nor is he required to pass any qualifying test. The situation is further complicated by the existence of two other circumstances. First is the existence of different authorities having the right to examine candidates appearing at the Law Examinations. So far as the two classes of Advocates (A.S.) are concerned, there are two different authorities which have the right to examine. One class is examined by the Bombay University and the other by the Bar Council. With regard to the Advocate (O.S.) and the Solicitors, the examining body is the High Court. It must be noted that none of these examining bodies undertakes the responsibility of teaching those whom they examined. The second circumstance which adds to the complexity of the situation is the difference of status among the legal practitioners in the Presidency. The Advocates (O.S.) and the Barristers have the whole field open to them. They can practise in any Court and on either side of the High Court though they can only plead and cannot act. The Advocate (A.S.) is restricted so far as the High Court is concerned to the Appellate Side. But he can plead as well as act. The Solicitor, on the other hand, can practice anywhere and so far as the High Court is concerned, on the Original Side he can only act while on the Appellate Side he can act as well as plead.

That, there should be such a diversity is the matter of qualifications, in the matter of Examinations and in the matter of Status among persons practising the same profession is a very unfortunate fact. But while it may be admitted that all this is very unsatisfactory and even deplorable, I do not think it can be argued that all this constitutes a problem. Because I am not convinced that the system complicated and illogical as it produces any injurious results. That, there are anomalies in the situation is beyond doubt; but there are anomalies also in other Departments of Education. To take only two examples, one from the Medical and the other from the Engineering Profession. The University of Bombay has instituted a course of Medical studies on the passing of which a person becomes entitled to the M. B. B. S. Degree. Parallel to it and alongside, there is the L.C.P.S. course conducted by the Government on the completion of which a person becomes entitled to a Diploma. The University of Bombay has prescribed a course of Engineering at the end of which the Degree of B.E. is conferred on the successful candidates. The Victoria Jubilee Technical Institute has also a Course of Engineering at the end of which the student gets a Diploma. Both the person who gets the University Degree as well as the person who gets his Diploma in Medicine or Engineering practise the profession and find employment both under Government and also outside Government. No one complains about this because each class finds a place that is suited to its training. This is exactly what happens in the Legal Profession if one cares to understand the way it functions. The Mykhtyars are confined to Criminal Courts of the lowest order and take up petty cases. The Advocate (A.S.) of the Bar Council who has become an eyesore to many practitioners practise in the Mofussil Courts of Sub-Judges and Sub-Divisional Magistrates in Taluka. It is the Advocate (A.S.) and the Advocate (O.S.) who alone practise in the District Courts and the High Court. Turning our attention to the way in which the profession functions in practice it cannot be said that there is anything very seriously wrong with the system for Legal Education. That the system is complex and asymmetrical is true but mere complexity and absence of symmetry can not be taken to constitute a problem especially when by the law of gravitation so to say each person settles down to the position and the class of work which is but commensurate with his training.

Assuming that there is a problem, it is necessary to make certain distinctions to avoid confusion of the issue. The problem of overcrowding of the Legal Profession must be separated from the problems of legal education. It would be indefensible both from the stand-point of education and also from the stand-point of social justice to frame a scheme of Legal Education on a basis which would make legal profession the preserve of the few. The question what sort of Legal Education should be given so as to produce an efficient lawyer is a purely educational question and must be settled by the Educationist without being influenced by what might ultimately happens if the number who took to law as a profession was so great that it exceeded the point of saturation. Another distinction which I think must be made is this : the question of Legal Education has no inherent connection with the question whether the Institutions charged with legal instruction should be whole-time or part-time. It is possible to conceive and to frame a system of legal education tolerably good and easily workable with a Law School or a Law College working part-time.

With these preliminary observation, I address myself to the considerations of the problem of reform of legal education. There are four questions that emerge for consideration:—

1. At what stage of his education student should be permitted to commence his study of Laws?
2. What should be the period for a complete course of legal education?
3. What subjects should be curriculum for a complete course of legal education include?
4. How should the Law College be organised so that the curriculum prescribed is dealt with in the most efficient manner?

Question No. 3 seems to me to be pivotal. On a correct answer to this question depends the solution of the remaining three questions. The best approach to the subject is furnished by the reports made from time to time by the Examiners appointed by the Bombay University at the LL.B. Examination containing the impressions formed by them of the work of candidates. The perusal of these reports will show that the examiners have along emphasised the following defects in the work of the examinees.

1. The absence of any indication of a correct understanding of the fundamental principles underlying the laws which he is required to study.
2. Absence of any grounding in general knowledge.
3. Want of orderly presentment of the subject?
4. Absence of any sense of relevancy of the answer given to the question asked.
5. Absence of any sense of precision in stating facts, arguments and opinions.
6. Inability to express in clear language what the student has in his mind.

These are undoubtedly very serious defects in a student of Law and something must be done to remove them. How can these defects be removed? We must first of all understand what these defects are due to. In my opinion these defects are due to two things, viz. a faulty curriculum and a faulty method of instruction.

From the educationist's point of view the study of Law requires a study of certain other auxiliary subjects without which the study of Law alone would be incomplete equipment for the practice of the Profession. What these auxiliary subjects should be will not be difficult to enumerate if we remember that a lawyer must have a legal mind. In the opinion of a keen observer whom Augustine Birrell quotes approvingly in his Obiter Dicta, a legal mind chiefly displays itself by illustrating the obvious, explaining the evident and explatiating on the common place. Disregarding for the moment, the quip conveyed in the observation, I think it contains an important bit of truth in so far as it suggests what the real business of a lawyer is. According to the observation, the business of a lawyer is to argue. So important a part does argument play in a lawyer's business that I am prepared to say that argument is the summum bonum of a lawyer's being. The essential requisites for the development of the argumentative ability are:

a. A knowledge of the individual and how he functions in society.
b. A knowledge of the working of the human mind.
c. A mind trained to drawing logical inferences.

In addition to those fundamental requirements of argumentative ability, there are other requisites, purely ornamental but none-the-less necessary, of grace of language and of orderly presentment. To put it in concrete terms, a lawyer's training apart from the study of law must include the study of the following subjects: (1) Sociology, (2) Psychology, (3) Logic, (4) Rhetoric and the art of public speaking, and (5) Command over language. None of these subjects form a part of the present curriculum of the Law course. The first step, therefore, is to reform the curriculum and to see that these subjects are included in it.

If the curriculum is expanded in the way suggested, then it seems to me that the one and the only answer to the second question namely what should be the period for a complete course of legal education is that it cannot be a two years' course as it is now. It must be more than two years. What exactly should the period be is a question on which there might be a difference of opinion. In my view, the period should be four years. I would divide this course of four years into two periods each of two years. At the end of the first two years, there is to be an examination to be held either by the University or by some other body appointed for the purpose, which examination to be called the First LL.B. Exmination. At the end of second two year's period, there is to be another examination held by the same authority and to be called the second LL.B. examination.

I will next deal with the question of dividing the curriculum between the first LL.B. and the Second LL.B. under my scheme. The course of the First LL.B. should include the following subjects:—

1. Sociology and Psychology. 2. Logic and Rhetoric. 3. English. 4. Law of Contracts. 5. Legal Philosophy and Legal Maxims. 6. Constitutional Law. 7. Government of India Acts. 8. Law of Crimes and Criminal Procedure.

The Course for the second LL.B. will include the course of study now prescribed for the First and the Second LL.B; minus Constitutional Law, the Government of India Acts, the Law of Crimes and Criminal Procedure and Contract which are under my scheme transferred to the First LL.B. I would, however, like to add the following Acts to the curriculum of the second LL.B.:—

(1) Provincial and Presidency Small Cause Court Acts, and

(2) Bombay Civil Courts Act.

I am not in favour of omitting the study of Civil and Criminal Procedures as is suggested in some quarters from the course of Collegiate studies especially as under my scheme there would be ample time for their study.

Having given my views on the questions relating to the course of studies and the period of studies, I take the consideration of the first question, namely, at what stage of his education, a student may be permitted to commence his study of law. I have no hesitation in saying that it should begin immediately after he passes his matriculation. I am driven to this conclusion by my inability to answer satisfactorily to myself the following two questions:—

(1) Why should the study of law be regarded as a postgraduate study.

(2) Does the undergraduate curriculum gone through by a boy in an Arts College gives him the training which is necessary as a preliminary for making him an efficient lawyer and the want of which has been a matter of constant complaint by the Examiners.

With regard to the first question, it may be pointed out that in the Bombay University no Degree in any Scientific subject, such as Engineering, Medicine, Chemistry and Physics is treated as a postgraduate Degree requiring the passing of the B.A. as a condition precedent for being admitted to the Degree Course. Why Law alone should be treated as an exception, I can see no good ground for justification. Secondly, what the boy studies during his four years in an Arts College for obtaining B.A. Degree. *Ex-Hypothesis* has been found as of no material benefit to him in the study of Law. It is the consideration of the matter from this point of view which has forced me, as I have said, to come to the conclusion that Law should not be treated as a post-graduate study but should be treated as a graduate study commencing right after the matriculation. There is nothing so inherently or particularly good in the present-day graduate course of the Bombay University which can be said to add to the make-up of a good lawyer as to compel us to hold that it must be a necessary prerequisite for the commencement of the study of Law. I may mention in passing that the Barrister's course is not a post-graduate course.

There is a view that a student may be permitted to take to legal studies after the Intermediate. The suggestion is a good one in so far as it implies a return to the old system when law was not regarded as a post-graduate study. Nonetheless in my view to adopt this suggestion would be a mistake and for two reasons. Experience has shown that a B. A. is not good enough. With this experience behind us, it seems to me somewhat odd to think that if we descend to the lower and inferior strata of the Intermediate, we could turn out a more finished product from the Law College than we do now when we draw our raw material from the higher and better strata of the B.A. If B.A. is not good enough, I cannot understand how it can possibly be maintained that the Intermediate would be better. Secondly, why leave the boy even though it be for two years in the hands of an Arts College which does not give him the preliminary training necessary for Law. If the boy is deficient in his preliminary training, why not take him in your own hands from the very commencement and give him the training? Why send him for two years to an Arts College which does not profess to give a course of instruction designed for the ultimate benefit of a lawyer?

I see three distinct advantages in my proposal of allowing a student to commence the study of law immediately after the Matriculation:

1. The first advantage to which I attach the greatest value is this. At present, a student who joins the Law Course has not the fixed objective of studying law for the purpose of qualifying himself for the profession. He comes there merely for the purpose of adding one more string to his bow. It is his last refuge to which he may or may not go for shelter. Probably, he comes to the Law College because he is unemployed and does not know for the moment what to do. Due to this unsteadiness in purpose, there is no seriousness in the Law student and that is why his study of Law is so haphazard. It is, therefore, necessary to compel him to stick to it. A boy,

who is a B.A., cannot have this fixity of purpose, because as a B.A. he has other opportunities in life open to him. My scheme has the advantage of compelling the boy to make his choice at the earliest stage at which every one in this country is required to make a choice of his career.

2. The second advantage of my proposal lies in its combination of economy and efficiency. A boy will be able to complete his legal education within 4 years. This is a saving of two years over the present system. The alternative suggestion also requires six years. From the standpoint of poorer students, it has no advantage over the present system. From the standpoint of training, I venture to say that the existing system as well as the alternative suggested by the Committee suffer in comparison with mine. The existing system allows only two year for the study which is undoubtedly very inadequate. The alternative scheme allots three years. But my scheme provides four full years. From the standpoint of efficiency, it is, therefore, superior to both.

3. The third advantage is that it will introduce a process of selection. Those who have not the definite object of entering the profession will be weeded out. Only those with the definite object will join. It will, thus, held to prevent the overcrowding of the profession.

There is only one objection which may be urged against it by some with whom I have discussed it. It is that a Matriculation student will not be able to follow lectures in law. My reply to this is twofold. My friend, Mr. S. C. Joshi, M. A., LL.B., Advocate of the Bombay High Court, assures me that there is no substance in the objection. He is conducting the classes for the Bar Council's Examination for the last several years with great credit as the results show. He has had first-hand experience of teaching Law to Matriculates and I attach much importance to his opinion in this connection. My second reply is that under my scheme, the course for the LL.B. is of two years and the study of Law need not commence from the first year. It may commence in the second.

Coming to the last question of the reorganisation of the Law Colleges, this question was considered by a Committee appointed in 1898 as also by another Committee appointed in the year 1915 known as Chandavarkar Committee and the proposal was rejected. I confess, I have a prejudice against the proposal of making the Law College whole-time. It is a fact that many of the students who are studying law at present are working during the day to earn their living. Indeed, Legal Education would not be possible to many a student and if he was not in a position to earn his living while he is studying. And if the total course of study were to extend over a period of six years as it happens today, I would still oppose the proposal of a full-time College. No educationist would be justified, in my opinion, in devising his scheme of education in such a manner as to impose upon the parent the burden of maintaining a student for six years assuming that there are no failures. But in view of the fact that my scheme requires only four years for the completion of the course and also in view of the fact that the boy is to be taken in hand in a somewhat immature state, I have brought myself as a matter of sheer necessity to favour the proposal of full-time College.

With regard to the staff of the College, I would organise it in two Divisions—the Tutors and the Professors. I am anxious that the actual teaching of Law should be done by persons drawn from the practising members of the Profession. In the absence of any touch with the practising members of the profession, a student in the Law College is likely to get into the academic groove so to say. He must be given a bias in favour of the practical. Only contact with the practising members can give a practical bias to his training. The professors, therefore, should not be required to be permanent members of the staff. Only the Principal and the Tutors should be permanent members of the staff. The work of the Tutors should be to give tuition to the boys and to coach them up, while the Professors and the Principal will do the lecturing.

The object of dividing the staff into two classes is primarily to remove the defects in the method of instruction. The faults in the method of instruction now in vogue will be obvious to any one who has any experience of teaching in Law College. Under the present system, the share which the student takes in his own legal Education consists merely in taking notes of lectures delivered by the Professors. This system at the most acquaints the students with the provisions of the different Acts. But it is doubtful whether the system of mere lecturing affords a sufficient training of the student's mind so as to enable him to apply legal principles to the complicated series of facts which arise in practice. There is also nothing in the system which can compel the student to follow up the lectures by reading the text-books prescribed with the result that student reads nothing till a few days before the date of the examination, when in order to work out the huge arrears he resorts to the notes and the cram books.

There are different views as to the proper method of giving instruction in Law. Some prefer the case method; others prefer the text-book method, supplemented by lectures. No one can dogmatise as to which of the two is the correct method. Methods of instruction must, of course, be left generally to the discretion of the individual members of the Teaching Staff. But, I believe that some positive direction is necessary to the teaching staff to being to its notice the fact that the present system is faulty and that it is necessary to introduce some change in the method, which will demand a larger share of intellectual effort from the student and which will, while instructing him, also train him. I am of opinion that instead of mere lecture there should be a combination of lecturing work and tutorial work; unless the tutorial method is used to supplement the method of lecturing, there is not much hope of the new college producing a new and a better class of lawyers.

The reform in the system of legal Education should in my view be accompanied by reforms in three other directions :—

(1) All the different Examination in Law should be abolished and should be replaced by one Examination common to all practitioners and the distinction between Advocate (A.S.) and Advocate (O.S.) in so far as it is founded in difference in Examination should be done away with. If the distinction is to be retained, it should be founded on the choice of the practitioner who should be called upon to make his decision at the time he applies for the Sanad whether he would practise as an Advocate (A.S.) or as an Advocate (O.S.) or as a Solicitor.

(2) There must be one common Examining Body. As a part of this scheme of re-organisation, I think a Council of Legal Education for supervising Legal Education and also for conducting Examination in Law should be established. The body should consist of the following:—

(i) Representatives of the University.

(ii) Representatives of the Judges of the High Court

(iii) Representatives of the Bar.

(iv) Representatives of the Professors of Law Colleges.

(v) Representatives of the Public.

I am not prepared to hand over the function of the Examination to the Bar Council. There is a danger of the Council developing the Trade Union mentality. It would be fatal to the whole system of the Legal Education if such a mentality became an operative force in the conduct of Examination. Already the system of Examination has resulted in killing all interest in the study of Law. Care should be taken to see that there is no aggrevation of this unfortunate result.

(3) The granting of the Sanad should not merely depend on the mere passing of the Examination. It should be made dependent upon the passing on three conditions.:—

(a) The holding of a Degree in Law.

(b) Reading in Chambers of a senior for one year and passing of an Examination in the Law of Pleading and the Ethics of the Profession. And in addition

(c) (i) in the case of a person who wishes to take the Sanad of an Advocate (O.S.) the passing of an Examination in High Court Rules (Original Side).

(ii) in the case of a person who wishes to take the Sanad of an Advocate (A.S.) the passing of an Examination in the Appellate Side Rules of the High Court.

(iii) in the case of a person who wishes to take the Sanad of a Solicitor the passing of an Examination in (a) High Court Rules (Original and Appellate Side) and (b) Conveyancing.

(d) Production of a certificate of good moral character.

There is no justification left for the existence, diversities and anomalies when the system of education is made common to all and is extensive enough for any class of practitioners.

With respect to the question of practical training in the Chambers of a Senior Lawyer it is necessary to mention the following points which arise for consideration:

(1) Are there facilities for training?

(2) What would happen if no senior lawyer was prepared to admit a law student in his Chambers for training or those that were prepared demanded exorbitant fees?

All these points must be settled if the test of training is to be practicable. With regard to point No. 1, I cannot be absolutely certain. But, I think it is possible to find a sufficient number of Seniors in Bombay and in the District Towns to provide facilities for practical training. On the second point I am sure that unless the High Court was prepared to compel a Senior to admit student to his Chamber for training the system would fail. The habit of not showing the tricks of the trade to one who may be possible rival and the fear that the student while under training will get into touch with the clients and will run away with some of them is so ingrained in the mind of the Seniors that I am sure, they will never consent to take student in their Chambers unless they are compelled to. In relation to third point I think the High Court should lay down the fees for training in Chambers. Otherwise, the fees are likely to be prohibitive which would have the result of making the legal profession the preserve of the rich.[1]

Notes

* **College Notes:** We, however, note with satisfaction that Mr. Fyzee has handed over charge to no less a person than Dr. Ambedkar. A lawyer of repute, he is a close student of Economics, an authority on Constitutional Law and a personality known throughout India and elsewhere. To write more about him would be otiose. Expecting much from our Principal we shall not embarrass him now. We prefer to wait and see.

1 Govt. Law College magazine: Vol. VII; No. 1; January, 1936.

7

B. R. AMBEDKAR, 'MEMORANDUM OF ASSOCIATION OF THE PEOPLE'S EDUCATION SOCIETY, MUMBAI, 8TH JULY 1945', IN HARI NARAKE ET AL (EDS), *WRITINGS AND SPEECHES* VOL. 17, PART 2 (NEW DELHI: DR AMBEDKAR FOUNDATION, 2014), 429–438

6
Memorandum of Association
of
THE PEOPLE'S EDUCATION SOCIETY MUMBAI

(Estd. 8th July, 1945)

Founder:
Dr. B. R. Ambedkar
M.A. Ph.D., D.Sc,
LL.D., (Columbia). D. Litt., (Osmania) Barrister-at-Law.

Head Office:
Anand Bhavan,
Dr. Dadabhai Naoroji Road,
Fort, Mumbai-400 023.

Registered under the Society's
Registration Act XXI of 1860. Registration No. 1375 of 1945-46
Date 9th July, 1945 and the Bombay Public Trust Act, 1950 (Bombay XXIX of 1950) Registration No. F 303 (Bom.)
Dated: 2nd June 1953.

PEOPLE'S EDUCATION SOCIETY, MUMBAI.

Bard of Trustees

1.	Shri K. B. Talwatkar	(Trustee)
2.	Hon'ble Shri K. H. Ranganath	(Trustee)
3.	Shri S. S. Rege	(Trustee)

Members of the Governing Body

1.	Dr. S. P. Gaikwad, G.C.A.M.	(Chairman)
2.	Shri S. S. Rege, B. A., Dip. LIB. Sc.	(Dy. Chairman)
3.	Shri K. B. Talwatkar, M. A., LL.M., S.E.M.	
4.	Dr. P. T. Borale, B. A., LL.B., Ph. D. (Law)	
5.	Shri M. S. Moray, B. A., LL.M.	
6.	Prof. S. K. Mohagaonkar, M.Com.	
7.	Hon'ble Shri K. H. Ranganath, B.Sc, B.L.	
8.	Padmashri Dr. M. L. Shahare, M.Sc, Ph.D.	
9.	Prof. S. L. Khot, M. A., LL.M.,	
10.	Prof. Arun M. Donde, M.A., LL.B., Ex. MLC.	

Secretariate

Prin. D. J. Gangurde, M.Com., LL.M., Secretary

MEMORANDUM OF ASSOCIATION OF THE PEOPLE'S EDUCATION SOCIETY, MUMBAI.

Name and objects of the society

1. The society shall be called the People's Education Society and shall be managed and administered by the Buddhists.

2. The office of the Society shall be at Bombay or at such other place as may be decided from time to time.

3. The aims and objects of the society shall be:-

(a) To provide facilities for education, secondary, collegiate, technical, physical and the like;

(b) To start, establish, conduct and/or aid educational and Buddhist religious associations such as schools, colleges, vihars, hostels, libraries, playgrounds, Buddhist Institutes etc. at suitable places in the State of Maharashtra as well as any other parts of India;

(c) To provide facilities for education of the poor and the Buddhists;

(d) To create and foster general interest in education among the Scheduled Castes and Buddhists who are converted from amongst the Scheduled Castes and in particular to give them special facilities, scholarships and freeships for higher education;

(e) To promote science, Buddhist and other literature and fine arts and to impart useful knowledge in comparative studies of religion;

(f) To purchase, take on lease or otherwise acquire property for the Society and to invest and deal with the moneys of the Society in such manner as may from time to time be determined;

(g) to construct, maintain, rebuild, repair, alter, replace or reinstate houses, vihars, buildings or works for the purpose of the society;

(h) to sell, dispose off, improve, develop, exchange, lease, mortgage or otherwise alienate or deal with all or any property of the Society;

(i) to co-operate, or affiliate the Society or any Institution or Institutions run by or belonging to the Society with a view to securing further advancement of the aims and objects of the Society especially of Buddhists;

(j) to raise money with or without security for carrying out any of the propose, aims and objects of the Society;

(k) to procure the Society to be registered or recognized in any state in India;

(l) to do all other lawful things and acts as are incidental or conducive to the attainment of any of the aforesaid aims and objects.

II - Subscribers and patrons

4. Any person paying Rupees ten per year as subscription to the Society shall be eligible to be enrolled as a subscriber of the Society and shall be entitled to the privileges of the subscriber.

5. Any person paying a lump sum donation of Rs. 500 or more to the Society shall be eligible as a patron of the Society and shall be entitled to the privileges of a patron.

III - Control and management

6. The Sociey shall have:-

(i) A Governing Body;

(ii) A Bard of Trustees;

(iii) A General (originally managing) Council;

And

(iv) An Executive Committee for every College, Vihar, School or other institution or a group thereof as the Governing Body may decide for the Management of its affairs.

7. The Governing Body shall consist of eleven members. Out of these eleven not less than seven shall be persons from amongst the Buddhists who are converted from amongst the Scheduled Castes.

7. (a) The Governing Body shall have power to invite any person or persons to be *ex-officio* members of the Governing Body for per poses specified in a special resolution making such appointments. Such a person shall have no right to vote on any question which falls outside the scope or purpose for which he has been appointed.

Where any dispute arises as to whether the question falls within the scope or the purpose, the decision of the Chairman shall be final.

8. The Board of Trustees shall consist of three persons appointed by the Governing Body from among its own members. Of these, at least two shall belong to Buddhists converted amongst the Scheduled Castes.

9. All the properties and funds of the Society shall vest in the Board of Trustees, save as herein otherwise provided.

9. (a) The Board of Trustees shall have the rights to sue and be sued on behalf of the Society in respect of the properties and funds of the Society.

10. (1) There shall be a General Council to supervise and co-ordinate the work of all institutions of the Society. The General Council shall consists of not less than fifteen members nominated by the Governing Body. Out of these 15 members 11 shall be from the Governing Body of whom 8 shall be from the Buddhists who are converted from amongst the Scheduled Caste members of the Governing Body. The rest shall be from the subscribers and patrons.

(2) Unless otherwise provided by the Governing Body the head of every institution will be an *Ex-officio* member of the General Council.

(3) The Resolutions of the General Council shall be recommendatory only.

11. For every College, Vihar, School or Institution of the Society or a group thereof as Governing Body may decide there shall be an Executive Committee. The Executive Committee shall consist of not less than five and not more than seven members appointed by the Governing Body, one of whom shall be the Dean or Principal of the College or School or Institution, the Registrar of the institution, not less than two from the Buddhists who are converted from the Scheduled Castes and one who in the opinion of the Governing Body is an Educationist.

12. The Chairman of the Governing body, who shall be Buddhist, shall be an *Ex-officio* member and Chairman of the Board of Trustees, General (Originally Managing) Council and all Executive Committees. He will be a member of these Bodies in addition to the number of members specified in the above clauses.

12. (a) (1) The Executive authority of the Society shall vest in Chairman.

(2) All deeds, documents and assurances requiring to be executed by or on behalf of the Society may be executed by the Chairman alone and shall be binding on the Society.

13. The supreme control and Governance of the Society, its institutions, its property and its funds shall be vested in the Governing Body.

14. The first members of the Governing Body shall be:-

1. The Hon'ble Dr. B. R. Ambedkar, M.A., Ph.D., D.Sc, Barrister-at-Law, New Delhi.
2. Rao Bahadur, N. Shivraj, B.A., B.L., M.L.A., Madras.
3. Daulatrao Gulaji Jadhav, B.A., LL.B., Bombay.
4. Raja Ram Bhole, B.Sc, LL.B., Poona.
5. J. H. Subbiah, B.A., Secunderabad.
6. Hirjibhai Khushalbhai Patel, B.A., LL.B., Bombay.

7. G. T. Meshram, New Delhi.
8. Rao Bahadur S, K. Bole, Bombay.
9. M. V. Donde, B.A., Principal, Gokhale Eduction Society's High School, Parel, Bombay.
10. S. C. Joshi, M.A., LL.B., New Delhi.
11. M. B. Samarth, Barrister-at-Law, Bombay.

The Hon'ble Dr. B. R. Ambedkar shall be the first Chairman of the Governing Body and after him he shall always be a Buddhist.

15. The membership of the Governing Body and Board of Trustees may terminate either on death, incapacity, resignation or removal.

16. The term of the office of the members of the General (Originally Managing) Council and of the members of the Executive Committee other than the Dean or Principal and Registar shall be for three years unless terminated by death, incapacity, resignation or removal. A person whose term of office has expired will be eligible for renomination. The Dean or Principal and Registrar shall countinue as members of the Executive Committee so long as they hold office as Dean or Principal or Registrar.

17. The Governing Body shall have power to remove any member of the Governing body, of the Board of Trustees, of the General (Originally Managing) Council and of any Executive Committee from the body provided that three-fourth of the members of the Governing Body present at a meeting specially called for the purpose vote in favour of his removal.

18. The present Chairman of the Governing Body shall appoint or nominate his successor.

19. In case there is no valid nomination of the successor to the present Chairman, or the person so nominated refuses or fails to accept or ceases to hold the post of any reason whatsoever the Chairman shall be elected by the remaining members of the Governing Body.

20. Subject to the provision herein contained all vacancies in the Office of the other members of the Governing body, the Board of Trustees, the General (Originally Managing) Council or the Executive Committee shall be filled by the Governing Body provided that a vacancy of Buddhist converted from the Scheduled Castes member shall be filled by a person belonging to Buddhist who is converted from amongst the Scheduled Castes only and no other.

21. The Chairman of the governing Body shall be Executive Officer of the Governing Body and will act in consultation with the members of the Governing Body in matters of General Policy and finances.

22. (i) The Chairman may appoint a member of the Governing Body to act as the Deputy Chairman in his absence and delegate to him such authority as he may choose to do.
(ii) The Chairman may also appoint a person to act as the Secretary of the Society and prescribe in writing the duties of the Secretary, his salary and term of his office.

(iii) The Governing Body may also appoint from among themselves one member of the General Secretary of the Society. His term of office shall be three years.

23. The Governing Body may appoint necessary staff for carrying on its affairs and also for running its institutions, fix their scales or pay and service conditions and frame standing orders or rules for the guidance and directions of the staff, authorities and Bodies of the Society and may frame Regulations defining their functions, powers and duties.

24. For each college, Vihar, School or Institution or a group thereof as the Governing Body may decide, the Governing Body may appoint a Registrar.

25. Subject to the superintendence and control of the Chairman, the Registrar will work under the head of the institution. He will perform all the duties pertaining to the day to day administration of the institution in accordance with the standing orders and regulations of the Society.

IV - Funds of the Society

26. The funds of the society shall consist of grants, donations, subscriptions, fees, gifts, etc. received from time to time.

27. Secretary shall maintain proper books of accounts and other documents of the income and expenditure of the Society. The accounts of the Society shall be periodically audited by the auditors recognised under the Indian Companies Act and appointed by the Governing Body.

28. The Governing Body shall appoint from amongst the members of the General Council and Executive Committee, or Committee, a Secretary who shall carry on the general work of the Council and of the Executive Committee or Committee respectively. The tenure of the office of the Secretary shall be three years.

29. An annual statement of receipts and expenditure of the Society shall be drawn up by the Secretary of the Society and a consolidated statement shall be kept at the Office of the Society and shall be opened at all times for inspection of the members of the Governing Body, Board of the Trustee, General (Originally Managing) Council and Executive Committee, Patrons and Subscribers.

V - General

30. The Governing Body and other Bodies shall discharge their duties and exercise their powers, authorities and functions in accordance with the Articles annexed to this Memorandum (Schedule - A).

31. The Governing Body shall have power to alter, amend, add or modify the said Articles as may be required by circumstances, provided always that such alteration, amendments, additions, or modifications shall not be inconsistent with the provisions of this Memorandum.

32. This Governing Body shall have power to alter, amend, add or modify this Memorandum save and except provision regarding the composition of the

Governing Body, the Board of Trustees, the General (Original Managing) Council and the proportion of representation on each such body of the members of Buddhists who are converted from amongst the Scheduled Castes, the provision regarding the term of the office the first Chairman, the ex-officio membership of the other bodies of the Chairman, contained in clauses 7, 8, 9, 10, 11, 12, 14, 20, and 21 there of provided that three-fourth of the members of the Governing Body present at the meeting specially called for the purpose vote for such alteration, amendment, addition or modification of the Memorandum,

Signed
B. R. Ambedkar.
S. K. Bole.
M.V. Donde.
S.C. Joshi.
M. B. Samarth.
D. G. Jadhav.
H. K. Patel.

9th July, 1945.

8

B. R. AMBEDKAR, [1]'ON GRANTS FOR EDUCATION', BOMBAY LEGISLATIVE COUNCIL DEBATE, 1927, IN HARI NARAKE (ED.), *WRITINGS AND SPEECHES* VOL. 2 (NEW DELHI: DR AMBEDKAR FOUNDATION, 2014, 2ND EDN), 39–44

Dr. B. R. Ambedkar: Mr. President, I do not wish to take much time because I know that the time that we have at our disposal is very short. All the same, I wish to present certain points for the consideration of the Honourable the Minister for Education.

The first point that I wish to bring to his attention is the fact that we are making indeed a very very slow progress in the matter of the education of our children. The recent report issued by the Government of India on the progress of education makes a very sad reading. It says that if the progress of education goes on at the rate at which it is going on today it will take 40 years for boys and 300 years for girls of school-going age to be brought under education. I beg to submit, Sir, that that is a very dark-prospect for this House to contemplate. The Honourable the Finance Member on the day on which he presented his budget told us that from the year 1921 22 to the present day, the expenditure on education had increased by something like 39 lakhs. Sir, taking into consideration the amount of increase of expenditure on education and the increase in the number of pupils in the schools, I find that the increase in the number of pupils is certainly not commensurate with the increase of expenditure on education. If we take the statistics from 1916-17 to 1922-23, we find that the expenditure on education has increased by something like 100 per cent, while the increase in the number of pupils during the same period is only 29 per cent., Sir, I know that there is a great financial stringency in this presidency, and that we are not at present situated in a position to ask for a rapid increase in education, but we can certainly plead for one thing. We have in this presidency two departments, which if I may say so are working at cross purposes. We have the Department of Education, the purpose of which is to moralise and socialise the people. We have on the other hand the Department of Excise which is working, if I may say so, in the reverse direction. Sir, I think that it is not asking too much if I plead that we should at least spend on education the same amount that we take from the people in the form of excise revenue. The amount of expenditure that we incur per individual in this presidency on education is only 14 annas, but the amount of money that we recover in the form of excise revenue is Rs. 2-2-9 (Rs. 2.17), I think it is only fair that our educational expenditure should be so adjusted that we should spend on the education of the people as much as we take from them in the form of excise.

Another matter which is more or less analogous and to which I want to draw the attention of my honourable friend the Minister for education is that, at present the amount of money which we are spending on primary education is to a large extent really wasted. The object of primary education is to see that every child that enters the portals of a primary school does leave it only at a stage when it becomes literate and continues to be literate throughout the rest of his life. But if we take the statistics, we find that out of every hundred children that enter a primary school only eighteen reach the fourth standard; the rest of them, that is to say, 82 out of every 100, relapse into the state of illiteracy. What is the remedy for this state of affairs? Sir, the comments made by the Government of India in its report on the review of education, I think might, without much excuse be read to this House. The report says:—

> "The wastage in educational effort is immense and most educationalists are of opinion that there is no solution to this problem of wastage in educational effort in India, but compulsion. The total wastage of educational effort and its concurrent dissipation of educational funds in the primary classes is about fifty per cent of the total energy put forth."

I therefore request the Honourable the Education Minister to spend more money on primary education, if for nothing else at least for the purpose of seeing that what he spends bears some fruit ultimately. Sir, this argument is not very different from the argument that was urged from the official benches in the matter of Back Bay reclamation. We were urged to spend more money on Back Bay because we were told that if we do not spend more money on Back Bay what we have spent will be an utter loss. I think the same argument might be utilised in this case, as well, and we can say that unless we spend a sufficient amount of money, to see that every child that enters a school reaches the fourth standard, what we have already spent upon him is of no purpose whatsoever.

Sir, the third matter to which I wish to draw the attention of the Honourable Minister for Education is this. Going over the figures which give us information as to the manner by which we finance education in this presidency I find that out of the total expenditure which we incur on arts colleges, something like 36 per cent is financed from fees; out of the expenditure that we incur on high schools, something like 31 per cent, is financed from fees; out of the expenditure that we incur on middle schools, something like 26 per cent, is derived from fees. Now, Sir, I submit that this is commercialisation of education. Education is something which ought to be brought within the reach of every one. The Education Department is not a department which can be treated on the basis of *quid pro quo*. Education ought to be cheapened in all possible ways and to the greatest possible extent. I urge this plea because I feel that we are arriving at a stage when the lower orders of society are just getting into the high schools, middle schools and colleges, and the policy of this department therefore ought to be to make higher education as cheap to the lower classes as it can possibly be made. I therefore wish to draw the attention of the Honourable Minister for Education to this rather glaring fact in the administration of education in this presidency.

Sir, the fourth point that I wish to bring to the attention of my honourable friend the Minister for Education is the great disparity in the comparative advancement in education of the different classes in this presidency. But before I go to that, I wish to explain one fact, namely, that the census report of this presidency has, for the purpose of comparing the advancement of the different communities in the matter of education, divided the total population into four different classes. The first class is called "advanced Hindus", the second class is called "intermediate Hindus" and it includes those people who for political purposes have now been designated as non-Brahmins i.e., Marathas and allied castes.

There is a third class called the backward classes which includes the depressed classes, Hill Tribes and the Criminal Tribes. Then, we have the fourth class which covers the Mahomedans. Bearing these divisions in mind, one sees a great disparity in the comparative advancement of these different communities in the matter of Education. Comparing these classes of people, according to the order in which they stand on the basis of population and according to the order in which they stand on the educational progress, what do we find? I find that the intermediate class, namely, non-Brahmins, who are first in order on the basis of population, are third in college education, third in secondary education and third in primary education. The Backward classes who are second in order of population are the fourth in the order of college education, fourth in order of secondary education and fourth in order of primary education. The Mahomedans who are third in order of population are second in the order of college education, second in the order of secondary education and second in order of primary education. The advanced Hindus who are fourth in order of population are the first in order of college education, first in order of secondary education and first in the order of primary education. Now, Sir, I have given an idea of the comparative disparity in the educational advancement of the different communities. But the figures do not give us the range of disparity in the advancement of the different communities in our presidency. I will, therefore, present the following figures to the Honourable the Minister for Education for his serious consideration. Taking first the primary education, we find there are—

Advanced Hindus	...	119 students per 1,000 of their population.
Mahomedans	...	92 students per 1,000 of their population.
Intermediate Class	...	38 students per 1,000 of their population.
Backward Class	...	18 students per 1,000 of their population.

That is the state of the primary education. Coming to the secondary education, we find—

Advanced Hindus	...	3,000 in one lakh of their population.
Mahomedans	...	500 in one lakh of their population.
Intermediate Class	...	140 in one lakh of their population.
Backward Class	...	14 in one lakh of their population.

That is the state of the secondary education. Now, coining to the college education we find—

Advanced Hindus	...	1,000 in two lakhs of their population.
Mahomedans	...	52 in two lakhs of their population.
Intermediate Class	...	14 in two lakhs of their population.
Backward Class	...	Nil (or nearly one if at all).

That is the state of the backward class, as far as the college education is concerned, when their total population is something like 37½ lakhs. Sir, these figures show two things conclusively: one, that the different communities are not on a par in the matter of education. They also show another thing to which I should like to draw the attention of the honourable House, namely that the Mahomedans have stolen an enormous march in the matter of education. Sir, this is not an imaginary statement. The statistics I have given to this honourable House are from the Report of the Director of Public Instruction for Bombay for 1923-24, and in support of this argument I may cite the opinion of no less a person than Sir Ibrahim Rahimtoola who made the same remark from the presidential chair of the Mahomedan Conference. It may be remembered that I am not making this statement in any carping spirit nor grudge the efforts that Government have made in the matter of the education of Mahomedans. I must here emphasise that this country is composed of different communities. All these communities are unequal in their status and progress. If they are to be brought to the level of equality then the only remedy is to adopt the principle of inequality and to give favoured treatment to those who are below the level. There are some I know who object to this and adhere to the principle of equality of treatment. But I say Government has done well in applying this principle to the Mahomedans. For I honestly believe that equality of treatment to people who are unequal is simply another name for indifferentism and neglect My only complaint is that Government has not yet thought fit to apply this principle to the backward classes. Economically speaking or socially speaking, backward classes are handicapped in a manner in which no other community is handicapped. I, therefore, think that the principle of favoured treatment must be adopted in their case. As I have shown, their position is worse than that of the Mahomedans and my only pleading is that if the most favoured treatment is to be given to those who deserve it and need it most, then the backward classes deserve more attention of Government than do the Mahomedans. That is the question which I prominently, wish to place before this House, and I urge upon the Honourable the Minister for Education that he should adopt the same methods and principle towards the uplift of the backward classes as have been adopted towards the uplift of the Mahomedan community. Sir, I may refer the Honourable Minister to the instructions issued by the Government of India in 1885 on the Report of the Education Commission of 1882. There were several proposals put forward for improving the education of the Mahomedan community; the proposal on which the Government of India, however, laid stress was the appointment of a special inspecting staff to look to the educational wants of the Mahomedan community and to bring home to it the necessity of education. I think there is an equal urgency for special inspecting staff to look after the education of the depressed classes. I may mention, Sir, that the Primary Education Act is a great wrong. Perhaps honourable members may not agree with me, but I say it is a wrong, it is double wrong. It is wrong because the responsibility of education is transferred to the hands of those who are not enlightened enough to understand that education is a great necessity. If there are any people who realise the necessity for education they are not to be found in this Council. The members of the local boards are too uneducated to realize that education is a necessity. Therefore, I say this Council has done a great wrong in transferring the responsibility for education to the hands of those people who do not feel for education. Again, the transfer of education to local bodies is a wrong because the burden has thereby been transferred to shoulders less broad to bear it. Sir, education of the masses, we all realize, is a matter of great cost and if there is any body which can be said to be able to bear it, it is this Council with its revenue of 15½ crores and not the local bodies with their meagre revenues of a few lakhs. I feel, Sir, that this Council in transferring education to the local bodies has practically postponed the spread of education among the masses *sine die* and in doing so has gravely erred. But, Sir, this is only preliminary to, the point which I wish to make, namely that the people who are the greatest sufferers by this wrong are the depressed classes. With great respect to the Honourable the Minister for Local Self-Government, I am impelled to say that his local boards are conceived after the fashion of money houses in a museum where the aim of the curator is to make room for one individual of every species. Sir, there is only one representative of the depressed classes provided in each local body. What is the utility of having only one representative of these classes? I cannot understand. If, for instance, the representation of the depressed classes in a local board is intended to force upon the local board the policy which is in the interests of the depressed classes, it is futile. For, certainly, one man cannot count in a body of ten or twelve. I hear complaints from all parts of the presidency that, under the present regime, the depressed classes find themselves in a most helpless condition. They are surrounded by people who by no means share their aspirations or their desires for advancement and betterment. There is, therefore, all the greater necessity, I say that this Government should employ certain inspecting agency under their direct control which will see that the depressed classes are not neglected by the bodies to whose charge such an important subject like education has been entrusted.

The second thing that I wish to say about the depressed classes is that I find a certain sum has been set aside in the budget for scholarships for the backward communities. Now, Sir, I cannot understand the connotation of the words "backward classes" as used in the budget. I would have very much wished that the Honourable Minister had adopted the same-phraseology which the Director of Public Instruction adopts in his report, and I should very much like to see that he allocates a separate and distinct sum to each of the different communities which he proposes to include in the term "backward classes." We would then be in a position to know how the intermediate Hindus, backward Hindus, and the Mahomedans progress year by year. Now-a-days we are lumped together, when, as a matter of fact, there is no reason to lump us all together, because we are certainly different from one another however much we might wish to say we are one.

And the third thing which I wish to point out and which I hope the Honourable Minister will give his best consideration to, is the method of giving scholarships to the boys of the depressed classes. Now scholarship as an aid is better than no aid at all. But my honourable friend the Minister for Education will take it from me that my enquiries and my experience show that the method of giving scholarships is really a waste of public money. The depressed class parents are too poor, too ignorant, to understand that the help given by Government is really the help for the education of the child. The scholarship is looked upon by the parent as a family aid to meet their expenses. It is certainly not made available for the education of the boy as such, which is the primary object of the scholarship. Secondly, Sir, with the scholarship I have found that the boy is never able to reach the goal. There are a variety of reasons for that. First of all, a boy of the depressed classes is growing up in an evil set of surroundings. . . . . .

An Honourable Member: Who is responsible for that?

Dr. B. R. Ambedkar: God knows. He is brought up in circumstances which are by no means desirable, and when a boy gets a scholarship, he is an easy prey to all sorts of evil influences. Without proper direction he succumbs and gives up his education and money spent upon him is lost. I would, therefore, put it to the Honourable Minister whether it will not be better for him to spend this money in promoting hostels which either Government may open of its own accord or which may be opened by private agency for the promotion of the education of the backward classes. Sir, it will be a double saving. A hostel, first of all, weans the boy from evil surroundings. It provides effective inspection. And when a hostel is managed by private agency, it will mean some saving of money to Government.

Sir, these are the three suggestions which I wish to make in the very short time that is at my disposal. I hope that my honourable friend the Minister of Education will carefully consider them and do the needful in the matter.

Note

1 B.L.C. Debates, Vol. XIX. pp. 971-76, dated 12th March 1927.

9

B. R. AMBEDKAR, [1]'ON THE BOMBAY UNIVERSITY ACT AMENDMENT BILL 1', BOMBAY LEGISLATIVE COUNCIL DEBATE, 1927, IN HARI NARAKE (ED.), *WRITINGS AND SPEECHES* VOL. 2 (NEW DELHI: DR AMBEDKAR FOUNDATION, 2014, 2ND EDN), 45–53

Dr. B. R. Ambedkar: Mr. President, I have listened with great interest to the speech which was delivered by my honourable friend the member for the University of Bombay. He has so exhaustively covered the subject in his speech which it took him an hour and twenty minutes to deliver that I fear very little is left for me to say. However, I think it fortunate that there is a point of view which has not been so far presented before this House either by my honourable friend the representative of the University or by my honourable friend Prof. Hamill who was specially called in to advise us on this important bill which we are discussing to-day. Sir, my honourable friend Mr. Munshi devoted a considerable part of his speech to the organization of the University of Bombay. He talked with a great deal of intimacy as regards the relations of the syndicate, the senate and the academic council as laid down in the Bill. I have not the good fortune to be a member of the University. I cannot therefore say with the same authority as to whether the provisions that have been incorporated in this particular bill will produce the results which we all desire that it should produce. But, Sir, I must say with due respect to my honourable friend the member for the University that even if we succeed in establishing the relations between the three bodies in the way in which my honourable friend wants that they should be, I am afraid that in the end we will be getting only the shadow but not the substance. Sir, the bill is primarily intended, if I understand the Honourable Minister for Education correctly, to organize the University of Bombay into a better teaching university. That I consider to be one of the principal objects of this Bill. Now, Sir, when I come to analyse the provisions that are incorporated in this bill must say that I felt that in this particular matter we are sure to be disappointed. One of the greatest defects from which this

University has suffered ever since it was established was that it was primarily constituted as an examining body.

Sir, it must be realised that the University cannot succeed in promoting research or in promoting higher education, if it makes the examination system the be-all and end all of its existence. This fact was recognised by the University Commission of 1902 and the bill which followed the report of that Commission recognised that the statute which brought the University into being must be altered so as to enable the University directly to undertake teaching besides its usual task of examining the scholars appearing at its examinations. Now, Sir, when that particular Act of 1904 came into operation, the University, of course, was blocked in its path of undertaking higher education by the existence of a certain number of colleges which were already existing at that time. Obviously, therefore, Sir the only thing that the University could do was to appropriate to itself the field of what is called post-graduate work, and since 1912 the University of Bombay has been following along that line and has established what is called a School of Sociology and Economics to deal particularly with those students who care to take up post-graduate work in that department. I understand, Sir, that the University is also desirous of establishing certain other post-graduate faculties in order to carry out the mission which has been entrusted to it by the Act of 1904. With due respect to those who have framed this bill. I must say, Sir, that they have not paid any attention to the results of this policy of bifurcation that has been adopted by the University in carrying on its function as a teaching university. Sir, I think my honourable friend Prof. Hamill and my honourable friend Mr. Munshi will bear me out when I say that this bifurcation was brought into being by the Act of 1904, by which the University has appropriated to itself the post-graduate work and has relegated to the colleges the under-graduate work has brought about a certain amount of rivalry—I may almost say a certain degree of enmity—between the two institutions. Although my experience of this is limited, yet I was a Professor for sometime in one of the colleges, and even though I am no longer a Professor, I still have the chance of meeting my old colleagues and they tell me that the relations between the University Professors and the Professors of the colleges are not as cordial as they ought to be. Surely, Sir, that must be so. When, for instance, a University sets up itself as something higher, as something superior to the other colleges which are already carrying along similar education in their own way, one is apt to feel jealous of the other. Now, I submit, Sir, where a college professoriate is not on amicable terms with the professoriate established by the University, I think no research, no promotion of knowledge, can be carried on with any benefit either to the colleges or to the University, or to the public at large.

Secondly, I submit, Sir, that unless the University undertakes undergraduate teaching, any amount of super-imposition of post-graduate work will not be of any avail whatsoever. Sir, what is the position of the different colleges that we have to take? Apart from the Government colleges, I beg to submit, Sir, that most of the colleges are established as a result of private effort, and I do not mean any disrespect to those who are serving upon these colleges, when I take the liberty of stating that

I do not think that the colleges are able to cope satisfactorily with the training of the under-graduates. First of all they are inadequately staffed. Take, for instance the two subjects which were my special subjects, namely, history and political economy. I find that a college has generally two professors on its staff to deal with these subjects. Now, I think it would be absurd to believe that two professors in a college can adequately teach such a vast subjects as political economy or history. The result is and I think my honourable friend Prof. Hamill will bear me out when I say that every professor is obliged to lecture for something like thirteen hours in a week. I say that a professor who is made to work in that galley slave fashion can never be a teacher in the real sense of the word. He can only be a hack doing a task with the help of ready-made notes. We can expect no originality from him and he can give no inspiration to those who may have the misfortune to listen to him. The whole study is bound to be a merely mechanical process. Not only are the colleges under-staffed but they are generally staffed by men not because they have more to give to the colleges but because they are willing to accept less. With the help of the army of under-graduates, any adventurer can form a college and get the control of under-graduate to teaching. I say, Sir, if your under-graduate work is as bad as I have described it to be, a university which merely super-imposes postgraduate to work upon it cannot succeed in promoting real knowledge or real research. Thirdly, the present system involves absolute waste, and I think that by a better organization of the University and the colleges this waste could be easily avoided. Take, for instance, the question of teaching of political economy in the city of Bombay itself. There are, Sir, to my knowledge somewhere about six professors at the Sydenham College of Commerce who deal particularly with the subjects of history and political economy and commercial geography. There are two professors at the Wilson College who are also dealing with the same subjects. There are two at the Elphinstone ; there are two at the St. Xavier's. Altogether, Sir, in a city like Bombay we have, so to say, a faculty engaged in the teaching of history and political economy which is composed of twelve teachers. Surely, Sir, if these four colleges, with their twelve professors on them, could be organized in such a fashion that the lecturing system was pooled and the students in the different colleges were allowed to listen and attend to the lectures to be delivered in any one particular college, the professors who are lecturing would be easily released to do some other kind of special work. If that is done, I am absolutely certain that these twelve gentlemen, who are now lecturing on the same subjects in the different colleges, not only will be able to manage the under-graduate teaching, but also can manage the post-graduate teaching as well. So that the expenses which we now have to incur on the extension of the School of Sociology and Economics will certainly be saved for better utilisation on other subjects. Now, Sir, not only does this waste take place with regard to the post-graduate teaching of history and political economy; but I submit, Sir, that this waste will take place with regard to any other subject that the University might appropriate to itself as a subject for post-graduate research, for the simple reason that our colleges are, so to say, pocket universities in themselves. Each college is teaching almost every conceivable subject, and it has upon its collegiate staff, professors who teach all subjects which are laid down for the University examinations. That being so if the University establishes separate professors for post-graduate work there is bound to be duplication and waste in addition to the several disadvantages which I have mentioned in the earlier part of my speech. I therefore submit, Sir, that if the object of the bill is to promote higher education and research, the best method would be not to separate the colleges from the University as has been done now but to make a synthesis in which the University and the colleges would be partners on terms of equality and would be participating in promoting together, both the undergraduate and the post-graduate studies. Sir, what I have stated I must say is really not mine. It is what was recommended by the Sadler Commission which analysed a similar problem which faced the University of Calcutta. There is no doubt about it that the Sadler Commission was one of the most expert Commissions that could possibly be had in this country. I do not personally understand how, for instance, this Government can strut about with a report brought about by men who were absolutely inexpert in their job and pit it against the elaborate and considered judgment of experts who sat upon the Sadler Commission.

I have read with great care the report prepared by the University Committee for the reorganisation of the University of Bombay. But I have found nothing in it which can lead me to alter my opinion[2] that the recommendations of the Sadler Commission will be far more effective and beneficial than the recommendations of the Bombay University Committee. I, therefore, think that it would be far better if my honourable friend the Minister for Education could still in some way, either by introducing provisions in this bill itself or by giving powers to the Senate in the matter of making regulations, allow the University to localise teaching by giving greater control over colleges which may be called "constituent colleges" situated in geographically compact centres. The committee has, I think, admitted that Poona is a place which is ripe for establishing a separate university. There is no doubt that Bombay itself is ripe to have a separate university for itself and I think that if the colleges located in these two centres were separated and grouped into a university, we would be solving the problem of the promotion of higher education and research. As regards mofussil colleges which are scattered about in the Presidency we can very easily deal with them by adopting the suggestion of the Sadler Commission which recommended the establishment of a "Mofussil Board." I say that the scheme suggested by the Sadler Commission is a hundred times better than the scheme recommended by this Reforms Committee, namely, the appointment of a Rector. This is all, Sir, that I have to say as regards the organisation of the University itself.

Now, I wish to turn to the question of the composition of the Senate. A great deal of heat was generated yesterday by the speech of my honourable friend Mr. Jadhav when he said that the statement of objects and reasons does, not recognise/the necessity of the representation of backward communities on the Senate of the University of Bombay. I was somewhat surprised to see that my honourable friend, the member for the Bombay University, flared up at once. But I should like to point out, Sir, that we always kick the ladder by which we rise, and that my honourable friend, the member for the University, who has violently disclaimed communalism in himself is no an exception. Sir, I should like to remind him that he himself had issued a manifesto to the graduates of the University to support him on the ground of Gujarat was for Gujaratis. I would like to ask him now if that is not communalism, what is communalism? I should like him to answer that . .. .

Mr. K. M. Munshi: I am glad to say, Sir, that that statement is absolutely incorrect.

Dr. B. R. Ambedkar: It is not absolutely incorrect. I myself have read your manifesto. However, politicians are men with very short memories.

What I want to state on the floor of this House is this, that I do not think that the Hindus and Mahomedans, constituted as they are, can honestly say that they are non-communal in their attitude towards each other. No member in this House can say that he is non-communal in his attitude. I challenge any honourable member to deny it . .. .

Rao Bahadur R. R. Kale: I challenge that statement.

Honourable Members: We challenge that statement too.

The Honourable the President: Order, order. No conversation across the table, please.

Rao Bahadur R. R. Kale: But the honourable member Dr. Ambedkar said that he would challenge any honourable member to deny his statement.

Dr. B. R. Ambedkar: There can be no gainsaying about this, that every Hindu and every Mahomedan is born in a certain caste or a community. There is no gainsaying that we are brought up and bred up in a communal environment. We share the aspirations and the ambitions of that community ; we feel the disabilities of that community and consequently, there can be no doubt in my mind that every member in this House as well as outside is bound to look at every question consciously or unconsciously from a communal point of view.

Honourable Members: No, no.

Dr. B. R. Ambedkar: I refuse to believe in the "Noes" absolutely; I call it hypocrisy—It is absolutely hypocrisy to shout "No", Sir. I myself look at every question that comes up before this House—I honestly admit—from a communal point of view and I ask myself whether it would be good for the depressed classes or not.

Mr. K. F. Nariman: Sorry.

Dr. B. R. Ambedkar: Those who say "sorry" are themselves not free from communalism. It is very easy to talk about non-communalism, because it is only talk. We know, Sir, that we are so minded that we cannot, for instance, associate with other communities on terms of equality, that whenever we want to marry our daughters we begin to ask whether the bridegroom to be is a man Of our own caste or not (Laughter), when we want to invite guests for dinner we commence to enquire whether they are members of our own community. . . ..

Mr. B. G. Pahalajani: I challenge that.

Dr. B. R. Ambedkar: It is sheer hypocrisy to say that we do not do these things. I wish the honourable members to realise that this is a defect for which I do not accuse any one community. I say, Sir, that it is a blemish from which we all suffer.

That being so, it ought to be recognised that no one community, however intellectually advanced it may be, can be the guardians of other communities. This has been recognised even by the legislators who framed the Reforms Act. If that was not so, we would not see in this Council separate representation for Mahomedans, separate representation for backward classes and separate representation for the depressed classes. It is because we are constitutionally unable to take a larger view of the situation and in order that the operative forces of communalism may be checked, that this counter-check has been provided and I think very wisely provided by these legislators. I should like to be honest, Sir, and I do hope honourable members will be honest on this point. There is no use talking one thing and doing another. That is the reason, I submit, why there is a necessity for the representation of communities, which are not intellectually advanced, on the Senate of the Bombay University. I submit Sir, that I do not wish to accuse the Senate of any conscious bias at all, yet I say that the policy of the Bombay University hitherto has not been very encouraging to the backward or the depressed classes. I will cite only one instance. Take the instance of the system of education that has been adopted by the University. There is no doubt about it in my mind and I do not think that those who represent the University will deny the fact, that our system of examination is the severest possible that exists in India to-day. This is no doubt justified by certain educationists in India who believe that the raising of the standard of examination is equivalent to the raising of the standard of education. I beg respectfully to differ from them. Examination is something quite different from education, but in the name of raising the standard of education, they are making the examinations so impossible and so severe that the backward communities which have hitherto not had the chance of entering the portals of the University are absolutely kept out. But I do not wish to speak of that; because that system applies to all communities alike. But, Sir, just think of it. Has the University ever considered the effect of simultaneous examinations on the progress of education of the backward communities? I do not understand what virtue there is in demanding that a particular candidate who appears at an examination shall pass in all the papers at one shot. It may be a matter of indifference, for instance, for students whose parents are rich enough, who can spare time to attend the colleges during the day time and who can devote their whole time to education. But what about the poor, the poverty-stricken parent, who requires his son to earn in the day time to add to the family earnings in order to make both ends meet? What about the boy who finds very little during the 12 hours of the day to devote to university education? Surely, if the University was mindful of the economic condition of the backward communities, it certainly would not have persisted in a system of simultaneous examinations which in my opinion is absolutely unjustifiable and absurd. I will give you another instance which comes to my mind just now, because my honourable friend Mr. Munshi says that the University has been doing everything without showing any preference of any kind to anybody. One of my friends, who has been nominated to the University Senate, told me the other day he twice moved a resolution in the Senate that candidates belonging to the depressed classes who appear at University examinations should be shown some concession in the matter of fees. I understand from him that the proposition was twice turned down by the Senate.

An Honourable Member: There are poor people in all communities.

The Honourable the President: The honourable member should proceed without minding interruptions.

Dr. B. R. Ambedkar: It has been everywhere recognised, even by the Government, that there are communities which are economically poor and which do require certain special concessions from the Government, in order that they may come on the same level on which the other communities are. If this wise principle cannot be appreciated and understood by the Senate, then I submit such a Senate can never be the guardian of the interests of the backward classes at all.

My honourable friend Professor Hamill made certain remarks in the course of his speech, and I think it is necessary that I should deal with him, although I do not wish to take much of the time of the House. He said that the depressed classes and the backward classes could certainly get nomination on the Senate, if they can help the efficiency of the University. I think that was the line of argument that he adopted, that if the members of the depressed classes were experts in educational matters, they should certainly have a seat on the Senate of the University of Bombay. Now, I should like to say that my honourable friend Professor Hamill absolutely forgets, when he makes that statement, the true function of the Senate. The Senate is not an executive body of the University. No member from the backward classes has asked for any special representation on the Syndicate or on the Academic Council. I recognise, and I realise fully as well as my honourable friend Professor Hamill does, that these two bodies are no doubt bodies which are to be manned by experts, who will run the show of the University. But I have to remind him that the Senate is entirely intended to be a legislative body, a body which has to put forth the needs of the backward communities and to suggest the facilities that are necessary for meeting them. The Senate in my opinion, corresponds exactly to our Legislative Council, and we have in this Legislative Council members from the depressed classes, who are appointed not because they desire to displace any honourable members who are sitting here on the Government side but their only business here is to point out to the Government what are the needs of the communities which are suffering under disabilities. That is all we are asking, and I think when my honourable friend makes the point he absolutely forgets what the Senate is intended to be.

Now, Sir, before I close, I wish to state one thing most emphatically, Sir, there is a demand from honourable members belonging to the Swaraj party that we must have provincial autonomy. Sir, it is a demand which is a welcome demand. But, Sir, I beg to submit that when three-fourths of the population is drenched in ignorance and does not know its rights and responsibilities there can be no hope of autonomy. If we do get self-government notwithstanding the fact that three-fourths of the population is drenched in ignorance, our representative system will be a sham, and there would be a rule of wealth against poverty, of power against weakness. That is really what it will be. I, therefore, say, Sir, that if we desire to have provincial autonomy, we must ensure two things. One thing is that every access must be given to every grade of modern education to the communities which are educationally backward, in order that they may realise their rights and liabilities of citizenship, and secondly, in order that every access may be given to these communities, it is absolutely necessary, under the present circumstances, that special representation should be provided for them.

Before I sit down, Sir, I do wish one matter cleared up. You, Sir, have given us a ruling yesterday about which I am not quite clear. I understand, Sir, from your ruling yesterday that the principle of communal representation has been ruled out. Now, by that I understand that the principle of communal representation in the ordinary sense of that word, namely, that the voters of a particular communities are to be grouped together to elect a member from that community is ruled out. That is my interpretation of your ruling. So that, we are debarred now from raising the question of communal representation on the various bodies of the University in that sense of the term. But I do not think that your ruling goes so far as to say that we shall have no say in the matter as to how the 40 seats which are reserved for nomination shall be distributed. I submit that that particular matter is still open for the honourable members of this House to discuss in the select committee or at the second reading. I should like to ask, therefore, my honourable friend the Minister of Education that in his concluding remarks he should make his position clear is regards that point; because, I want to say most emphatically that unless the representation to these backward communities is provided for on the Senate, the bill would be of no value to us whatsoever, and I for one will vote against it.

Notes

1 B.L.C. Debates, Vol. XX, pp. 825-33, dated 27th July 1927.
2 Dr. Ambedkar's written evidence to the Bombay University Reforms Committee is printed as Appendix III.

10

B. R. AMBEDKAR, 'UNIVERSITY REFORMS COMMITTEE QUESTIONNAIRE – RESPONSES BY AMBEDKAR, 1925–26', IN HARI NARAKE (ED.), *WRITINGS AND SPEECHES* VOL. 2 (NEW DELHI: DR AMBEDKAR FOUNDATION, 2014, 2ND EDN), 292–312

[1]QUESTIONNAIRE

Of University Reform in Bombay Presidency

(The Bombay Government appointed a Committee to look into the problem of reform of the Bombay University. This Committee consisted of 13 members with Sir Chimanlal H. Setalvad, Kt. as its Chairman. Dr. Ambedkar was not a member of this committee but he was one of the 321 persons to whom the committee sent its questionnaire of 54 questions. Dr. Ambedkar replied only some of the questions which he considered worth replying. The questions replied by Dr. Ambedkar are alone reproduced here to be followed by his evidence.—*Editor*.)

1. What in your opinion should be the aim and function of University education in the Bombay Presidency? Do you consider that the existing system of University education in this Presidency affords the young Indians of this Presidency adequate opportunities of attaining this aim? If not, in what main respects do you consider the existing system deficient?

2. Do you consider that the defects pointed out by you mainly lie in or spring from (*a*) the spirit and methods of instructor or pupil; (*b*) the conditions of education, antecedent to the students' entrance of the University; or (*c*) the administrative or educational machinery of the University?

3. How far in your opinion has the University promoted knowledge of, and mutual interest in and sympathy for, the history and culture of the different

communities in this Presidency? Can you suggest means by which this can be further promoted?

II. Secondary and Intermediate Education

(Questions 4-7)

4. Do you consider the training and attainments of students coming out of our High Schools sufficient preparation for entering upon University education? If you consider this preparation inadequate, have you any suggestions for the improvement of the present conditions?

5. Do you consider the creation in this Presidency of (*a*) a new set of institutions in intermediate between High Schools and University; (*b*) a new Board of Secondary and Intermediate Education such as was proposed by the Calcutta University Commission necessary or desirable? If so, how should such institutions and such a Board be constituted and financed?

6. If you consider intermediate institutions, with or without an Intermediate Board, unnecessary or undesirable, how without them could the level, range and effectiveness of existing High School education in this Presidency be improved?

7. How may the University best secure the maintenance of efficiency in the institutions that send students to it for admission?

III. Functions of the University of Bombay

(Questions 8-24)

(*a*) *Teaching* (Questions 8-13)

8. In what directions is it necessary and practicable as well as advisable, in your judgment, to extend the function of the University of Bombay so as to make it predominantly a teaching University?

9. Do you consider that the University should, in addition to postgraduate teaching take any direct part in under-graduate teaching? If so, how would you reconcile and co-ordinate the teaching functions of the University with those of the existing teaching institutions?

10. If you do not consider the University should take any direct part in under-graduate teaching, how by proper co-ordination would you utilise to the best advantage the existing facilities for under-graduate study?

IV. Additional University in Bombay Presidency

(Questions 25-30)

25. Is it desirable to constitute any additional Universities within the Bombay Presidency? What Centres of higher education in the Presidency do you consider—

(*a*) ripe for immediate expansion into Universities,
(*b*) likely to be ripe in the near future, and on what grounds?

28. How would the institution of additional Universities affect the existing University of Bombay? How would you secure co-operation, co-ordination, and reciprocity between the University of Bombay and the new University? What arrangement do you suggest for the period of transition?

VII. Constitution

(Questions 36-40)

36. What defects do you find in the constitutional machinery of the University of Bombay?

37. What should be the strength, composition, duration of office, method of constituting and powers and functions of the Senate? Who, if any, should be *ex-officio,* life, and nominated members of the Senate? How does your method of constituting the Senate secure the representation of all interests and communities?

38. Do you consider that it is necessary or desirable to decentralise the powers and functions hitherto exercised by the Syndicate of the Bombay University? If so, what powers or functions would you remove from the Syndicate and to what new or existing bodies of the University would you assign them? How should the Syndicate so reorganised and any new bodies you may propose be composed?

39. What functions and powers would you assign to the Faculties and Boards of Studies? How should these bodies be constituted and appointed?

III. Functions of the University of Bombay

(Questions 8-24)

(*c*) *Prescribing Courses and Examining* (Questions 16-19)

16. How in your opinion has the University been discharging the functions of (*a*) conducting examinations, (*b*) prescribing courses of study, and (*c*) appointing text-books? Would you suggest any modifications in the exercise of these functions?

17. How far can University examinations be profitably replaced or supplemented by other means of testing proficiency, intelligence and competence?

18. On what branches of study should the Bombay University undertake the teaching immediately and in the near future?

19. In considering the extension of the teaching functions of the University of Bombay and bearing in mind the special requirements of the people of Bombay, would you suggest the institution of any more faculties e.g. of Fine Arts or Technology so as to make the scope of the University broader, more liberal and more comprehensive?

(*d*) *Post-Graduate Courses and Degrees* (Questions 20-21)

20. When the Bombay University further develops its teaching functions, what should be the duration of studies for post-graduate degrees? How would you award such degrees, whether by examination, thesis, original research or a combination of one or more of these?

21. Do you wish to institute any new degrees *honoris causa* and, if so, on what grounds would you have them awarded?

(*e*) *Promoting Research* (Questions 22-23)

22. How Can the University best encourage and guide independent investigation of Indian and especially Bombay's problems, whether historical, economic, sociological, industrial, or other?
23. Is there any need for the creation of a University Press and Publication Department? How might such Department be organised and financed?

(*f*) *Appointing University Teachers* (Question 24)

24. In a Bombay Teaching University what should be the method of selecting and appointing University Professors, Readers, Lecturers etc.? What qualifications are requisite in them? What range of salaries do they require? What should be the conditions regulating their appointment and tenure of office?

IV. Additional Universities in Bombay Presidency

(Questions 25-30)

30. What principles or policy should be followed by (*a*) the Bombay University, (*b*) any new University within this Presidency in permitting the opening of any new College or Institution, constituent or affiliated?

V. Relation of the University and the Public

(Questions 31-34)

31. How far do you consider the curricula of the Bombay University satisfy the needs of Agricultural, Industrial, Professional and Public-life in the Presidency, and especially in the City of Bombay?
32. Can you suggest method of promoting cordial relation and co-operation between the University and other public bodies whether industrial, commercial, professional, municipal or Government?
33. What measures should be taken to bring the University and its working into closer relation with the industrial and commercial life and interests of the City?
34. What should be the extent and purpose of the University's contribution to the education of the adult non-collegiate population? How should the University organise extension lectures, vacation terms and other measures to this end?

VI. Relation of University and Government

(Question 35)

35. What should be the relation of the Government of India and of the Government of Bombay to the University of Bombay and to any new Universities that may be created? What modifications, if any, do you think necessary in

the existing powers of the Chancellor and of Government to control University finance, legislation, appointments of University Officers and Teachers and membership of University bodies? What should be the relation, if any, of the Director of Public Instruction and the Minister in charge of Education to the University?

VIII. Curricula

(Questions 41-44)

41. Are you generally satisfied with the subject and curricula at present prescribed for the various University Examinations? If not, can you indicate the changes you desire?

42. Are you in favour of establishing (*a*) an absolute or (*b*) a greater differenciation of the pass and honours courses? How would such differenciation affect the Colleges and Students?

43. Would you approve of an absolute exclusion of science from the Arts Courses? Do you approve of the present dissociation of Literature and Arts from the study of science?

44. Do you consider the existing courses for the Bachelor's and Master's degree provide a sufficient variety of options and satisfactory combinations and correlations of Courses of Study?

IX. Use of the Vernacular

(Questions 45-46)

45. To what stage and to what extent do you consider the vernacular, can and should be used to replace English as the medium of instruction and examination (*a*) in Bombay, (*b*) in any newly constituted University? What safeguards do you suggest to secure that the standard of English required by students does not suffer from such replacement?

46. What do you consider the best method of promoting the scientific study of the Vernaculars of this Presidency and for encouraging the production of good vernacular literature of all kinds?

XIII. Special Communities

(Question 52)

52. Do you consider any special measures are required for the promotion of University education in any particular community?

[2]WRITTEN EVIDENCE BY DR. B. R. AMBEDKAR

Question 1: I agree with the Inspectors of the Board of Education in England that the aim and functions of University Education should be to see that the teaching carried on there is suited to adults; that it is scientific, detached and impartial in character; that it aims not so much at filling the mind of the student with fact or theories as at calling forth his own individuality, and stimulating him to mental effort; that it accustoms him to the critical study of the leading authorities, with perhaps, occasional reference to first hand sources of information, and that it implants in his mind a standard of thoroughness, and gives him a sense of the difficulty as well as the value of reaching at truth. The student so trained should learn to distinguish between what may fairly be called matter of fact and what is certainly mere matter of opinion. He should be accustomed to distinguish issues, and to look at separate questions each on its own merits and without an eye to their bearing on some cherished theory. He should learn to state fairly, and even sympathetically, the position of those to whose practical conclusions he is most stoutly opposed. He should become able to examine a suggested idea, and see what comes of it, before accepting it or rejecting it. Without necessarily becoming an original student he should gain an insight into the conditions under which original research is carried on. He should be able to weigh evidence, to follow and criticise argument and put his own value on authorities.

I see no reason why the aim and functions of the University Education in the Bombay Presidency should be different. Judged by the quality of the students it turns out it must be said that the existing system of University Education in this Presidency has totally failed to realize the aim and functions of University Education.

Question 2: It is possible that this failure springs partly from the spirit and methods of the instructor, partly of the pupils and partly from the conditions of education antecedent to the students' entrance to the University. In my opinion, however, the failure springs mainly from the administrative and educational machinery of the University. Before a University can be in a position to fulfil the aims and functions of University Education it must be so organized that it becomes essentially a place of learning, where a Corporation of Scholars labour in comradeship for the training of men and the advancement and diffusion of knowledge. In the light of these remarks it will be obvious that the Bombay University in the first place is no true University. It is not a Corporation of Scholars. It does not undertake the training of men and it is not directly interested in the advancement and diffusion of knowledge. On the other hand, the Bombay University in respect of its administration and educational machinery is what a University ought not to be. It is a Corporation of Administrators. It is only concerned with the examination of candidates while the advancement and diffusion of knowledge is outside the ambit of its interests.

Question 3: The University of Bombay has not promoted knowledge of and mutual interest in and sympathy for the history and culture of the different communities in this Presidency. A purely examining University that does not concern itself with inculcating the love of learning cannot achieve this object. And it seems to me that the only way of success along this line is first of all to convert the University into a Teaching University.

Questions 4-7: I do not feel I am competent to answer these questions satisfactorily. I agree that a great deal depends upon what kind of "stuff" the University gets from the high schools. How to get the right kind of stuff is a problem with every University. But I cannot understand why a University should be required to enter upon the control of high schools in order to compel them to produce the required kind of stuff. I know of no University that has undertaken this responsibility. All that the Universities do is to hold their own entrance examination whereby they select the kind of stuff they want by their test papers. I do not see why the Bombay University should be called upon to do more.

Questions 8-10: There are in my opinion two distinct problems that must arise in any attempt that may be made for converting the University of Bombay into a Teaching University. They are (*i*) how to convert it into a Teaching University and (*ii*) how to organize its teaching. With the first problem I will deal when I come to questions 36-40. Here I will deal with the second problem. In the Incorporation Act of 1857 no provision was made for allowing the University to undertake teaching functions. The Act of 1904 for the first time described the University as being incorporated for the purpose (among others) of "making provision for the instruction of students", a phrase which might seem to have been intended to include undergraduates in putting into practice this clause all the older Universities have followed the University Commission which recommended that the Universities might justify their existence as teaching bodies by making further provision for advanced courses of study. As a result of this we find today that the undergraduate teaching has been separated from the postgraduate teaching, the former being taken up by the University and the latter left to the colleges.

I am totally opposed to any such sharp division between post-graduate and undergraduate training. My reasons are as follows:—

(1) The separation of post-graduate work from undergraduate work means the separation of teaching from research. But it is obvious that that where research is divorced from teaching research must suffer. As has been well observed by the Commissioners of 1911 on University Education in London.

> "69. Teaching will, of course, predominate in the earlier work, and research will predominate in the advance work; but it is in the best interests of the University that the most distinguished of its professors should take part in the teaching of the undergraduates from the beginning of their University career. It is only by coming into contact with the junior students that a teacher can direct their minds to his own conception of his subject, and train them in his own methods and hence obtain the double advantage of selecting the best men for research, and getting the best work out of them. Again it is the personal influence of the man doing original work in his subject which inspires belief in it, awakens enthusiasm, gains disciples. His personality is the selective power by which those who are fittest for his special work are voluntarily enlisted in its services and his individual influence is reproduced and extended by the spirit which actuates his staff. Neither is it the few alone who gain; all honest students gain inestimably from association with teachers who show them something of the working of the

thought of independent and original minds. 'Any one', says Helmholtz, who has once come into contact with one or more men of the first rank must have had his whole mental standard altered for the rest of his life'. Lectures have not lost their use and books can never fully take the place of the living spoken word. Still less can they take the place of the more intimate teaching in laboratory and seminar, which ought not to be beyond the range of the ordinary course of a university education, and in which the student learns, not only conclusions and the reasons supporting them, all of which he might get from books but the actual process of developing thought, the working of the highly trained and original mind."

"70. If it is thus to be desired that the highest university teachers should take their part in undergraduate work and that their spirit dominate it all, it follows for the same reasons that they should not be deprived of the best of their students when they reach the stage of post-graduate work. This work should not be separated from the rest of the work of the University, and conducted by different teachers in separate institutions. As far as the teacher is concerned it is necessary that he should have post-graduate students under, him. He must be doing original work himself, and he often obtains material assistance from the co-operation of advanced students. Their very difficulties are full of suggestions, and their faith and enthusiasm are a pay source of refreshment and strength. He escapes the flagging spirit and and the moods of lethargy which are apt to overtake the solitary worker. There can be no question of a higher class of teachers than the professors of the University, or the whole position of the University will be degraded. On the other hand, a university teacher of the highest rank will naturally desire to have as his post-graduate students those students whom he has already begun to train in his own methods, though his laboratory or seminar will, of course, be open to students who come from other universities, and to some perhaps who come from no university at all, as well as to some who come from other teachers of the University of London. There must be a great deal of give and take, and students may often gain by studying under more than one teacher of the same subject; but that is an entirely different thing from separating the higher work from the lower. We do not think it would be possible to get the best men for University Professorship it they were in any way restricted from doing the highest work or prevented from spreading their net wide to catch the best students."

"71. It is also a great disadvantage to the undergraduate students of the University that post-graduate students should be removed to separate institutions. They ought to be in constant contact with those who are doing more advanced work than themselves, and who are not too far beyond them, but stimulate and encourage them by the familiar presence of an attainable ideal."

The disastrous consequences which follow to advanced research work where it is separated from teaching have become patent at least to me. It is a notorious fact that many Indian students who have returned with post-graduate degrees from the University of London and other universities have been failures in the sense that they have failed to master their subjects although some of them occupy the highest posts in the educational line. The reason for this is to be found in the fact that their under-graduate training was utterly insufficient for advanced research work. The Committee will remember that post-graduate training is very modern in its origin and conception. There were men at Cambridge and Oxford who did a great deal of excellent work although those universities did not have post-graduate departments. Even now the men at the head of post-graduate departments at Oxford, Cambridge and London are only graduates and yet they are doing their work of directing post-graduate research remarkably well so as to attract students from all parts of the world. The reason is that their undergraduate training was of a high order. I am, therefore, bound to emphasise that the University must undertake the training of the undergraduates if it intends to rear a structure of a sound system of post-graduate work.

(2) Secondly, the assumption by the University of direct responsibility for teaching in the post-graduate sphere by its own staff which is regarded as a great reform tends to produce the unhappy effect of placing the university staff in antithesis and in opposition to the college staff which feels that its status is unreasonably reduced by the formal and practically permanent limitation of the colleges to an inferior sphere of work.

(3) Thirdly, the establishment of a distinct University Professoriate for post-graduate work is a sheer waste of the resources of the University and can be easily avoided by a proper husbanding of the resources of the colleges. In our system of University education the colleges are the only places of learning. But they are at present the property of separate bodies and the management of each college is vested in a separate governing body. The income derive from a college goes to its own fund. If there is any surplus after the necessary expenses it only serves to swell this fund. Each college teaches the same subjects as the rest and is so to say a 'pocket' university obliged to maintain a competent staff to teach all the subjects and to provide separate libraries and laboratories for their own use. Autonomous as these colleges are none of them is financially a wealthy institution to be able to engage a first class and adequate staff and to provide a first class and adequate equipment in the form of libraries and laboratories. Owing to their slender resources the college staff is handicapped and overburdened. Being obliged to teach too many subjects specialization becomes impossible and a college professor under these circumstances has neither the inducement nor the opportunity to become the master of a small branch of a great-subject. As an inevitable result of this system of autonomous self-sufficing colleges we have scattered here and there poor professoriates, poor libraries and poor laboratories. But because the existing resources seem insufficient when looked upon as attached to or dissipated among the different colleges it does not follow that the resources of the colleges in the aggregate are not great enough to cope with the teaching of the post-graduate and undergraduate work of the Bombay University. Take for instance the resources of the colleges situated in the City of Bombay for the purpose of teaching economics.

We have in the City of Bombay the following colleges providing training in Economics for the B.A. Course of the Bombay University:—(1) Elphinstone College, (2) Wilson College, (3) St. Xavier's College and (4) Sydenham College,

There are two men teaching economics at the Elphinstone, two at the Wilson, two at the St. Xavier's and some six or so at the Sydenham College. Together there are about 12 men in the City of Bombay engaged in the teaching of economics. I know of no university in the world which has such a large number of men engaged in the teaching of one subject and yet all this plethora of professors is running to waste merely for the want of a better organization. And the University instead of attempting to stop, this waste had added to it by the appointing of two more professors of its own to the existing lot.

It is however obvious that if these colleges could be induced to pool their teaching and library resources it would not only produce a strong specialized professoriate but it will produce a professoriate adequate to deal with both undergraduate and post-graduate work and thus obviate the waste of university resources on the two university chairs of economics. To bring this about one has only to arrange that these twelve men do combine together to distribute among themselves the work of carrying out the economics curriculum of the University and agree to lecture to all students taking that course irrespective of the colleges in which they are enrolled. The same plan could be easily adopted in organizing the teaching of other subjects in the colleges in the City of Bombay. The only difficulty probably in the way of this plan is of the students having to run from college to college to attend these lectures. This difficulty can be easily met. I should say that all lectures on Political Science shall be delivered at the Sydenham College. All lectures on Philosophy and Psychology shall be delivered at the Wilson College and all lectures on Literature and languages shall be delivered at the Elphinstone College. By this arrangement the frequent run of students between colleges will be entirely obviated. The colleges should be declared to be halls of lectures on a particular subject and the lectures while remaining on the foundations of their respective colleges will coalesce together so as to form a homogeneous group and will have rooms at the college which is assigned for the subject they will be dealing with, and which will contain the portions of the libraries of the colleges on that particular subject.

I agree that University should be a centralized institution and if the plan of a new University were to be laid down *ab integro* it would be better to rule out the type in which a university was to be composed of affiliated colleges. But it must be recognized that universities cannot be sown broadcast and that where a number of institutions of collegiate status have come into being they cannot be lightly abolished in order to promote the success of centralizing institution. Under the plan I have outlined neither the standard of university education nor the independence of colleges is sacrificed. Administratively the colleges remain independent. Educationally they become integral parts of the University. In short the position becomes somewhat like the position at Oxford and Cambridge where the university is the colleges and the colleges form the university. Such an organization makes the most of the existing colleges and eliminates the waste.

Question 25: My scheme of organizing University Education applies only to those centres where the colleges are situated in close proximity. If this scheme is to be utilized on a large scale the first thing to do is to control the location of colleges so that they shall be established in close proximity. In other words it is necessary to prevent adventurous educationists from opening individual autonomous colleges in all sorts of unseemly and unpromising towns. When one recalls the waste, duplication and dissipation of resources involved in the existence of such separate and scattered colleges one is surprised to see that such anarchical situation should have been tolerated so far. I regard it a great piece of good fortune for the Bombay Presidency that the growth of these isolated colleges has not as yet become so rank and wild as in Bengal. But steps must be taken at once to counteract the establishment of scattered colleges at random if the standard of University Education is to be maintained. For this purpose I should lay down the centres of University Education in this Presidency and should not allow any college to be started at any other place. In my opinion the following places should be marked as actual or potential centres of University Education:—

I—Bombay.
II—Poona.
III—Ahmedabad.
IV—Surat (potential).
V—Karachi
VI—Hyderabad (potential).
VII—Dharwar (potential).
VIII—Sangli (potential).
IX—Nasik (potential).
X—Amalner (potential).

Having defined the centres of University education the next thing to do is to organize the teaching at those places. At most of the above University centres there is as yet only a single college providing education in Arts. Only in Bombay and Poona are there groups of colleges in close proximity. There the problem of University teaching can be easily solved by permutation and combination of the various college staffs into departments. At those centres where there are as yet only a single isolated college the problem of providing education of the university type can be solved in two ways (1) by allowing the foundation of new colleges in close proximity of the existing ones for the purpose of teaching one particular subject or (2) by recognizing the existing college as a university and to allow it to expand by starting new departments of study. The former plan seems to be easier of success. But the latter would be better from the standpoint of efficiency. By adopting this policy, instead of having a number of colleges scattered through the different parts of the Presidency to meet the educational demands in those parts of the Presidency we would be able to have other universities in other parts of the Presidency to meet the educational demands in those parts. By this we may not have achieved the ideal of a centralized university. But we may at least be achieving the next best, of having all the colleges which are affiliated to a university situated in the university town in close proximity of one another to combine together in intellectual co-operation and make the university so to say a living personality.

Question 28: Bombay and Poona are the only places ripe for immediate expansion into universities and I suggest that these be at once incorporated into separate universities. Ahmedabad is likely to be ripe in the near future. It has already an Arts College and a Science Institute and may be converted into a University.

Pending the establishment of universities in the centres marked above the three universities of Bombay, Poona and Ahmedabad should have an external side like the University of London whereby arrangements could be made to grant degrees to students of the other colleges appearing at their examinations.

If the future universities to be established in this Presidency shape themselves into centralized institutions then the problems raised in these questions will not arise. For, then, the university will be in full control of its staff and teaching arrangements. But I will assume that our future universities will be a cluster or constituent colleges independent in their organization. At any rate it will be so of the new universities of Bombay and Poona. Under the scheme of having constituent colleges, the colleges will still continue to be places licensed by the university to provide University education. The plan of inter-collegiate teaching will remove the waste duplication and dissipation of resources by the constituent colleges. But will that arrangements be sufficient to ensure that the standard of university education will be maintained at a high level. That depends upon the standing of the teaching staff engaged in imparting University education. At present the teachers are attached to the colleges and their pay and status are regulated by the authorities governing the colleges. But the colleges do not seem to be making the appointments solely from the sense of obtaining the most qualified persons nor regulating their grades, tenure, pay and promotion in such a manner as to open a career to the best and most qualified member of the staff. The whole educational work carried on by Government is entrusted to the educational services in the three grades of which are included all the administrative and inspecting officers, and all the teachers in Government colleges and schools from the most responsible to the most junior. As in all services the principle of seniority is so deeply rooted that it has become a sacred convention that all superior posts should go by seniority. The principal drawback of this system so far as the work of University education is concerned is that rewards are regulated not by depth of scholarship but by the length of service. Teachers of a college who are subject to be transferred from place to place as is the case with the members of the Government service cannot but feel that the body corporate which claims their loyalty and obedience *is* not the college but the service and more often than not their ambition is directed to securing service promotions than that of creating a school of learning with which their names will be identified. The invidious distinction drawn between the I.E.S. and P.E.S. is another weakness of the service system in that it tempts even the very junior members of the former to regard themselves as the superior of the most senior and distinguished members of the latter. This introduces an element of friction among the members of the college staff rendering difficult that free and friendly co-operation which is so indispensable to promote the intellectual life of any educational institution. Last but by no means the least in importance is the fact that under the present circumstances the professors in the Government colleges by reason of their being servants of the Government have lost the confidence of their students. The students instead of regarding their professors as their intelectual leaders regard them as the agents of Government and the professors receiving no response from their students drudge on without kindling their interest and winning their allegiance. In the colleges maintained by Missionary bodies the leading members of the staff are European Missionaries. The rest of the staff consists of Indian teachers. The distinction between the I.E.S. and P.E.S. is reproduced there on a small scale though it is not quite so emphasized as to produce open friction. In the private colleges maintained by Societies, such as the Deccan Education Society all the members of the staff are the members of the Society. The staff here is therefore more homogeneous and has nothing in its organization to lead to any cleavage. But the constitution of these colleges restricts them to the appointment of men who care to become life members of the Societies which control them. I cannot speak very definitely about the prospects offered by these private colleges but it is certain that they are very poor even when compared with the lowest grades in the Government colleges and indeed they are so poor that they cannot attract men of moderate attainments unless the same can afford to maintain a large margin of disinterestedness. But it is not the private colleges alone that fail to procure proper persons to fill their vacant posts. Even Government colleges with the best of prospects seldom succeed in hitting upon the right sort of a person. The reason is that neither have any proper machinery for making a judicious selection. In the case of Government colleges it is the Director of Public Instruction or the Secretary to Government that makes the choice. But as a matter of fact they are the most inexpert people for this task. Similarly the appointments in the private colleges are mostly in the hands of the heads of the colleges and they too are incapable of making proper choices. The fault lies in not recognizing that to assess the merits of a person one must belong to his kind. It will take an economist to judge an economist.

Quite apart however from these difficulties and drawback there is no possible means of bringing a University staff thus recruited by the different colleges into a due relation, as regards either its members or its distribution, to University needs. The University might find itself supplied with half a dozen professors of one subject and without a single in another equally important branch of knowledge. University organization cannot proceed on these lines, and the difficulties described above can be removed only by placing the appointments of all teachers of the University in the hands of the University itself acting through the Academic Council (*see* constitution of the new University) or at least by giving the University an effective voice in their appointment.

I therefore propose that the collegiate branch of the Educational Service should be separated from the Administrative branch and should be placed under the University with proper safeguards. In other words the teachers' posts at the different colleges should be converted into chairs attached to and supported by certain foundations in the present case by the private colleges and Government. But the appointments to these chairs should be controlled by the University.

I attach the greatest importance to the control of the University over the appointment of its teaching staff. Hitherto the University of Bombay has attempted to maintain the standard of University education by means of its power to test it by a rigid system of examination. The result has been a gradual lowering of the calibre of its graduates. This is principally to be attributed to the egregious error committed by the fathers of our University education in not at all recognizing that the only means of maintaining the standard of University education are the rigid exclusion of students who are unfit for University studies and the existence of a body of highly qualified and productive teachers, organized in departments adequately equipped. In other words they attempted to maintain the standard of the University degrees without attempting to maintain the standard of the teachers and the taught. When events are moving us in the direction of making the University of Bombay a teaching University, it must be clearly realized that "the power to control teaching is of more importance than the power to test it by granting degrees". A University cannot become a teaching University unless its academic affairs, i.e., teaching and examination are left to the uncontrolled discretion of those engaged in teaching. But it will be fatal to the standard of a University degree if the University reposed such a large trust in a body of teachers in whose calibre it has no confidence. I therefore propose that the University should have the power of purse over the colleges. All Government grants to the colleges should be made through the University, so that the University will have a voice in the appointment of the staff of teachers and their equipment in the matter of libraries and laboratories.

Questions 36-39: If a University as a corporation of learning is to serve the community, then its constitution must provide (*a*) for a body which will keep it in touch with all varied requirements of the community ; (*b*) for a body which will give the University a statesman-like guidance in the provision and also in accommodation of means to ends so as to bring about a working comprise between the possible misconceptions of the public and the possibly too narrow outlook of the scholar ; and (*c*) for a body of scholars engaged in the work of teaching to give an authoritative direction to the academic business of the University.

I want to impress upon the Committee that a University does not become a teaching University merely by engaging in the work of teaching through the agency of its own staff. That is not the criterion of a teaching University. A University may undertake teaching and yet may not be a teaching University. Whether or not a University is a teaching University depends upon whether or not the scholars engaged in the work of teaching have the authoritative direction of the academic business of the University in their hands. If it is in their hands then the University is a teaching University. If it is not in their hands then the University is not) a teaching University. A teaching University is a teachers' University.

I am led to make these preliminary remarks because I feel that the Committee in inviting answers to its questions on the constitution is motivated by the desire to obtain such suggestions as will help to make the University of Bombay a teaching University. The existing constitution of the University of Bombay does not provide in any adequate or clear cut manner any of the three bodies I have said to be necessary for a University to function properly. The Senate of the University is not sufficiently representative of the life and interests of Bombay. The Syndicate has not the responsibilities and powers which should devolve upon the Executive

Council of a great University and often has devolved upon it duties which it is absolutely unfit to perform. While the teaching staff which is really the heart of the University has practically no voice, let alone authoritative direction, in the academic affairs of the University.

To make the University of Bombay a teaching University I would first of all proceed to the constitution of faculties. For this purpose I will take it that my scheme of inter-collegiate teaching between the colleges situated in the City of Bombay is adopted. Under that scheme the several studies pursued in the colleges will naturally have to be grouped into Departments, e.g., Economics. History, Politics, Administration, Law, Literature, Languages, Chemistry, Physics, etc. It will be admitted that students are receiving at a University their final systematic preparation for one or other of the several occupations of life for which a University education is necessary at any rate, the most advantageous preliminary.

To succeed in this it is necessary to group together certain branches of knowledge which students pursue. Not only do the needs of students require such a grouping but the needs of the teachers point in the same direction, for it is obvious that certain studies have a closer relation between them and there is a greater similarity in the point of view from which they are approached. These forces emanating from the teachers and the taught have led everywhere the grouping of the several departments of study into what are called Faculties. I suggest therefore that the Departments in the new University of Bombay should be grouped into Faculties and the Faculties should be made the basis of the University organisation if our University is to be a teaching University. A faculty should consist, either wholly or mainly of the Professors and Assistant Professors of the subjects comprised within the Faculty ; and of such other teachers and officers appointed by the University as the Faculty may co-opt. The Vice-Chancellor should *ex-officio* be a member of every faculty. A Faculty should have the power to make Regulations—

(i) to appoint Committees consisting of the Faculty together with other persons to act as Board of Studies and for other purposes ;

(ii) to determine generally the conditions for the award of degrees, diplomas, and other distinctions within the purview of the Faculty ;

(iii) to determine generally the course of study to be pursued by students of the University in the subjects within the purview of the Faculty ;

(iv) to determine generally the method and manner of teaching and examination with regard to the subjects within the purview of the Faculty.

I must say again that if the Faculties are to be entrusted with the powers set out above and the teachers are to be freed from the restrictions imposed by a common syllabus of instruction and a general quasi-external examination, it is necessary to make sure that the teachers are worthy of the trust imposed in them.

The Faculties should be the constituent bodies of the University. Having constituted our Faculties to take charge of the academic and educational work of the University, we must constitute a Central Governing Body to take charge of the administrative work of the University. This body should correspond to the existing Senate of the Bombay University but should be entirely different in character and composition. In my opinion the Senate as a supreme governing body should be comparatively a large body mainly non-professional in character but including representatives of graduates and the teachers. The advantages of such a mode of government are obvious. By mean of a large Senate a number of influential citizens, chosen because of their individual capacity, and of representatives of the great interests of the town, municipal, administrative, commercial, legal, scientific, etc., and of members of Legislative Council, the Assembly and the Council of State are brought into touch with the University and serve as channels between the University and the community as a whole. Such a Senate will be able to ask for support to the University with greater authority and success and the whole city will feel interested in the success of the University.

But the Universities Commission of 1902 regarded it as a fault of the system and reported that the Senates of the Universities were too bulky in numbers (in 1900 the Senate of the Bombay University consisted of 305 fellows) and incapable of exercising proper control in educational matters. That Commission did not understand that the proper function of the Senate was not to control the education but to keep the University in touch with all the varied requirements of the community. That being the function of the Senate it must necessarily be large and varied in its composition. I propose that the Senate of the University of Bombay should be composed of 150 members. One of the most important changes effected under the Universities Act of 1904 was the provision that two-fifths of the Ordinary Fellows should be associated with the profession of teaching. As a preventive of the system in which Fellowships were bestowed by way of compliment without due regard to the qualifications of the recipient this proviso was a salutary proviso. But in view of the proposal I advocate of giving greatly increased statutory powers to the Faculties, I do not think that the teachers in the University need more representation on the Senate than is sufficient to enable each of the Faculties to have a spokesman. I, therefore, propose to restrict the representation of the teachers to the Deans of the Faculties. The rest of the Senate should be composed of persons in the political or commercial world and interest in education may be able to render the University substantial service.

The chief function of the Senate would be legislation—

(1) to make statutes affecting the Government of the University and pass resolutions,
(2) to confer all honorary degrees,
(3) to approve of the admission of constituent colleges or University departments,
(4) to institute any new degree, diploma, or certificate,
(5) to decide disputes between Faculties.

Having provided for the two bodies one to look after the Government of the University and the other to take charge of the academic business of the University, we have now to provide for third body charged with the provision and also the accommodation of means to ends. In other words there must be a Central

Executive of the University. This body should correspond to the existing Syndicate of the Bombay University but should be entirely different in character and composition. The Syndicate appears, both as to its composition and the conditions of its work, the least satisfactory of all the University bodies. As a supreme executive the Syndicate should have the custody and use of the Common Seal, the management of the whole revenue and property of the University and (except as otherwise provided) the conduct of all the affairs of the University. But instead of this the work of the Syndicate has been extended over a wide field of business much of which might be conveniently entrusted to other and more appropriate bodies. The existing system concentrates in a so-called executive the work rather of discussion than of deliberate decision. I, therefore, propose to abolish the Board of Accounts and transfer its functions to the Syndicate which shall have power to determine—

(1) The finance, investments and accounts of the University.

(2) The amount and payment of fees to be exacted within the University, or in relation to the enjoyment of privileges therefrom.

(3) The terms and mode of appointment, tenure of and removal from office, duties, emoluments, allowances, salaries and superannuation allowances of the officers of the University, including its professors, teachers, registrars, librarians and permanent servants.

(4) The tenure of office and terms and manner of appointment and the duties of the Assessors, Examiners and Examining Board.

(5) The provisions and tenure of fellowships, scholarships, prizes, rewards, and pecuniary and other aids.

(6) The provision, maintenance, and supervision of halls, hostels or other premises for the residence of students.

(7) The admission of students as under-graduates of the University.

(8) To deal with the real and personal property of the University.

(9) To provide buildings, premises, furniture and apparatus and other means needed for carrying on the work of the University.

(10) To borrow money for the University and to mortgage University property if necessary

(11) To enter into, vary, carry out and cancel contracts on behalf of the University.

(12) To entertain, adjudicate upon and if thought fit redress any grievances of the officers of the University, the professors, the teaching staff, the graduates, under-graduates and the University servants who may feel aggrieved otherwise than by an act of the Senate.

(13) To regulate the Government grants to the constituent colleges.

These three bodies, the Senate, the Syndicate and the Faculties should be constituted by the Act of Incorporation and together they are enough to supply all the necessary organs of a great teaching University. But there seems to be a want for one more body for the new University of Bombay, particularly for the transition period that is bound to be very long before the mother colleges at the centre of University education ripen into Universities pending which they must remain affiliated to one or other of the newly organized teaching Universities in this Presidency. But even if this problem of making provision for the transition period was not there, the need for a fourth body in the management of a great teaching University would be felt nonetheless.

The plan of organization I have proposed is based more or less on the principle of separation of powers. The centre of legislative power is the Senate. The centre of executive power is the Syndicate and the centre of academic power is the Faculty. But if these separate powers are exercised independently and without any co-ordination, the result is bound to be injurious to the best interest of the University. A Faculty is here taken as the basis of University organization and is given complete autonomy in prescribing courses of study and arranging the teaching of and the examining work. But provision must be made for the control of all matters not expressly assigned to the Faculties, the settlement of matters affecting more than one Faculty, and for a final decision when differences arise between one Faculty and another. There is not only a need for a body for co-ordinating the Faculties but there is also a need for a body for co-ordinating the Faculties and the Syndicate, otherwise the Syndicate by the exercise of its executive powers may seriously interfere in the academic freedom of the Faculties. The control of the purse must ultimately mean the control of all else and it is therefore necessary to ensure that the Syndicate shall not take any action having a direct educational bearing on the University as a whole without consultation with a body representative of the teaching staff as a whole. Thus whether as a feature of the transition period or as a permanent feature of University organization there is a clear necessity for the establishment of a fourth body in the act of incorporation. That body I propose to call the Academic Council. Its functions will be partly advisory and partly executive.

Its executive functions would include the determination by regulation or otherwise of all matters relating to—

(1) The quorum to be required at meetings of the Faculties or at meetings of any Committees appointed by the Faculties.

(2) The duties and powers of Advisory and other Boards, including Boards and Committees to be appointed by the University jointly with any other University or Body touching any educational matter.

(3) The qualifications for honorary degrees and distinctions to be awarded by the University and the means and steps to be taken relative to the granting of the same.

(4) The visitation of affiliated colleges.

(5) The affiliation and disaffiliation of colleges.

(6) The tenure of fellowships, scholarships, exhibitions and pecuniary and other aids.

(7) The discipline to be enforced in regard to the graduates and undergraduates in so far as they come within the jurisdiction of the University.

(8) The removal from membership of the University of graduates and undergraduates and the withdrawal of degrees, diplomas, certificates and distinctions, subject to an appeal to the Senate. The advisory functions of the Academic Council shall be as follows:

(*i*) The Syndicate shall not make any decision in regard to any matter relating to the organisation, improvement, and extension of University education, both under-graduate and post-graduate without first inviting and receiving a report thereon from the Academic Council.

(*ii*) The Syndicate shall not issue general directions to the Faculties, or review any act of any Faculty or of any Committee or Board of a Faculty, other than the election of an officer or representative of such body, upon the appeal of any other Faculty or give directions for their future action without first inviting and receiving a report thereon from the Academic Council.

(*iii*) The Syndicate shall not make any appointment to the teaching staff without first inviting and receiving a report from the Academic Council.

The composition and strength of the Senate, the Syndicate and the Academic Council should be the same as proposed by the Calcutta University Commission for the new Calcutta University. I think it might be better to change as well the nomenclature and call the Senate, the Court and the Syndicate the State of the new University. I also propose that the Viceroy should be the Visitor of the University.

Question 16: The University of Bombay may have been discharging the functions of (*a*) conducting examinations, (*b*) prescribing course of study, and (*c*) appointing text-books very well. But the University never seems to have paid attention to the pernicious effect of all this on the teacher and the taught. How to secure freedom for the University teacher to teach as he thinks best and not to restrict him by a hard and fast syllabus is a problem which should be in the forefront of the problems to be solved by this Committee. If freedom for the teacher can be obtained then freedom for the learner will follow. For this purpose the teachers of the University ought under proper safeguards to have entire control of the education and examination of their students and the University ought to be so constituted as to make this possible.

Question 17: Besides examination, students' work in colleges ought to be taken into account. For the higher degrees there should be thesis and oral examinations.

Questions 18 and 19: The University of Bombay should have the Faculties of Engineering, Agriculture, Fine Arts, Technology and Music to make it a complete University.

Question 20: The duration of studies for post-graduate degrees should be four years (I am speaking only for social sciences). There should be two stages of two years each. At the end of the first stage the candidate should be entitled to the M.A. degree. He should specialize in one subject only which should be the subject of his major interest. The test should consist of a written examination accompanied by an essay of some 75 typewritten pages showing his familiarity with the art of using original sources and commenting upon them. At the end of the second stage the candidate should be entitled to the Ph.D. degree. There the test would include an oral examination and a thesis of a respectable size fit for publication. The thesis will embody the investigations of the candidate in a particular field lying within the scope of the subject he had taken at the M.A. as being of major interest to him. Beside this the candidate will present himself for an oral examination in two subjects to be known as subjects of minor interest which will be allied to the subjects of his major interest. This arrangement will allow specialization with a broad base.

Question 21: It may be well to have a few such degrees.

Question 22: By means of subventions, studentships and fellowships.

Question 23: Most essential to have a University press and publication department. Without this the post-graduate work will be considerably hampered.

Question 24: See answer to questions Nos. 11-13.

Question 30: Bombay University should confine itself to Bombay. New Universities should open their own departments. But if the new University is to be composed of colleges, then each college must confine itself to the teaching of one subject only.

Questions 31-33: See answer to questions Nos. 36-39.

Question 34: Spread of education should be a proper function of the University. But this cannot be achieved unless the University adopts vernacular as the medium of instruction which in the present circumstances is a far cry.

Question 35: Government should have no control over the academic affairs of the University which must be entirely entrusted to the Faculties. But Government should have some control over the legislative and administrative affairs of the University. This they should have by means of nominations to the Court and the Senate of the University.

Questions 41-44: I should leave these questions to the newly constituted Faculties. My opinion is that the curriculum even of the Honours Course provides a poor fare to the students.

Questions 45-46: I hold a very strong affirmative view on the use of vernacular as a medium of instruction. But I feel that the problem cannot be solved unless Indian public opinion decides which vernacular it selects for common intercourse.

Question 52: I think special measures are required for the promotion of University education among the Backward Classes and particularly the Depressed Classes.

Before closing my replies to the questionnaire I beg to express my surprise at the absolute disregard the Committee has shown in the matter of organizing a good Library. I cannot see how any University can function without a first rate library attached to it.

15th August 1924.

Notes

1 Report of the Committee on University Reform appointed by Government, 1925-26, pp. 226-31.

2 University Reforms Committee-Written Evidence No. 103, pp. 1-17, dated 15th August 1924.

INDEX